CONRAD'S DECENTERED FICTION

What are the fingerprints of Joseph Conrad's fiction? This richly illustrated book argues that Conrad's vibrant details set him apart as a writer and brings them from the margins to the center for study. With recently discovered primary sources – including drawings and maps in Conrad's own hand – this book travels widely across Conrad's fiction and explores its interest in marginal voices, characters and details. It produces a new picture of Conrad as a writer, and the first picture of Conrad as an amateur sketch artist. Introducing new critical vocabulary and applying new names from art history to Conrad studies, the book ranges across cartography, fashion, analytic philosophy, manuscript studies and animal studies to discover Conrad as an artist operating across and between different media. Offered as a complement to the abstract approaches of much literary theory, this detail-driven and margin-focused monograph mirrors the characteristic granular nature of Conrad's fiction.

JOHAN ADAM WARODELL's articles on Joseph Conrad have appeared in *Cambridge Quarterly, Conradiana, The Conradian, English* and *Journal of Modern Literature*, and won prizes from both the British and American Joseph Conrad Societies. He translated Olof Lagercrantz's monograph on Conrad and has also published on Woolf, Nabokov and Melville.

CONRAD'S DECENTERED FICTION

JOHAN ADAM WARODELL

CAMBRIDGE
UNIVERSITY PRESS

CAMBRIDGE
UNIVERSITY PRESS

University Printing House, Cambridge CB2 8BS, United Kingdom

One Liberty Plaza, 20th Floor, New York, NY 10006, USA

477 Williamstown Road, Port Melbourne, VIC 3207, Australia

314–321, 3rd Floor, Plot 3, Splendor Forum, Jasola District Centre, New Delhi – 110025, India

103 Penang Road, #05-06/07, Visioncrest Commercial, Singapore 238467

Cambridge University Press is part of the University of Cambridge.

It furthers the University's mission by disseminating knowledge in the pursuit of education, learning, and research at the highest international levels of excellence.

www.cambridge.org
Information on this title: www.cambridge.org/9781316512197
DOI: 10.1017/9781009057905

First published 2022

A catalogue record for this publication is available from the British Library.

Library of Congress Cataloging-in-Publication Data
NAMES: Warodell, Johan Adam, 1985– author.
TITLE: Conrad's decentered fiction / Johan Adam Warodell.
DESCRIPTION: First edition. | New York, NY : Cambridge University Press, 2022. | Includes bibliographical references and index.
IDENTIFIERS: LCCN 2021044727 (print) | LCCN 2021044728 (ebook) | ISBN 9781316512197 (hardback) | ISBN 9781009060868 (paperback) | ISBN 9781009057905 (epub)
SUBJECTS: LCSH: Conrad, Joseph, 1857–1924–Criticism and interpretation. | BISAC: LITERARY CRITICISM / European / English, Irish, Scottish, Welsh | LCGFT: Literary criticism.
CLASSIFICATION: LCC PR6005.04 Z9215 2022 (print) | LCC PR6005.04 (ebook) | DDC 823/.912–dc23/eng/20211203
LC record available at https://lccn.loc.gov/2021044727
LC ebook record available at https://lccn.loc.gov/2021044728

ISBN 978-1-316-51219-7 Hardback

To Philippa, Hugo and Lucy

I don't care for writing at all. What interests me is the creative work.

Joseph Conrad, Letter

Contents

Figures

Acknowledgments

One can write only for friends

Joseph Conrad, *A Personal Record*

Michael Greaney's tireless work and thoughtful guidance on this project span a longer time period than Conrad spent on most of his books. I am also grateful to Robert Hampson, John G. Peters and Philippa Warodell for reading many versions of my work; to Laurence Davies for pointing out the existence of an unpublished drawing; and to Keith Carabine for generously scribbling on every page and footnote of the manuscript. However, if there are any occasional mistakes in the writing, I have added them to make sure that the work can be distinctly attributed to me.

I happily acknowledge the work done by anonymous reviewers on earlier versions/sections of chapters that appeared in the *Cambridge Quarterly, Conradiana, The Conradian* and *Modern Fiction Studies.* I am indebted to the many Conradians who have helped my work over the years, often exhibiting the patience and understanding of Winnie to Stevie in *The Secret Agent.* Richard Ambrosini, William Atkinson, Debra Romanick Baldwin, Katherine Baxter, Helen Chambers, Mark Deggan, Stephen Donovan, Hugh Epstein, Jeremy Hawthorn, Brendan Kavanagh, Owen Knowles, Mark Larabee, Yael Levin, Nic Panagopoulos, Jay Parker, Kim Salmons, Allan Simmons, Peter Villiers, Cedric Watts. Thank you.

Lastly, I apologize for turning my family into involuntary Conrad experts.

Abbreviations

Conrad's works are cited from The Cambridge Edition of the Works of Joseph Conrad (Cambridge University Press, 1990–2016) or, in the case of *The Arrow of Gold, An Outcast of the Islands, Chance,* "Falk," *Typhoon,* "Amy Foster," "To-Morrow," *Nostromo, The Nigger of the 'Narcissus', The Rescue* and *Victory* from Dent's Collected Edition (London, 1946–55). The following abbreviations are used:

AG	*The Arrow of Gold*
C	*Chance*
CL	*Collected Letters of Joseph Conrad*, ed. Frederick R. Karl and Laurence Davies, 9 vols. (Cambridge University Press, 1983–2007)
HD	*Heart of Darkness*
I	*The Inheritors*
LJ	*Lord Jim*
N	*Nostromo*
NLL	*Notes on Life and Letters*
NN	*The Nigger of the 'Narcissus'*
OI	*An Outcast of the Islands*
OP	"An Outpost of Progress"
PR	*A Personal Record*
R	*The Rescue*
S	*Suspense*
SA	*The Secret Agent*
SL	*The Shadow-Line*
SS	"The Secret Sharer"
T	*Typhoon*
UWE	*Under Western Eyes*
V	*Victory*

Introduction

There are ways to start an introduction on Joseph Conrad's works other than by discussing Rembrandt's sketch of an elephant (Figure 0.1). But what a beautiful elephant this is. It is stamped as a masterful work by the quick interplay of overlapping lines, the sense of ease in its accurate portrayal of movement, and the large signature that signals the artist's pride. In no obvious way is the depiction of this elephant reminiscent of *The Anatomy Lesson*, *The Night Watch*, *Belshazzar's Feast*, one of Rembrandt's self-portraits, or any other of his canonical works. The tired label of chiaroscuro is difficult to apply here. The picture's material, size, motif and origin as a noncommissioned work preclude it from being classified among the masterworks. Its position on the margin of Rembrandt's artistic output, however, is unrelated to its inherent artistic skill (it has a more unified display of perspective, light and shadow than *The Anatomy Lesson*, for instance). Given this marginal position, we can approach Rembrandt's elephant with fresh eyes: allowing Rembrandt's art to talk to us directly rather than through the mediation of an established critical response.

An elephant, of course, is seldom in the position of being marginal. Margins themselves are of central importance for establishing artistic identity. The Italian art historian Giovanni Morelli (1816–91) catalogued depictions of ears, noses and fingers to establish the authenticity of paintings by Raphael, Botticelli, Mantegna, Titian and others. Going against a tradition that was "addicted to philosophical crotchets" and relying heavily on intuition as a means of interpretation, he published his work under a pseudonym, acutely aware that the "German and French critics would inevitably ridicule you if you were to tell them that even the nails were characteristic of a great master."[1] Apart from developing a technique that was verifiable and reproducible, he brought his readers close to the artwork itself. He variously referred to this as the "experimental method" and "the scientific study of art."[2] Rather than concerning

Figure 0.1 Rembrandt van Rijn. 1637. The Albertina Museum, Vienna.

himself with chronology, tradition, cultural history, the definition of beauty, or a picture's placement in the history of painting, he urged us to look at the painting itself and fondle its details: "Look at this Raphaelesque type of ear in the children. See how round and fleshy it is; how it unites naturally with the cheek and does not appear to be merely stuck on, as in the works of so many other masters."[3] Morelli was not particularly interested in ears as such but sought to identify forms that were distinctly Raphael's: the fingerprints of an artwork, the artist's handwriting: "the characteristic features in a work of art."[4]

For Conrad's fiction, many critics have taken anything but a Morellian approach to his detail-rich writing. The tendency of Conrad criticism has been, in Cannon Schmitt's formulation in a recent essay on the tide in *Heart of Darkness* (1899), to "read through the manifest details of a text to some sort of veiled or latent level of significance."[5] Thus David Leon Higdon and David Galef, respectively, complain that Conrad criticism routinely ignores significant elements of the text that are secondary to the "main action" and overlooks the "whole supporting cast" of the "minor characters."[6] The result of this macroscopic approach, Albert Guerard seems to maintain in a discussion of *The Nigger of the 'Narcissus'* (1897), is that as a critic, one "may even never get around to mentioning what are, irrespective of structure or concealed meaning, the best-written pages in the book."[7]

Whether the aforementioned statements represent Conrad criticism in moments of healthy self-awareness or ill-founded objections by a few contrarian Conradians, Conrad's texts have always been seen to encourage a type of selective reading for something outside the texts. According to E. M. Forster (1879–1970), himself influenced by the detail-oriented focus of analytic philosophy, Conrad "is always promising to make some general philosophical statement about the universe and then refraining in a gruff disclaimer."[8] In all of Conrad's stories, argues Wilson Follett (1887–1963), there is "a sense of seeking and not finding."[9] More recently, Ian Watt found that "Conrad's fiction was to remain dense with concrete images that impelled the reader's imagination to look for larger meanings"[10] and David Leon Higdon notes that in *Under Western Eyes* (1911) patterns "encourage us to rush blindly ahead of the story to certain conclusions."[11] "The structure of *Heart of Darkness* is the structure of the endlessly deferred promise," writes J. Hillis Miller.[12]

The sense of deferred promise is present in more writings than *Heart of Darkness* and relates to the way many texts appear to withhold crucial facts, such as Falk's cannibalism, Razumov's espionage, Captain Whalley's blindness and that the *Patna* – "sunk at sea" (*LJ* 66) – made it safely back to harbor. The sense of deferred promise is also related to the temptation to approach Conrad's texts with an overarching question, like: "Who is Kurtz?"; "Is Lord Jim 'one of us'?"; "Is Jimmy Wait an impostor?" Yet these focused questions that the texts pose may, paradoxically, be directly at odds with the stated aim of Conrad's primary and detailed investigations.[13] In response to Elsie Hueffer's "attack on my pet Heart of Darkness," Conrad admits, somewhat patronizingly, "the fault of having made Kurtz too symbolic or rather symbolic at all. But the story being mainly a vehicle for conveying a batch of personal impressions I gave the rein to my mental laziness and took the line of the least resistance. This is then the whole Apologia pro Vita Kurtzii" (*CL* II.460). There are two main ways to read this explanation, where Conrad playfully equates his defense of Kurtz with the cardinal John Henry Newman's defense of his life and his religious beliefs in *Apologia pro vita sua* (1864). Either, Kurtz is no more than one personal impression, among many others. Or, Kurtz's intended function is like a cookie jar or plastic bag – a container, nothing more, which holds distinct, eclectic elements together.

In the "Author's Note" to *The Nigger of the 'Narcissus'*, Conrad stresses that the crew is the protagonist – not Jimmy Wait, the title character.

Jimmy, like Kurtz, is the vehicle of the story: "he is nothing; he is merely the centre of the ship's collective psychology and the pivot of the action" (xi), the book is "written round him" (vii). Likewise, Conrad writes to Hugh Clifford that "the whole story" of *Lord Jim* (1900) is made up of "side shows just because the main show is not particularly interesting – or engaging I should rather say" (*CL* II.226). Instead, what appears to hold a central position is often described indirectly, frequently outside of direct experience and present tense, like Kurtz's words in *Heart of Darkness*, the cargo in *The Nigger of the 'Narcissus'*, the treasure in *Nostromo* (1904), Napoleon in *Suspense* (1925), Lord Jim's jump from the *Patna*, sexual activity in *Victory* (1915), and the bomb explosion at the Greenwich observatory in *The Secret Agent* (1907) (neatly placed in the empty space between two paragraphs). Another way of putting this is that Conrad uses the same description for multiple "central" things: an absence.

Is there meaning in these empty spaces in the narrative? At times, this notion of indirect writing is explained from the perspective that Conrad was keenly aware of the need for suggestiveness in a work of art ("Explicitness, my dear fellow, is fatal to the glamour of all artistic work, robbing it of all suggestiveness, destroying all illusion," *CL* VII.457), and of the limits of language, as if his texts were the product of an impossible attempt to asymptotically approach incommunicable experience. Stephen Skinner usefully connects this mode of writing with the rhetorical concept of apophasis, an "artistic method that seeks to express the inexpressible in such a way that its unsayability directs the imagination towards it while remaining beyond speech and comprehension."[14] As useful as this explanation of the function of an absence is, it places the focus and center of a story outside the text: on the inexpressible or the "otherwise present."[15] It can also suggest, if taken as a blanket answer, that the words that make up a story are subservient to a larger image and can "be referred back docilely to an idea that stands above it and explains it," to borrow Edward Said's expression.[16] Such a starting point, however, makes it difficult to read a story like "The Return" (1898), which lacks a main idea but "consists for the most part of physical impressions; impressions of sound and sight, railway station, streets, a trotting horse, reflections in mirrors and so on, rendered as if for their own sake" (7), as Conrad explains in the "Author's Note" to *Tales of Unrest* (1898).

Impressions rendered "as if for their own sake" may serve a main theme, plot, or idea, but they can also be understood as autonomous narrative units. For instance, "the splashy trotting of a horse" (118) that Alvan Hervey registers during an idle moment in "The Return" is unconnected to the story's overarching theme of infidelity, or connected in such a circuitous manner to the theme that this connection is not its primary or intended function. These types of element are, then, distinct from those rare details on which an overarching story pivots: without the rivets in *Heart of Darkness*, for example, Marlow would not get to Kurtz and without the piece of calico labelled "32 Brett Street" (*SA* 99) – "an incredible little fact" (*SA* 110) – the police would not get to Mr Verloc's residence in *The Secret Agent*

In my reading, Conrad's fiction exhibits a fascination with details that have significant value exclusive of their service to an overarching narrative. To varying degrees, the texts poke fun at their public writers for the ease with which they engage in generalizations – like Carleon Anthony, Julius Laspara, Peter Ivanovitch, Professor Moorsom, Avellanos, Decoud, Michaelis, Ossipon, Callan, Sevrin, Mrs Fyne, Mr X and Kurtz, who write about justice, revelation, feminism, morality, love and "queer politico-amorous rhapsodies" ("The Informer," 100). Conrad's own writing style instead echoes in the young captain's diary entries in *The Shadow-Line* (1917), Decoud's writing in his pocket-book in *Nostromo*, Marlow's writing to "The privileged man" (254) in *Lord Jim*, and Razumov's writing in his journal in *Under Western Eyes*. It is private, individual, distracted and occasionally discursive.

Modernism itself can, of course, be conceived of as an assorted collection of private impressions: a plotless segment of literary history. And, after the canonical studies on Conrad's impressionism by Eloise Knapp Hay, Ian Watt, Bruce Johnson and John G. Peters, it is far from an original claim to stress the importance of the individual impression for Conrad's texts.[17] Even so, there is the possibility that Conrad scholarship has lagged behind its own findings. Gregory Ulmer argues convincingly, in "The Object of Post-Criticism" (1983), that the criticism of modernism has only belatedly become modern; it is still concerned with categories, labels and structures rather than with collage and montage.[18]

Counting the advances in biographical and historical criticism in the 1930s; psychological criticism and New Criticism in the 1940s and 1950s; existential philosophy and New Criticism in the 1960s and 1970s; post-structuralism, postcolonialism and gender studies in the 1980s and 1990s; and many later developments,[19] Conrad criticism places the details of his fiction in the background: in the service of something else. To be fair, this is a large claim given the overwhelmingly large scale of Conrad criticism, leaving one with the feeling that you "could spend the rest of your life just reading secondary literature on Conrad."[20] Yet, while the close reading practices of New Criticism and other fields are certainly detail-oriented, and while there are numerous detailed studies on Conrad – no one states that his or her studies are primarily about details. If Conrad is a writer of detail, the primary elements of Conrad's prose have not been claimed as the primary focus of study. Indeed, if one had only read secondary literature on Conrad's writing, rather than Conrad's own writing, one would form the mistaken view that Conrad's texts were predominantly concerned with defining categories, taking positions, declaring ambivalences and arguing stances. In other words, impressions "rendered as if for their own sake" – to requote Conrad's phrase for the ingredients of "The Return" – are not studied as such.

But can one study impressions rendered for their own sake? Or does the study become a type of arational criticism of merely registering observations? In a chapter titled "Animals as Art Historians," Arthur Danto relates an experiment where pigeons were taught to distinguish between Bach and Stravinsky. That achieved, the next step was to see if they would classify Buxtehude, Scarlatti, Walter Piston, Eliot Carter and Vivaldi as Stravinsky-like or Bach-like. They agreed with the critical consensus that Buxtehude and Scarlatti were Bach-like, Walter Piston and Eliot Carter, Stravinsky-like. But they found Vivaldi Stravinsky-like, "leaving it up to us to decide whether they were in error or instructing us in how to think about and listen to Vivaldi."[21] I think the pigeons were right. They had the advantage of approaching the question without being art historians and without an awareness of critical concepts like dissonance, staccato, the Baroque and contrapuntal texture: they were paying attention to the individual form of the music without filtering it through established critical categories.

Categorization, in any form, is always an attempt at summary and simplification; apart from the implicit argument provided by these unwittingly philosophical pigeons, Hume, Locke, Bergson, Russell and Nietzsche – responding to Platonism and its outgrowths – contend that abstract concepts bundle incompatible particulars. In a paragraph that could work as a manifesto to Conrad's own type of detail-rich writing, Nietzsche strikes a cautionary note about the formation of concepts. He explains how even a simple concept like "the leaf" is a tremendous abstraction:

> In particular, let us further consider the formation of concepts. Every word instantly becomes a concept insofar as it is not supposed to serve as a reminder of the unique and entirely individual original experience to which it owes its origin; but rather, a word becomes a concept insofar as it simultaneously has to fit countless more or less similar cases – which means,

> purely and simply, cases which are never equal and thus altogether unequal. Every concept arises from the equation of unequal things. Just as it is certain that one leaf is never totally the same as another, so it is certain that the concept 'leaf' is formed by arbitrarily discarding these individual differences and by forgetting the distinguishing aspects.[22]

A more concrete example of a blunt word than "leaf" which constantly fails to explain a particular feeling or situation is "love." Nietzsche's *Morgenröte* (1881) explains that the word "love" (*Liebe*) is actually a superlative and that our misunderstanding derives from excessive usage. In a letter written during the composition of *The Rescue* (1920), Conrad explains that he has consciously avoided the word "love" in the story: "Attempting to tell romantically a love story in which the word love is not to be pronounced, seems to be courting disaster deliberately" (*CL* II.122). Despite the occasional reference to the word in the story, the readers of *The Rescue* are left to create their own vision of "love" – rather than let the blunt word flatten and discolor the unique narrative.

This avoidance of summary words and large categories can be classified as distracted writing. A distracted focus is one explanation for why, like the crew of the *Nigger of the 'Narcissus'* or the anarchists in *The Secret Agent*, Conrad's writing is eclectic – constituted by "books so fundamentally dissimilar as, for instance, 'Almayer's Folly' and 'The Secret Agent'" ("Preface," *PR* 18). Even with an interest in the political, moral, historical and philosophical values of Conrad's texts, I find it difficult to subsume his eclectic and detail-rich authorship under large narratives or large categories; it rather presents itself in the form of Sir Ethelred's handshake of a "glorified farmer" (*SA* 112), how from "behind that structure came out an impression of pale plumpness in a frock-coat" (*HD* 51), and how the "perforated pipe gurgled, choked, spat and splashed in odious ridicule of a swimmer fighting for his life" (*LJ* 138). Or what better way to introduce anyone to Conrad than with this sentence on Cornelius from *Lord Jim*: "His slow laborious walk resembled the creeping of a repulsive beetle, the legs alone moving with horrid industry while the body glided evenly" (*LJ* 214). Or take this paragraph from "Falk" (1901): "The night came upon him and buried in haste his whiskers, his globular eyes, his puffy pale face, his fat knees and the vast flat slippers on his fatherly feet. Only his short arms in respectable white shirt-sleeves remained very visible, propped up like the flippers of a seal reposing on the strand" (214). This paragraph, on fatherly feet and short arms like seal flippers, is certainly one of the most remarkable in Conrad's fiction – yet, it is neither discussed nor mentioned in secondary literature. For these and many other reasons, both quantitative and qualitative, it is tempting to argue that there is a significant gap between the criticism and the reading experience.

In Conrad studies, sentences are frequently discussed not on the basis of their inherent exuberance, brilliance, or strength but whether they fit an overarching critical category: a situation where "reading has been displaced by a project of sorting by theme."[23] A rejection of an overarching category as a guiding principle of primary interest prevents a situation of repeating established facts; introducing a new category allows for a situation where the same facts are repeatedly arranged in new combinations. Like Heyst's mind, which was as if constructed of "a white-walled, pure chamber, furnished with, say, six straw-bottomed chairs, and he was always placing and displacing them in various combinations. But they were always the same chairs" (*V* 202). What is needed is not a new seating plan – a new category – but attention to the minute, independent and eclectic details that characterize Conrad's writing. Similarly, by shifting our interest to the details, and decentering our gaze, we can pay more attention to the content of books rather than, say, entertain an idea about an overarching and superseding argument.

Yet, if Conrad scholarship were to cease to enlighten us with abstractions – what Nabokov calls "the academic purpose of indulging in generalizations"[24] – the change from a focus on large narratives would invite accusations of triviality and misdirected attention. This, in the spirit of Razumov in *Under Western Eyes* who, when lectured on the horrors of Russian feudalism, "went on studying the stripes of the grey fur of the cat" (171); like Adolf Verloc in *The Secret Agent*, who when lectured on the philosophy of bomb throwing, focuses his mind on the material and color of a sock – "Mr Vladimir's hand clasped the ankle reposing on his knee. The sock was of dark blue silk" (*SA* 22); like Marlow in *Heart of Darkness*, who in haste toward the Company's station, finds his attention drawn to a bit of white worsted tied round a native's neck: "Where did he get it? Was it a badge – an ornament – a charm – a propitiatory act? Was there any idea at all connected with it? It looked startling round his black neck, this bit of white thread from beyond the seas" (58–59); or, like Conrad who in the midst of attempting to finish an autobiographical text cannot seem to help stating how, regarding his writing desk, his eye "was attracted by the good form of the same drawer's brass handles" (*PR* 37).

These details about the grey fur of a cat, a blue silk sock, a bit of white worsted and a drawer's brass handles indirectly relate to larger themes. On one level, however, these details' function and value as autonomous units are more apparent than their relation to the direct and larger questions we as readers might have about autocracy, anarchism, colonialism and Conrad's life. Indeed, there is no further reference to these details in their respective narratives so it is difficult (but not impossible) to see how they function in a larger context – and why they are not trivialities. "Yet this discursiveness is not so irrelevant to the handful of pages which follow" (17), Conrad writes in "A Familiar Preface" to *A Personal Record* (1912); with these words he seeks to excuse his penchant for digressions and forewarn about the nonlinear narratives that make up this attempt at autobiography – that is mainly an eclectic collection of observations on (a) his grand uncle Mr Nicholas B, (b) a Bali pony, (c) the physical characteristics of his writing pen, and (d) a diatribe against Rousseau.

Faced with this type of reading experience, where the descriptive details do not always seem to support the main structure, Conradian scholarship has two main options: (1) impose order on eclectic detail, or (2) explain the disorder (re-evaluate our idea of disorder). If we seek to explain the disorder – rather than explain it away – we should engage with the *mot juste*, an idea developed by Flaubert and frequently invoked by Conrad. This idea that every element of a text should be composed of an adequate word is potentially problematic. The result of the *mot juste* applied indiscriminately is a horizontal narrative, without a hierarchy of aesthetic importance. This implies that the reference to a dark blue silk sock in *The Secret Agent* is a detail articulated with as much care and patience as the details that make up Stevie's explosive end or Winnie's implied suicide; the author's focus is evenly distributed across the words, whether they describe "the gorgeous perambulator of a wealthy baby" (*SA* 24) or the explosive effects of the Professor's X2 green powder.

In other artistic media, this type of horizontal approach is not considered equally abnormal. Speaking about the paintings from Picasso's early period, John Loughery explains how

> a bare foot is rendered with the same gravity as a facial expression. The patchy sand of an empty fairground says as much about loss and exhaustion as the look in the eyes of the artist's saltimbanques. The wrinkles in the face of *The Old Fisherman* (1895) are as finely calculated as the lesbian kiss, or the position and body language of each dancer, in *Le Moulin de la Galette* (1900).[25]

By paying attention to all elements of a painting, Loughery is following in Morelli's tradition.

By looking at the margins of previous research and Conrad's texts, I wish to offer a new approach to reading Conrad in monograph-form: where the particularity of the reading experience is directly reflected in its scholarship. Phrased in relation to the current critical landscape, this can be seen as an experiment in what I want to call "distracted reading": a type of reading where you allow yourself to pay attention to all aspects of a text, regardless of their ranking as more or less important by secondary literature. This is similar to "surface reading," which, in its focus on what is "evident, perceptible, apprehensible," aims to "bypass the selectivity and evaluative energy that have been considered the hallmarks of good criticism."[26] The primary focus of my monograph is simply to write on what Conrad writes about. This is a surprisingly controversial idea since it means allowing the minute, independent and eclectic details of Conrad's prose to guide the critical enterprise. It is from this perspective that a descriptive list becomes a contentious argument, and why it is significant that there are more than 25 types of hats and more than 150 different species of animals in Conrad's fiction, more than 400 ellipses in *The Nigger of the 'Narcissus'*, and 109 doodles in the *Shadow-Line* manuscript. Apart from large segments of texts that have not been discussed in secondary literature, there are nonlinguistic texts – his drawings and doodles – that are in the position of being an untapped primary source; treated as a marginal and minor detail of Conrad's authorship. At times, however, these visual and verbal texts overlap in content, technique and existence: the doodles and the writings are created with the same paper and ink, by the same mind and pen, in the same time and space continuum. In addition, Conrad's doodles and drawings are of especial interest in his role as a writer of verbal impressionism.

In *Conrad and Impressionism* (2001), John G. Peters cautions "that any similarities between impressionist art and literature result from similarities in philosophy – not technique."[27] This distinction is tremendously useful for opening up the discussion about Conrad's impressionism to writings on philosophy. However, the distinction strategically downplays the possibility that philosophy and technique can overlap – in the same way that content and form overlap.

Philosophy is not necessarily an independent, autonomous activity that stands above art and explains it. A painting can be a manifesto. Seeing technique as indistinguishable from philosophy, I take a perspective more similar to that of the French art historian Henri Focillon (1881–1943):

> a work of art exists only insofar as it is form. In other words, a work of art is not the outline or the graph of art as an activity; it is art itself. It does not design art; it creates it. Art is made up, not of the artist's intentions, but of works of art. The most voluminous collection of commentaries and memoirs, written by artists whose understanding of the problems of form is fully equaled by their understanding of words, could never replace the meanest work of art.[28]

Details, Doodles, Drawings, Delayed Decodings

The nine chapters in this monograph explore situations where the marginal is in the center, when the reader, the text, Conrad or I prioritize the detail above the thematic, categorical, topical and conceptual. Meanwhile, the chapters embrace the idea that Conrad's authorship is unified by its eclecticism, like Stein's garden in *Lord Jim*, which lacks an overarching aesthetic purpose, or commitment to a bigger picture, but where "you can find every plant and tree of tropical lowlands" (263).

Partly from the belief that too much energy has been spent on investigating categories, the aim is not to define the marginal. Neither is the marginal used with the meaning it has gained in criticism today, most prominently to refer to minority literature. In my monograph, the marginal is more of a necessary misnomer – the marginal is of central importance for Conrad's authorship; the marginal is filled with revealing 'details' (itself a complicated term perhaps most fittingly investigated in a footnote).[29]

The central importance of the marginal for Conrad's philosophy, writing and working method is made clear by both his preprint documents and published texts. From doodles in the margin of the manuscript, to the granular texture of his writing style, to writings about marginal voices and characters, the marginal is ever-present. Chapter 1 consequently starts at the literal margin of Conrad's writing: the manuscript page. By discussing doodles, Chapter 1 deals with a paradigmatic marginal aspect of Conrad's writing that is telling about his working method. Although doodling is a break from putting words on the page, it is not necessarily a pause from writing, because the process includes reflection. This chapter explores the ways doodling and writing may have intertwined for Conrad, who – like his characters Blunt, Razumov and Stevie – doodled. By moving his doodles from the margins of the manuscript to the center of discussion, a visual portrait emerges of an artist for whom "procrastination" and productivity worked in delayed symbiosis.

Similarly, Chapter 2 gets close to the text by tracing it to its original handwritten beginnings. The chapter explores why there are symbolic depictions of space from above – maps of the fictional environment – in many of Conrad's manuscripts. While these maps have routinely been marginalized and classified as insignificant, I suggest that Conrad constructed and used hand-drawn maps as part of his creative writing process, as if he needed a map to navigate his own fictional world. Indeed, these maps share certain qualities with the navigational maps in

Conrad's "Up-river Book." Three of Conrad's manuscript maps are linked to passages in his fiction that contain factual mistakes; it is unclear whether the maps led him astray or whether he produced the maps because of the complicated geography. A few of the doodled maps were produced after the text, while other maps likely served as visual drafts or predetermined plans to be translated by the author into verbal form. The maps' existence can be attributed to more than attempts at understanding the coordinates of the fictional environment. Among twentieth-century writers, Conrad was one of the artists most involved with maps and charts, both in his literary and especially in his professional life. However, although Conrad needed maps to write, it is not apparent that we need them to read – unless we seek to better understand the genealogy of the text and the creative process.

Chapter 3 continues the exploration of Conrad's working method by investigating another so-called marginal detail of Conrad's authorship: his drawings. An author associated with verbal impressionism is expected to have had his drawings discussed at length, especially if they are produced with a technique that is characteristic of visual impressionism. This is not the case with Conrad. For example, Peters's monograph *Conrad and Impressionism* speaks exhaustively and competently about the Conradian connection between verbal and visual impressionism, without mentioning Conrad's own drawings. Still, many of Conrad's drawings demonstrate uncommon skill and sedulous effort; they are mainly drawn in the painterly technique, a method that is conceptually difficult and that defines visual impressionism. Conrad's drawing technique is, furthermore, similar to aspects of his writing style. The drawings, like his texts, demonstrate a capacity for describing things indirectly using "negative space," focusing on the background to illustrate the subject. This is significant since painting in a specific style is more than a question of manual dexterity – it reflects a way of seeing the world.

By dating two newly discovered Conrad drawings, Chapter 3 connects Conrad's unfinished novel about a painter – *The Sisters* – to his interest in drawing. *The Sisters* is a much more complicated fragment than hitherto acknowledged. It is not an anomalous product to be placed on the margins of Conrad scholarship. The text relates to contemporary debates, Conrad's life and many of his works, both visual and verbal. While the critical consensus critiques *The Sisters* for dealing with a subject matter Conrad was not intimately familiar with, Stephen's role as a painter aligns with the author's interests: Conrad pursued drawing as a pastime, took drawing lessons for several months, sketched one of *The Sisters*' characters

(Doña Rita), continued to mention visual art and painters in his books, and produced multiple drawings the year he started the unfinished story. Written during the advent of modern visual art, *The Sisters* is of further interest in its portrayal of Stephen as a modern artist. The metaphors on painting Conrad used in the Preface to *The Nigger of the 'Narcissus'* relate to this discussion: they contextualize and oppose Stephen's thoughts about what it means to be an artist, and delimit the extent to which Conrad embraced all notions of modernity and the so-called end of art.

The next section goes beyond the manuscript and preprint documents toward the published texts, for a more philosophical understanding of how Conrad's fiction is linked to the marginal. Chapter 4 investigates a foundational concept of Conrad studies: delayed decoding. In its focus on fleeting sensory data, delayed decoding, like Conrad's painterly drawings, is connected to verbal impressionism. I also see delayed decoding as a major argument for the importance of the minor and marginal details of Conrad's prose. Chapter 4 connects Conrad's narrative strategy of delayed decoding with Bertrand Russell's concept of logical atomism, and argues why and how delayed decoding is Conrad's attempt to unbundle concepts – an important reason for why Conrad pays so much attention to detail. In my reading, delayed decoding gradually describes the quasi-atomic ingredients of a sensory experience rather than trying to distill the sensory experience, in its final rationalized shape, with one word or sentence. To this extent, delayed decoding feeds into the understanding of Conrad as the literary equivalent of a visual impressionist: he is concerned with pictorial, private, and phenomenological reality – not conceptualized, symbolic, and figurative reality. The chapter connects Conrad's delayed decoding with Russell's logical atomism, arguing that what the latter sought to do for philosophy, the former attempted to do in literature. Both delayed decoding and logical atomism communicate elementary sense-impressions; they construct a truth hierarchy where the particular is above the abstract. The chapter analyses how the language use of each concept corresponds to a host of assumptions about how we experience reality and what constitutes truth, assumptions that aid in explaining their extraordinary friendship (and why this monograph avoids large categories).

The chapter continues by more explicitly calling into question Ian Watt's concept of delayed decoding using my category, "delayed miscoding." The chapter contains a lengthy demonstration showing that the most quoted example used to illustrate this hallmark of Conrad scholarship is inconsistent. The need for such an exhaustive discussion on one example is motivated by the wide acceptance of Watt's theory of delayed decoding, a term most completely spelled out in *Conrad in the Nineteenth Century* (1979) and referenced in most introductory texts on Conrad. My reading is not an attempt to discard Watt's delayed decoding but an attempt to show that there is a discrepancy between what it names and what it explains. Delayed decoding's binary structure and bivalent logic are limited ways for analyzing a text that is paradigmatically ambiguous.

Watt's aforementioned monograph, *Conrad in the Nineteenth Century*, followed his magisterial opus *The Rise of the Novel: Studies in Defoe, Richardson and Fielding* (1957), which outlines the distinctive ways in which the novel differs from earlier literary forms. Contrary to the preceding literary tradition, the novel places a marked emphasis on the particulars of experience and the immediate facts of consciousness. In this, the novel, a modern invention, mirrors the anti-Platonic truth hierarchy of the modern philosophy of Descartes, Locke, Berkeley, Thomas Reid and others. In many ways, Conrad, who is not part of the discussion in *The Rise of the Novel*, represents the culmination of the novelistic form with his detail-rich technique of delayed decoding and its focus on the particulars of immediate experience. Conrad's connection to logical positivism is of course limited; a mechanistic, formulaic, scientific worldview that assigns truth to elementary sense-impressions cannot fully explain his imaginative authorship. Neither can logical positivism, with its focus on sense-impressions as the ultimate form of truth, be seen to dictate the form of the novel. This element of Conrad's writing technique is not really a dominant, guiding principle, but more of a defiant approach to the literary tradition. For example, Conrad's writing challenges the literary conventions of his time by demonstrating an affinity with modern philosophy in more ways than one. Thus, multiple statements unwittingly illustrate David Hume's rejection of cause-and-effect; in *The Secret Agent* a constable surges out of a lamp-post, a face rises out from a collar, a carriage crawls behind an infirm horse, a cat issues "from under the stones" (17), houses glide past "slowly and shakily" (121). With a title that hints at causation – *The Secret Agent* – its characters act independently.

Alfred North Whitehead, the British mathematician and American philosopher, famously described Western philosophy to be a series of footnotes to Platonism. With the advent of modern philosophy, Platonism can be said to have become a footnote to philosophy. During this marked change, the hierarchy of knowledge was turned upside down and suddenly the transient, changing and temporary was given the status of "true."[30] Modernism, in all its parallel manifestations, took this seriously – yet it is still easy to disregard a discussion on transient, changing and temporary details as one about trivialities rather than one of fundamental truth. Still, as Watt observes in *The Rise of the Novel*, "the novel's realism does not reside in the kind of life it presents, but in the way it presents it."[31] From this perspective, the description of a round hat in *The Secret Agent* can theoretically be more revealing of Conrad's ideas of truth than the engagement with the views of the Professor of philosophy in "The Planter of Malata" (1914).

Placing Conrad in this modern era, defined by its defiant attitude to established tradition and order, Chapter 5 takes the "trivialities" of Conrad's texts seriously. The chapter moves away from logical positivism and proposes that his detail-rich technique can also (and perhaps more aptly) be understood as a product of willful distraction; itself a clear digression from traditional narrative form. Conrad eloquently wrote about his inability to write; he stuttered his way through his texts with nonlexical grunts, snarls, howls, murmurs, gurgles, snorts and hems; and he sought to stay true to "the stammerings of his conscience" (xliii), a working method alluded to in the Preface of *The Nigger of the 'Narcissus'*. In Chapter 5, I argue that distraction – usually a writer's enemy – is another one of these unexpected features that Conrad used to propel his writing; his seemingly rambling digressions are part of a quest for verbal precision. Although he is frequently conceived of as a methodical and philosophical writer, distraction was a fundamental and serious part of his literary enterprise. By allowing distraction, inattentiveness and absentmindedness to become part of his fiction he was able to stay productive, steal the reader's attention and add a level of everyday realism to his texts. Conrad, I maintain, writes *in medias distractionis* and consistently pays attention to those who do not pay attention.

Chapter 6 approaches marginality and distraction as ways to structure a novel. Unlike previous readings of *The Secret Agent*, which have structured this novel around an overarching theme or argument (anarchism, terrorism, time, place and so on), Chapter 6 explores the unity of this novel from the perspective of its scattered and eclectic details. By looking at the scattered details for structure, the aim is to explore the way this novel is knitted in an overlapping pattern of interweaving sequences and temporal criss-crossings. Put differently, there are multiple links and connections across the chapters beyond the march of time. In my reading, *The Secret Agent* is not a sustained discussion of one topic, but a manifesto of marginality or manifest marginality: a novel written in the margins.

The next section in the monograph moves from a fairly abstract discussion of technique – delayed decoding, delayed miscoding, *in medias distractionis* – to detailed examples. If you will, the monograph takes Conrad's distraction to heart and allows itself to become distracted by specific examples, from hats to bats. These last three chapters are case studies in marginality. They explore marginal voices and characters.

Chapter 7 explores voices at the margin of society in *The Nigger of the 'Narcissus'*. To the extent this novel on seafaring is autobiographical, it also explores Conrad himself as a marginal subject. The novel is one of the most sympathetic portrayals of a class of people frequently considered to be marginal: a multinational group of physical laborers paid a meager wage, living in harsh and deadly conditions, executing their menial jobs heroically (with notable exceptions). To move from the margin to the center, take up the pen and write a compelling story about this life for the middle-class literary establishment – first published in the conservative W. E. Henley's *The New Review* – is the part of Conrad's achievement I focus on in this chapter. The chapter explores how Conrad makes his readers listen to the voice of the sailors, reflect on the value of their work, and appreciate the importance of seemingly menial, physical labor – like the heroism of serving coffee, which the novel discusses.

The next chapter considers another set of marginal characters of topmost importance: hats. The insouciant exploration of merchant sailors alongside hats as marginal characters is not made to equate the two, but to highlight a distinct aspect of Conrad's writing technique: his persistent and radical focus on the marginal. Like the chapter on Conrad's marginalia and doodles, the marginality of hat study is all too apparent; it smacks of esoteric trivia. In Chapter 8 I argue that such a commonsensical assumption is at odds with Conrad's fictional hats: their variety, number and position in the texts. Indeed, even though abundant secondary literature demonstrates that one can write on Conrad without writing on hats, Conrad himself did not seem able to write without including a full range of hats: from the bowler to the Bersagliere, there are more than twenty-five types of hat in his fiction. They are used for fiddling, collecting nails, catching butterflies, transporting cakes, holding strips of beef, carrying secret messages, and saving a "homeless head from the dangers of the sun" (*SS* 118). Conrad leaves us with the idea that while we may think that we wear hats, hats are clothed in meaning and may even wear us; there is no clear boundary between object and person; an everyday material object can be a key to understanding a complex individual and vice versa.

Exploring another crowning achievement of Conrad's literary enterprise, Chapter 9 argues that whereas individual references to nonhuman animals are frequently marginal within one specific text, the accumulation of these references forms a vast, unexplored textual segment: I have counted more than 150 different species of animal in his texts, ranging from the albatross to the yearling. Regardless of whether this is a high, low or average number of animals in an author's corpus, there is sufficient biodiversity in Conrad's fiction to deserve investigation. One hundred and fifty, as it happens, is Dunbar's Number, a suggested number of individuals by which a primate can maintain a social relationship – knowing both who each individual of the group is and how they relate to every other individual in the group. Guided by this cognitive limit, we will give these animals central attention. Enlarging a marginal element, this first comprehensive study of Conradian fauna redirects our gaze toward what has been considered unimportant. The result is a closer look at animal metaphors that invite reflection on human–animal relations, and demonstrate that an author can write attentively, sympathetically and thoughtfully on animals, despite primarily mentioning them in metaphors.

Conrad's animal metaphors are structured as idiomatic clichés, but appear to be Conradese – and serve to create what I designate as an "unreality effect." While the Barthesian reality effect advances the idea of superfluous detail in a text – a type of filler that only serves to say "*we are the real*"[32] – the unreality effect, which I argue unites Conrad's unconventional animal metaphors, has the opposite purpose: it confronts the reader to question the reality of the fictional construct. The unconventional sayings that produce this unreality effect all say: we have the appearance of a marginal, incidental detail but we are one of the most complicated structures in the text.

Taken together, the nine chapters move from an exploration of a so-called detail of Conrad scholarship – Conrad's doodles and drawings – to a discussion about why Conrad is a writer of detail – delayed decoding, delayed miscoding, timely distraction – to an investigation of specific details. Put differently, the monograph's wide-ranging chapters – on Conrad's philosophy of language, doodled manuscripts, and published texts – present layered evidence for the major significance of details and margins for Conrad's writing. If the ideas in this monograph are convincing, however, you will rightly call me out on the fact that "detail," "margins" and "marginality" are misnomers: inappropriate terms for dealing with significant elements of Conrad's authorship.

PART I

Preprint Documents

Paper, Pen and Ink

CHAPTER I

Doodles and The Shadow-Line

> Pardon the blot. This damnable pen.
>
> Letter

> [Marlow:] look at the ink blot resembling the head of an arrow under these words . . . The pen had spluttered, and that time he gave it up.
>
> *Lord Jim*

> [George:] The ink was thick, pale, and sticky; the pen spluttered. I wrote furiously, anxious to be done with it.
>
> *The Inheritors*

> 'Can't write?' said the clerk, shocked. 'Make a mark, then.' Singleton painfully sketched in a heavy cross, blotted the page. 'What a disgusting old brute,' muttered the clerk.
>
> *The Nigger of the 'Narcissus'*

In that rare thing, an essay on doodles, Matthew Battles argues that literary researchers operate with the belief that "if a doodle has anything to tell us about the creative work of its author then it isn't a doodle."[1] If one accepts this belief as a valid premise, discussing Conrad's doodles becomes a vain attempt to reach for originality by engaging with the insignificant. Indeed, doodles are presumably disregarded by scholars on reasonable grounds: they differ in form and intention from the verbal text; they represent a break from the creative process – a product of absentmindedness, like the wringing of thumbs characteristic of certain Conradian characters. In this reading, Conrad's many doodles are not of more literary significance than the cigarette stains in the manuscripts of *The Shadow-Line, Nostromo*, and *The Secret Agent* or the bread pellets that occasionally went flying at his dinner table.[2]

Yet Conrad's wife/occasional typist stresses that his doodled manuscripts are "valuable," as if they reveal something integral about his mind or modus operandi: "Some of the early fragments of his manuscripts would be valuable to-day. I do not refer to the complete ones, bought by

Mr. John Quinn, but to the greatly treasured fragments bearing on their wide margins some queer little sketches of human faces, allegorical designs, coiled ropes, anchors, and capstans."[3] These fragments have not been identified, but the visual appearance of the *Shadow-Line* manuscript testifies to Conrad's practice of sketching in the margins. Regarding *The Shadow-Line*, Conrad himself wrote to John Quinn: "From a literary point of view it will be curious for critics to compare my dictated to my written manner of expressing myself" (*CL* IX.543).

Despite these invitations to examine Conrad's marginalia and the *Shadow-Line* manuscript, its unofficial decoration of 109 doodles has been left as an untapped primary source, unpublished and unexplored. The Oxford edition, by Jeremy Hawthorn, and the Penguin edition, edited by Jacques Berthoud, discuss the variance between the text of the printed edition and the manuscript; they do not mention the doodles. With over 200 pages of critical commentary, the 2013 Cambridge edition, with explanatory notes by Owen Knowles, devotes three sentences to the doodles. Among Conrad connoisseurs, this minimal attention to doodles extends into epistolary research. In his overview of 3,500 letters, Frederick Karl excludes the doodles from discussion since they "are of minimal interest" (*CL* I.xlvi). Indeed, Battles observes that "bibliographers, who have learned to count and classify the meaningful marks of authors, printers, readers, and redactors, largely pass over the doodle in silence."[4]

The assumption is that doodles are insignificant and separated from the text. For *The Shadow-Line*, this intuitive, categorical and unexamined assumption is problematic. As I will show, there is a connection between the story, its dedication to Conrad's son Borys, and the eight upper-case 'B's in the manuscript. Indeed, the surprising and revolutionary claim would be that the story and its doodles were created with the same paper and ink, by the same mind and pen, in the same time and space continuum, but stood unconnected to one another – created by a divided self under diametrically different rubrics of relevance. We therefore have to shift the burden of explanation and ask not whether *The Shadow-Line* and its doodles are connected in any significant way, but how.

Regarding *The Shadow-Line*, the doodles demonstrate how intimately connected the writer was to the story's meditation on impatience and inaction. Partly autobiographical, concerning the transition from youth to adulthood and a captain's first command of a sailing vessel, *The Shadow-Line* records the twenty-one-day challenge of hesitant progress: wind, propulsion, thought, sleep and time halt; disease reigns. By reading the doodles in *The Shadow-Line* (see Figure 1.1) in this context of stagnation

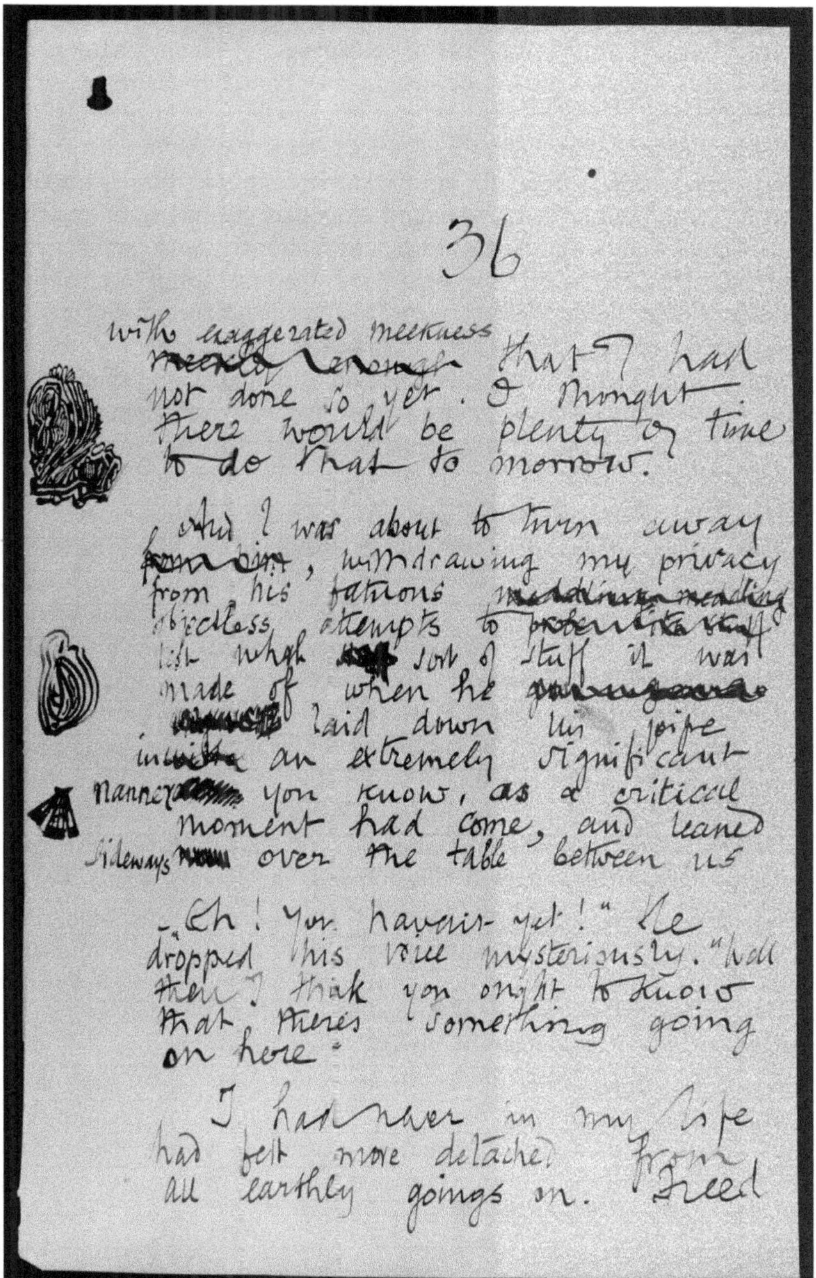
36

with exaggerated meekness
that I had
not done so yet. I thought
there would be plenty of time
to do that to-morrow.

And I was about to turn away
, withdrawing my privacy
from his fatuous
objectless attempts to
which sort of stuff it was
made of when he
laid down his pipe
in an extremely significant
manner you know, as a critical
moment had come, and leaned
sideways over the table between us

"Eh! You haven't yet!" He
dropped his voice mysteriously. "Well
then I think you ought to know
that there's something going
on here."

I had never in my life
had felt more detached from
all earthly goings on. Freed

Figure 1.1 *The Shadow-Line*, holograph manuscript, page 36. Beinecke Rare Book Room and Manuscript Library, Yale University.

and as an element of his writing, I hope to show that, like Kurtz's marginal comment in his writing on colonial expansion – "Exterminate all the brutes!" (95) – what exists at the margin may be highly telling about the central message.

Battles's general understanding of doodles as art – "Preliterate, primordial, the doodle is at once the most common and the most ignored art form"[5] – is at odds with the standard dictionary definition. A doodle is there defined as a rough drawing, made idly, carelessly, or absentmindedly. Etymologically, the word is rooted in a German noun for "a fool" (*Dudeltopf*) and in the English verb "to dawdle." Today, and on the shoulders of the vast literature of self-styled handwriting experts, the doodle is associated with the subconscious. Although Freud doodled, he never wrote about doodling, and no study has ascertained whether doodling is connected to the subconscious, a concept that itself is elusive and empirically unverifiable.

The status of doodles as the product of Freudian fidgeting relates to William James's empirical research on the stream of consciousness, where constant, unfettered writing is code for the ever-present consciousness. The focus there, however, is on consciousness as a unified stream, without gaps for absentmindedness. Indeed, empirical research has continued to reject the everyday assumptions about doodling as an absentminded activity.[6] It is, then, unsurprising that many of the small drawings we encounter in *The Shadow-Line* contradict the commonplace assumptions about doodling. Since Conrad's intentions behind his creation of drawn marginalia are unknown, we cannot with certainty classify them as senseless scribbles. Although the etymological parentage of the English word 'doodling' would insist on this classification, the French *gribouiller*, the Polish *gryzmoli* and the German *kritzeln* translate into scribble rather than dawdle or simpleton. Conrad's (marginal?) languages, then, do not accept all the negative associations of 'doodling' on which English insists. For lack of a better English word, I shall describe Conrad's marginalia as doodles throughout, but I do so without assumptions about whether they were produced (a) absentmindedly or (b) subconsciously or (c) can all be classified under one identity.

To categorize them under one label is difficult, partly due to their number. Occurring more than a hundred times in *The Shadow-Line*, the monochromatic and indelible doodles form a visually central paratext at the margins of its holograph's rectos, materializing as persistently as Ransome's servings of coffee in the story. The 187 pages of *The Shadow-Line*'s holograph have an average of 0.6 doodles a page, most of them highly detailed in nature. It is tempting to speculate on the time that was put into their production, and on how Conrad divided his time between writing and doodling (or question whether these activities are necessarily distinct).

First, let us get a sense of the doodles' visual presence in the manuscript. In common with those in his other manuscripts, the doodles in *The Shadow-Line* are compact; every line of the doodle is connected to the rest, as if the pen that created it did so *al primo*, in one motion, without leaving the paper. The doodles often appear in a set, and a couple of the doodles form a narrative where they build upon one another. Certain consecutive doodles show such continuity that if you were to cut them out from their pages, an impartial observer could arrange them in approximate succession, similar to their original placing. Candidates for this experiment could be the circular doodles on the pages numbered 105, 154, 158 (see Figure 1.2), 165 and 185, or the doodles of squares on pages 91, 105 and 152. Development can also be seen in Conrad's many illustrated 'B's in the margin of the manuscript on pages 7, 84, 90, 150, 155, 181 and 187. These are not mere letters, but doodled drawings that recall a letter Doña Rita sent to Monsieur George, "signed with an enormous, flourished exuberant R" (*AG* 339). In general, as the page numbers increase, so do the frequency, density, and complexity of the doodles. The 'B's are part of this generalization, but looked upon as an independent chain, apart from the other doodles, they decrease in detail as the page number increases.

It is difficult to say whether there is a pattern that unites Conrad's doodles. Whereas one can always uncover patterns of no importance, by, say, incessantly studying a list of a lottery's winning numbers – as Massy does in *The End of the Tether* (1902) – doodling is not a random process. There is a logic/consistency in Stevie's doodling in *The Secret Agent*. By strictly drawing circles, Stevie follows a strict geometric logic. His circles in turn are created and limited in their eccentricity by his painting tool: a compass. Similarly, Razumov in *Under Western Eyes* exclusively draws squares and triangles. Conrad's doodles are, however, not limited to one geometric shape, though like Razumov's and Stevie's drawings they are mainly abstract. Although about 7 percent of Conrad's doodles in the *Shadow-Line* manuscript are calligraphic, they are not mimetic in a strict sense. Many of his other doodled manuscripts, including the ones of *An Outcast of the Islands*, *The Secret Agent*, *Lord Jim*, *Nostromo* and *Almayer's Folly*, contain mimetic sketches of real-life objects: flowers, boats, maps, animals and feathers. The typical Conradian doodle in *The Shadow-Line* is abstract.

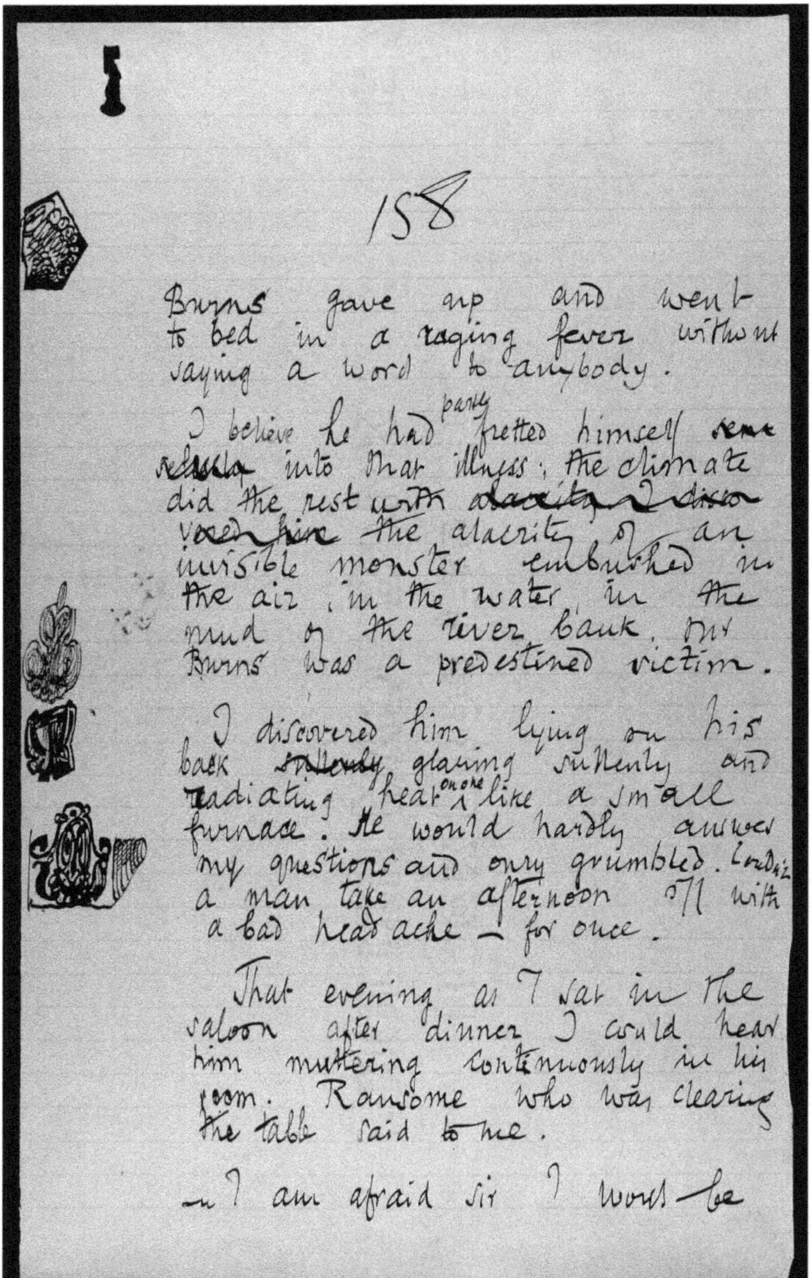

158

Burns gave up and went to bed in a raging fever without saying a word to anybody.

I believe he had partly fretted himself into that illness; the climate did the rest the alacrity of an invisible monster ambushed in the air, in the water, in the mud of the river bank. Mr Burns was a predestined victim.

I discovered him lying on his back glaring sullenly and radiating heat on one like a small furnace. He would hardly answer my questions and only grumbled. Couldn't a man take an afternoon off with a bad headache — for once.

That evening as I sat in the saloon after dinner I could hear him muttering continuously in his room. Ransome who was clearing the table said to me.

— "I am afraid sir I won't be

Figure 1.2 *The Shadow-Line*, holograph manuscript, page 158. Beinecke Rare Book Room and Manuscript Library, Yale University.

Do these doodles communicate something beyond their mere image? The eight 'B's in the manuscript hint at Conrad's connection to Borys during the writing of the story. The story itself is, in part, dedicated to Borys, and in Conrad's letters, written during his work on the manuscript, he frequently refers to Borys with a 'B'. Analogously, when Captain Blunt of *The Arrow of Gold* (1919) uses his forefinger to doodle an upper-case 'R' in the pipe ash and spilt wine, his mind is occupied by Doña Rita (occasionally referred to as 'R' in the text). That said, to read the eight 'B's in the manuscript of *The Shadow-Line* as code for Borys, while no doubt of critical importance, should not be at the expense of reducing calligraphic drawings to letters. (There are also 'B's in "Amy Foster," *Nostromo* and *The Secret Agent*: stories that are difficult to connect with Borys.)

In an otherwise very subtle essay on the "six dozen" 'K's in a manuscript of *Under Western Eyes*, and how these 'K's demonstrate personal involvement in the story, David Smith speculates that the doodles refer directly to Kirylo Sidorovitch Razumov.[7] In this reading, all doodled 'K's – no matter how disparate in visual complexity – have one meaning. This literal reading is problematic since there is an abundance of 'K's in multiple manuscripts without a Razumov – *Almayer's Folly, Lord Jim, Nostromo*, "The Warrior's Soul," *The Shadow-Line* and *The Secret Agent.*

Since Conrad's doodles show similarity in shape across different manuscripts belonging to different stories, the visual shapes of the doodles are unlikely to relate to the structure of the specific story they accompany. There are, for example, doodled letters in squares in manuscripts belonging to *Nostromo, Under Western Eyes, The Secret Agent* and *The Shadow-Line*. What is unique for *The Shadow-Line* is its high number of doodles, unparalleled in any other preserved manuscript. (A contender for second place on this list of most doodled manuscripts is "The Warrior's Soul," counting thirty-nine doodles in fifty-seven pages of manuscript and finished a year before *The Shadow-Line* reached publication.) Let us now focus on the mere fact of the existence of 109 doodles in the *Shadow-Line* holograph. There are many competing ways to account for the aggregate existence of these doodles. By a process of exclusion, I will now approach the idea that the doodles were part of the writing process.

The Shadow-Line was written under peculiar circumstances. At the time of composition, Conrad's letters complain of a gouty right wrist. After the completion of the story, he catches up on letter writing. In the opening lines, he excuses the delay on the basis of his wrist. During the ten months he spent writing the story, he complained about this wrist in letters to Hugh Clifford, Richard Curle, John Galsworthy, André Gide, Violet

Hunt, Jack London, W. M. Parker, J. B. Pinker, Arthur Symons, Harriet Mary Capes, John Quinn, and E. L. and Helen Sanderson. In one letter he notes that the pain caused by the gout was inconstant and came in waves: "My gout got into my wrists and gave me but short respites. These were occupied in writing MS of course" (*CL* v.543). He was composing *The Shadow-Line* in a state of unpredictable pain, marked with occasional pain-free moments. Do the doodles testify to this pain? Were they produced when, due to the pain, he could not muster the energy to write? Frederick Karl observes that "when Conrad suffered from severe gout, he grasped in his fist an oversized pencil."[8] However, doodling and writing both require similar hand movements and gout is worsened by movement, not reduced.

Paul Eggert suggests that the doodles in *Under Western Eyes* may partly have arisen due to "the need to clear a clogged nib as Conrad wrote."[9] It is not implausible that Conrad at times doodled to clear the nib (working perhaps with "some sloppy, inky quill pens," *N* 237), but this should not be overemphasized. The doodles in the holograph of "Amy Foster" (1901) demonstrate that when Conrad wrote in pencil and had no nib to clear, he still doodled. There is also likely to be one efficient way of clearing the nib, yet Conrad's doodles display variety. For instance, the page numbered 36 in the manuscript of *The Shadow-Line* has three doodles that are very different in shape (see Figure 1.1).

Ian Watt considers the doodles in the margins of *Almayer's Folly* to be proof of Conrad's distraction, and Owen Knowles classifies the doodles in *The Shadow-Line* as "a pause in composition."[10] These explanations are intuitive and in agreement with the standard definition of doodling, an unproductive act of absentmindedness. Yet the claims feed into the conception that every word written is progress, and that the time spent in the writing studio not plotting words on the paper is a distraction or pause from work. The conception is misguided since it conflates the final product (the words on the page) with the production process, thereby excluding reflection that is not immediately concurrent and overlapping with the written text. Yet when the Marlow of *Lord Jim* ceases to write – "when the scratching of my pen stopped for a moment" (123) – thought does not come to a standstill, but forces itself upon him, albeit in an unproductive form: "I suffered from that profound disturbance and confusion of thought which is caused by a violent and mechanic uproar" (123). And after Jukes in *Typhoon* momentarily finds himself with an "arrested pen" (19), thought is alive: "He paused, and thought to himself" (20). Similarly, Cosmo in *Suspense* "dropped his pen and thought" (131).

For Conrad, the equation between progress made and words produced is disproved by his own working method, which involved prewritten reflection. In "Books," he classifies the novelist as a worker in the "fields of thought" (12). Many of his letters stress that he had a mental picture of the story before he wrote it down or that a large part of writing was about translating a mind-image into words. "It's an old subject," he writes about *The Shadow-Line*, "I have carried it in my head for years under the name of First Command" (*CL* v.441). The first preserved letter that mentions *First Command* is dated February 14, 1899 – the year when the first edition of *Heart of Darkness* appeared, fifteen years before *The Shadow-Line* made it into manuscript form.

Although doodling is a break from putting words on the page, it is not necessarily a pause from writing, a process that includes reflection. Put differently, plotting words on the page can itself be an act of procrastination and a break from writing. When Callan in *The Inheritors* produces journalistic pieces at a fast pace without giving his own thoughts room on the page, he is procrastinating about his higher artistic ambition of being a writer of note. Indeed, employing the pen is not the same as writing any more than playing music can be equated with picking up an instrument: Mr Burns in *The Shadow-Line* explains that his former captain was not playing the violin but "made continuous noise" (52). And in *Victory*, "The Zangiacomo band was not making music; it was simply murdering silence with a vulgar, ferocious energy" (55). So if Conrad's artistic allegiance was to creativity and reflection, merely jotting words on the page without reflecting would have formed an act of procrastination regarding his definition of writing – resulting in a state where "Pages accumulate and the story stands still" (*CL* II.83).

As if Conrad's artistic goal lay beyond mere quill driving, a marginal note to himself on a manuscript page of *Nostromo* places a notable space between "I will write" (written four times in close succession) and "very well" (written three times). In Conrad's fiction, doodling is not directly or exclusively associated with distraction or absentmindedness. Instead, throughout his imaginative writing reflection appears as the common denominator. Apart from the introductory note about how Captain Blunt thinks about Doña Rita as he doodles an 'R', there is reflection in the act of Stevie's and Razumov's doodling. When Razumov in *Under Western Eyes* is in the process of producing an "aimless drawing of triangles and squares" (42), he has an epiphany: "And suddenly he thought: 'My behaviour must appear to him strange. Should he take fright at my manner and rush off somewhere I shall be undone completely'" (42).

There is also the case of Stevie's doodling in *The Secret Agent*, which in its intensity seems to exclude any external reflection that is not related to the actual drawing at hand. Stevie sits at the table and draws "circles, circles, circles; innumerable circles, concentric, eccentric; a coruscating whirl of circles that by their tangled multitude of repeated curves, uniformity of form, and confusion of intersecting lines suggested a rendering of cosmic chaos, the symbolism of a mad art attempting the inconceivable" (40). It is with full intensity that he devotes himself to doodling (and illustrates the inadequacy of the word "doodling" to account for small drawings produced with focus and interest): "The artist never turned his head; and in all his soul's application to the task his back quivered, his thin neck, sunk into a deep hollow at the base of the skull, seemed ready to snap" (40). This intense level of concentration, like an overfilled boiler approaching a violent explosion, foreshadows Stevie's fragmented final form. Oddly, Stevie – the passive, domestic animal – becomes an agent of change as the X2 green powder detonates prematurely. His doodling is therefore a marginal action invested with symbolic significance and of central importance for the novel as a whole. On the assumption that Conrad would not leave a significant detail unmeditated, the association between doodling and reflection is significant.

The variation in detail and intensity of Conrad's own doodles indicates that he identified with Blunt's, Razumov's, and Stevie's doodling practices; at times, Conrad may have put his soul and all of his reflection into the doodling effort. As I shall contend, even when doodling appears to be a break from writing, it was likely to be part of Conrad's creative process.

When writing, Conrad frequently played chess with his two sons. He would play a couple of moves, then write a couple of words, then make a further move, and so on. At first sight, it appears that Conrad played chess to procrastinate, just as the captain in *The Shadow-Line* shirks his duty by playing the violin. But his son John argues that this activity was not a break from the creative process: "I realised fairly soon that the mental effort of playing chess helped my father to realign his thoughts so as to overcome an 'impasse' for the arrangement of words or the construction of a phrase to convey some subtle meaning."[11] If all intermittent writing breaks are created equal, doodling would have fulfilled a similar function.

At first glance, doodling appears to be at odds with the content of *The Shadow-Line*. The delicate and dainty doodles contrast with the notion of the sea as a test of manliness. The story's praise of fidelity, duty and work commitment contrasts with the doodles in the margins of its manuscript – creations that people associate with the activity of uncommitted schoolboys. Yet the doodles' difference from the text may be the link to the text: a response.

Looking for similarity between doodling and the text, we can observe that doodling is associated with boredom, impatience and procrastination, experiences that correspond to the sentiment aboard the stagnant ship on *The Shadow-Line* and its narrating captain's accurate premonition, "as if a sort of composite soul, the soul of command, had whispered suddenly to mine of long days at sea and of anxious moments. 'You, too!' it seemed to say, 'you, too, shall taste of that peace and that unrest in a searching intimacy with your own self'" (53). These experiences of inaction were also essential to Conrad's productivity and success as a writer. John Batchelor has suggested how Conrad was able to write about his inability to write. For Batchelor, Conrad's method of work comes close to what has later been termed "positive procrastination" or "structured procrastination": the tendency to get a lot done by doing what one is not supposed to do. To produce his best work, Conrad needed obligations that he would habitually fail to fulfill: he "needed to disobey the secure, responsible people in his life who believed in obligation, contracts, and money in the bank, and to strike defiant, heroic, and romantic attitudes."[12] Unlike Captain Hagberd in "To-morrow," then, Conrad is active and productive when he tells himself that he will do something the next day.

"[T]he more perfect the artist," T. S. Eliot writes in "Tradition and the Individual Talent," "the more completely separated in him will be the man who suffers and the mind which creates."[13] According to Batchelor, Conrad succeeded in "splitting off the mind which suffers from the mind which creates";[14] his relatively persistent fears about writing blocks, unproductiveness, inadequacy and inability were channeled into his prose. Batchelor spells out the counterintuitive fact: "The remarkable thing is that Conrad can write all this down"[15]: he can reflect verbally on his writing blocks (I "rang the bell violently, or perhaps I should say resolutely, or perhaps I should say eagerly, I do not know," *PR* 70). In short, Conrad's prose production rested on a dialectic that shifted between requirement, obligation and truancy – a situation echoed in the interplay between doodles and words in the *Shadow-Line* manuscript.

This working method can also be seen in the ship's and narrator's struggle with propulsion, which many have read as an analogy to Conrad's struggle with writing. The idea is that Conrad's creativity and production were not linear, advancing predictably like a steamship, but came in stochastic bursts, like the wind on the sailing vessel in the story. This analogy is imperfect: the story continues despite the wind. Or, the wind that carries Conrad's prose forward could be his experience of a writing block. Doodling can, then, be constructed as an engagement with, or reflection on, inaction. And of course, as many have pointed out, the apex of action in *The Shadow-Line* orbits around inaction.

It is also tempting to search for a close connection between the text and the doodles, by comparing their placement in the manuscript with the adjacent text: its structure, form or theme. For example, the 'B's in the manuscript could be close to passages that have a direct relationship to Conrad's concern about Borys's present occupations and his crossing of the shadow-line in the First World War. The assumption here is that the doodle would be adjacent in space and time to the passage it decorates. But we have no evidence that the doodles were produced next to the passages on which Conrad was working. Many doodles tend to be placed at the very bottom of the page, as if he preferred this space for doodling. Eggert comes to a similar conclusion about the structure of the holograph of *Under Western Eyes*: "As the Ks are usually in the same position (around the mid-point of the left-hand margin, often at the extreme edge of the sheet rather than against the text), they are unlikely to be a symbol for passages to which Conrad needed to return."[16] If the doodles constitute a reflective aspect of writing, the outcome of this reflection may come as the story progresses – or be seen in the overall quality of the story, rather than in individual passages. Since Conrad frequently spoke about his stories as monolithic wholes – hyperreal mind-images that were clear and lucid to his understanding – it does not follow that his reflection was about a certain detail, word or passage.

"The close, neat, regular handwriting was not attractive . . . it was a dull-faced MS, each line resembling every other line, in their close-set and regular order. It was like the drone of a monotonous voice" (110), an unnamed narrator exclaims in "The Inn of Two Witches." To get a full sense of how dull the appearance of this manuscript is, and what he had to overcome to read it, he specifies: "A treatise on sugar-refining (the dreariest subject I can think of) could have been given a more lively appearance" (110). In accordance with their verbal content, Conrad's manuscripts are, in contrast, lively and interesting: doodled and blotted (see Figures 1.1 and 1.2). To the question asked in *A Personal Record*, "Would it bore you very much in reading a MS. in a handwriting like mine?" (28), the answer is no – for more than one reason.

By being nonverbal, Conrad's doodles have independence and break the equation between writing and plotting words on the page: they form visual evidence for why doodling and writing intertwine in productive ways.

They demonstrate how stagnation was not only part of *The Shadow-Line*'s content, but also, as his letters testify, part of his experience in writing the story. Given Conrad's unique relationship to writing – expressed once as "I don't care for writing at all. What interests me is creative work" (*CL* VIII.338) – the doodles are important. They complicate our understanding of Conrad's writing process so that progress and procrastination overlap: they hint at the extent to which Conrad was true "to the stammerings of his conscience and to the outspoken consciousness of the difficulties of his work" (xi), as he maintains in the Preface to *The Nigger of the 'Narcissus'*. It is therefore not a mistaken ambition to move the doodles from the margins of the manuscript to the center of discussion, where not only Blunt, Razumov and Stevie are recognized as doodlers, but also Conrad himself.

CHAPTER 2

Maps and Victory, *"Geography and Some Explorers," "The Secret Sharer" and* An Outcast of the Islands

> "I just saved it by proficiency in map-drawing. It must have been good, I suppose."
>
> "Geography and Some Explorers"

Speaking about Conrad's maritime career and how this offered almost daily engagement with maps and charts, Robert Hampson's article "'A Passion for Maps': Conrad, Africa, Australia, and South-East Asia" concludes by noting that Conrad "probably was more involved with maps and mapping than any other major nineteenth- or twentieth-century British novelist," an involvement that "leaves its mark on his fiction."[1] No less daring in its claims, Florence Clemens's essay "Joseph Conrad as a Geographer" argues that there are clear parallels between land described on official Malaysian maps and land described in Conrad's texts. "No one writing on the Indies," Clemens declares, "has possessed a more sensitive and receptive mind, a mind of more photographic accuracy."[2] The maps of real places included in the Cambridge, Oxford and Penguin editions of Conrad's work testify to similar beliefs, on behalf of the editors, in the dependence of Conrad's fiction on maps. On multiple occasions, scholars and editors have even attempted to map the geography of *Nostromo*, the only one of Conrad's novels "whose action takes place in an imagined country."[3]

Conradian scholars, editors and Conrad himself have, then, shown a fascination for maps. This fascination is further motivated by the recent emergence of "critical cartography," which demonstrates that maps are a type of text open for readings.[4] With the aim to contribute and expand on this cartographic research, this chapter will look at Conrad's own maps, many of which have been neither discussed nor reproduced, until now.[5] On the few occasions when scholars have briefly mentioned a hand-drawn map in the margin of a manuscript or in a letter, they have primarily labeled it as a doodle, sketch or "conjectured plan."[6] Maps can certainly take the form of a sketch or a doodle: the word "map" comes from the Latin *mappa*, which roughly translates to napkin – indicating the casual, sketched nature of the first maps. Yet all of the sketches and doodles I discuss here are symbolic depictions of topographical or two-dimensional space from above, which is a quality of maps that many doodles, sketches and conjectured plans do not share. I therefore follow Allan Simmons's example by calling these doodled depictions of fictional space maps.[7]

While these sketches may have been an element of Conrad's working method and can be explained in relation to Conrad's extraordinary engagement with maps in his fiction – like the focus on the practice of map drawing in the essay "Geography and Some Explorers" (first serialized as *The Romance of Travels* in 1924) – critics have focused on other worthy topics. Even the book editions of Conrad's notebooks "The Congo Diary" (1926) and the "Up-river Book" (1972), containing more than twenty-four maps and sketches from the Congo, only reproduce five sketches in total.[8] And even when the details of Conrad's manuscripts are discussed in minute and extensive detail, the doodled maps are overlooked. With 604 pages of commentary on the emendations and variations in the manuscript and typescript of *Victory*, the 2016 Cambridge Edition of the novel overlooks Conrad's own attempt at navigating the text: a monochromatic, two-dimensional geographic survey in the margin of a page numbered 760, in part four, chapter one. However, as has become customary, the edition reproduces an official map of the historical setting – "The Far East in the late nineteenth century" (919). Similarly, the 2016 Cambridge Edition of *An Outcast of the Islands* reproduces the same map of "The Far East in the late nineteenth century" (477) rather than Conrad's own.[9]

I reproduce a newly digitized map for the play of *Laughing Anne*, and newly digitized maps in the manuscripts of *Victory, Almayer's Folly, Nostromo* and *An Outcast of the Islands*, hoping to gain some understanding of the way Conrad used map drawing for his fiction, and partly to contextualize Conrad's and Marlow's "passion for maps" (*HD* 48). After all, the maps' placement in the manuscripts alongside the stories and correspondence to factual content of the stories, show that Conrad used them when writing – but not how so. However, since I have only been able to personally access about thirty of Conrad's book-length manuscripts and a selection of the holograph letters, and have had to rely on secondary sources for the remaining, there may be more doodled maps in his manuscripts and the letters that I have overlooked.[10] Nevertheless, my sample size is sufficient to suggest that while Conrad sketched at least three maps after the text had been completed, he also produced the maps in his manuscripts before the written text, as a type of draft or test case for an idea. As Proust used train tables, Melville consulted whaling charts, James Joyce referenced ordnance surveys of Dublin, and Faulkner sketched his own maps – Conrad constructed and used maps as part of his creative writing process. As I will show, discussing these doodles as maps implies looking upon maps from the perspective of "critical cartography": as incomplete, abbreviated and imaginary versions of the territory they portray.

Mapping Fact and Fiction: Overview and Background

In his 5,500 word essay "Geography and Some Explorers" Conrad recalls the moment "the Great Lakes of Africa" had been "discovered" (12), and how this was the impetus for him – a boy less than thirteen years old, living in Warsaw and named Józef Teodor Konrad Korzeniowski – to do his "first bit of map-drawing" and pay his "first homage to the prestige of their first explorers" (12): "It consisted in entering laboriously in pencil the outline of Tanganyika on my beloved old atlas which having been published in 1852 knew nothing of course of the Great Lakes" (12). The anecdote illustrates that geography is a dynamic field of knowledge, underpinned by adventure and travel – a stark contrast to the way Conrad claims he was taught the subject as a schoolboy. The author-to-be nevertheless passed the yearly examination in geography, apparently not by writing any apt responses to the examiners' questions, instead: "I just saved it by proficiency in map-drawing. It must have been good, I suppose; but all I remember about it is that it was done in a loving spirit" (11).

Map drawing in a loving spirit continued throughout his life, and, according to his own account in "Geography and Some Explorers," he recorded and improved on navigational maps during his seafaring career in the Merchant Service, where it was his "duty to correct and bring up to date charts of more than one ship, according to Admiralty notices" (12).

Despite this interest in maps from his boyhood and through adult life, unlike the many maps reproduced in Robert Louis Stevenson's and Thomas Hardy's fiction, Conrad only authorized the publication of one map alongside or as part of his fiction. (It does not necessarily follow that Stevenson's and Hardy's fiction is more geographical or cartographic; it could be the opposite. A text that reads as a map does not need a map.) The map Conrad authorized showed the locales of his fiction and was compiled by Eugene F. Saxton, an editor at Doubleday, and his wife,

Martha Plaisted Saxton, for the end papers of the first American edition of *Victory*. Conrad corrected some of the inferences and was, according to a letter to the Saxtons, "really touched by the skill and care you have put into this emminently [*sic*] successful piece of work" (*CL* v.433). Writing to F. N. Doubleday in 1923, he suggests that they should enlarge the Saxtons' map as the frontispiece of *The Nigger of the 'Narcissus'* for the Concord edition.[11]

Conrad could also be skeptical about attempts at linking his fiction to places on maps. In a letter to Richard Curle on the publication of a short piece that would link Conrad's "Youth" to specific places Conrad had visited, he writes: "The paragraph you quote of the East meeting the narrator is all right in itself; whereas directly it's connected with Mintok it becomes nothing at all." The name "Mintok" makes the story about "a damned hole without any beach and without any glamour" – "robbing it of all suggestiveness, destroying all illusion" (*CL* vii.457). Illusion, it seems, is easier to uphold if places in a story can only be found in the story – nameless and mapless outside of the fictional universe.

Linking fiction to places on real-life maps for the reader is different from using maps for support when writing, or as an instrument for discussing writing. Conrad habitually used maps when writing, such as in "The Congo Diary," a record of Conrad's twenty-eight-day journey on foot from Matadi to Nselemba, and the "Up-river Book," the continuation of the same journey on the Congo River on the steamer *Roi des Belges*. For the "Up-river Book" Conrad relied on the maps by Ludvig Rasmus Koch, the original commander of the *Roi des Belges*. Koch, in turn, likely used George Grenfell's ten-panel map (1884–89). In "The Congo Diary," the verbal accounts are accompanied by "regular sketches of the day's journey, with place names, geographical features, items of interest, the general direction of the journey and the distance covered."[12] Hampson observes that the notations in the "Up-river Book" hint "at the trained eye of the sailor, and the sketches with their apparatus very clearly suggest a professional practice."[13] In the "Up-river Book," Hampson continues, both "text and maps record times, bearings and soundings, leaving the trace of a range of professional practices."[14] For instance, sections of land are numbered, depth fathoms are given ("1 fat." and so on) and the steamer's course is marked with a dotted line. (One fathom, 6 ft; 1.83 meters, was considered the minimum safe-distance for the stern-wheel steamer.) These sketched maps served as navigation tools. It is tempting to believe that the handwritten maps in his fiction also served to orient Conrad's writing – as navigation tools to assist the author's memory – as a holdover from his seafaring days where incorrect locations could mean the difference between life and death.

The sketches are descriptive rather than artistic, concerned with spatial relations and locations, with individual sections mapped out and named. Since multiple preserved drawings demonstrate Conrad's skill as an amateur visual draftsman (see Chapter 3), the symbolic nature of these maps cannot be due to insufficient artistic skill. Indeed, one reason for the professional cartographic look of the maps in the "Up-river Book" is their similarity to charts Conrad used during his seafaring career, as if it were built on the same logic of that of the Great Britain Hydrographic Office. One of these charts that Conrad used is located at the Beinecke Research Library and contains a penciled note by his wife: "'This chart formerly belonged to Joseph Conrad and was used by him at sea' Jessie Conrad." The chart portrays the Gulf of Siam from 1857. It is a noteworthy record in Conrad studies since it documents Conrad's first command, and thereby charts the same route that Conrad described in *The Shadow-Line*, his "exact biography" (*CL* v.543).[15]

Apart from the maps in the Congo notebooks and in his manuscripts, and the two stage diagrams in his letters to acquaintances, Conrad doodled and sketched characters, buildings and the natural environment from his fiction, like the San Tomé mine in *Nostromo* and Nelson's bungalow in "Freya of the Seven Isles," which he sketched twice on holograph leaves numbered 10 and 66. The argument for paying scholarly attention to the maps that Conrad sketched is therefore partly based on the connection between Conrad's doodling and writing (see Chapter 1). It is also based on the fact that these descriptions of space form a coherent category – a list of two stage diagrams for two plays and at least eight maps across six books (or more than thirty maps, if you include the sketches in the "Up-river Book" and "The Congo Diary").

In letters to acquaintances, Conrad sketched the scenes for the stage plays of *The Secret Agent* (written 1920) and *Laughing Anne* (written 1920; Figure 2.1), and sketched at least eight maps in his fictional manuscripts – private acts of composition never intended to be published that form part of the unacknowledged paratext, alongside stains, sketches, calculations and cigarette marks. There is a possible representation of Higuerota in the manuscripts of *Nostromo*.[16] *An Outcast of the Islands* contains a map, as does *Romance*, and the "Author's Note" for *Almayer's Folly*. On the recto and verso of a page dated 1924 and concerning "The Secret Sharer" there is a sketch of the captain's cabin and a sketch of the officers' quarters

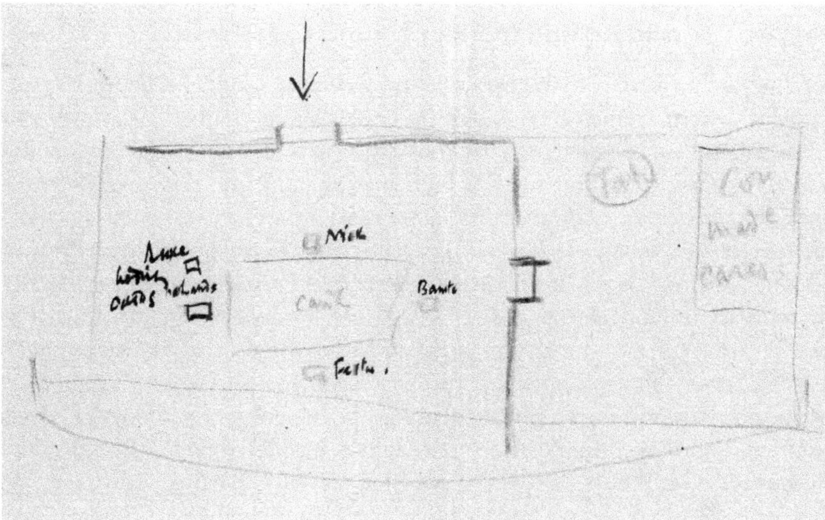

Figure 2.1 Conrad's doodled map on a copy of *Laughing Anne and One Day More*. Image courtesy of Sotheby's.

> Four men were sitting by the light of a solitary candle. There was a bottle, a jug and glasses on the table, but they were not engaged in drinking. Two packs of cards were lying there too, but they were not preparing to play.
>
> "Because of the Dollars"

(reproduced in the Cambridge Edition on pages 531 and 532 – but not discussed, either there or elsewhere).

The sketch is tipped-in on page 18 of Gérard Jean-Aubry's personal copy of *Laughing Anne and One Day More*. In blue crayon, the sketch shows the stage layout for Act II, scene I of *Laughing Anne*: two independent rooms in a house connected by a door with one of the rooms having a door to the outside. In Conrad's handwriting, the positioning of the characters is marked with black ink: "Anne holding cards stands," "Mick," "Bamtz" and "Fector." Anne assists Bamtz by holding his cards since Bamtz has stumps for hands. There is also indecipherable writing in blue crayon. On the verso is a less detailed sketch of the final scene with the writing: "A summary description of personages in the play." In a letter to Jean-Aubry on December 1920, Conrad describes *Laughing Anne* as "a play for Grand Guignol (English), 2 acts, 3 scenes. It will play forty minutes. Subject: Laughing Anne (Because of the Dollars)."[17] Grand Guignol was the name of a theatre in Paris, which became known for its naturalistic horror shows.

From Mind to Map: Critical Cartography

At first sight, a map may appear to be whatever Conrad's fiction is not: straightforward, transparent, scientific and without double meanings. For instance, the maps sketched for the stage plays of *The Secret Agent* and *Laughing Anne*, the short story "The Secret Sharer," and the novels *Victory, Almayer's Folly, An Outcast of the Islands* and *Nostromo*, represent an aerial perspective: the maps are not placed among the characters and their field of vision, but from above. It is easy to see the links here with "cartography as a form of scientific illustration,"[18] especially as Conrad's navigational maps in the "Up-river Book" are also made from above. But is this link deceptive?

The study of maps now incorporates "information theory, linguistics, semiotics, structuralism, phenomenology, developmental theory, hermeneutics, iconology, marxism, and ideology" and refers to thinkers like "Cassirer, Gombrich, Piaget, Panofsky, Kuhn, Barthes and Eco."[19] According to Franco Moretti, maps are "analytical tools: that dissect the text in an unusual way, bringing to light relations that would otherwise remain hidden."[20] There is no clear distinction between text and map; it is difficult to establish where one starts and the other ends. Harley, in "Deconstructing the Map," describes the map as a "graphic text."[21] With the rise of "critical cartography," a map is no longer just an element of a positivist project – involving teleological development toward a complete and final geographic knowledge. Individual maps are not primarily, if at all, neutral contributions toward a universal geography, but individual artistic achievements that can be read from multiple perspectives. Harley defines the map as inherently rhetorical: "a graphic language to be decoded."[22] Another way of saying that maps are geographic, rhetorical devices is to stress that there is such a thing as cartographic thinking involved in the act of mapping: it is a specific language that Conrad employed with specific associations, preconditions and presumptions. Yet readers frequently understand a map as a neutral, scientific object, "akin to chronologies, dictionaries and encyclopedias."[23] As such, the map is a complicated and promising element in Conrad's fiction open to readings, especially since Conrad used the maps privately – in manuscripts and in letters rather than in his published fiction.

The doodled maps in Conrad's manuscripts do not function as neutral, scientific objects. The sketched map in *Victory* is a fictional representation of a fictional space, lacking referential value to the extratextual world. The map, then, corresponds to something which does not exist any more or less than the text – it is ultimately grounded in fantasy, memory or imagination rather than physical space. Research on how maps work in the fiction of Robert Louis Stevenson, Thomas Hardy, J. R. R. Tolkien, Agatha Christie and others, where the maps are reproduced alongside the text in accordance with the author's original intention, suggests that the text makes the map real and the map makes the text real – a type of created, circular correspondence, where "text and map are self-protectively linked"[24]: authenticating each other. The map allows the elements of the text to become verifiable facts.

What I find more interesting, however, is not the relative epistemic status of the map and the text – whether one is more real, whether one mimics the other, and so on – but why there is a map in Conrad's manuscript at all. The stage diagrams for the stage plays of *The Secret Agent* and *Laughing Anne* are in line with the visual medium of theatre and the historical practices of dramaturgy, but the maps in his fictional manuscripts are more difficult to understand. Did Conrad need a map to navigate his own fictional universe? Was a map an impetus for the text – a creative ingredient? An alternative reading? A retrospective reflection? A map, like a cooking recipe or an instruction manual, is generally created with a specific purpose; it is the exception when a map exists as the ultimate source of reality – for its own sake rather than as a copy of reality. A map provides direction and guidance. By "its very nature," explains Sally Bushell, "a map is a thing of use."[25] But a thing of use for whom? Can we, as readers, use Conrad's maps? Or are the maps, like a private language, only accessible by Conrad?

Map and Text Correspondence

There is some similarity between Conrad's texts and his maps. His maps are not arbitrarily assembled lines that could equally well be found in other writers' texts, but deliberate reflections on his unwritten or written texts. Consider the sketch in the "Author's Note" to *Almayer's Folly* (Figure 2.2). The fourth side of the verandah on Almayer's house is open and faces the river, as in the sketch. In cursive, Conrad has written 'River' opposite a rectangular box – the verandah – placed within a larger rectangular box, representing Almayer's "new, but already decaying house – that last failure of his life" (5). There are five small rectangular boxes placed between the river and the house; they may symbolize the general disarray, the unkempt grass growing by the bank and the "four wooden armchairs" (14) scattered about the verandah that "straggled forlornly as if ashamed of their shabby surroundings" (14). The "Author's Note" itself, however, contains no

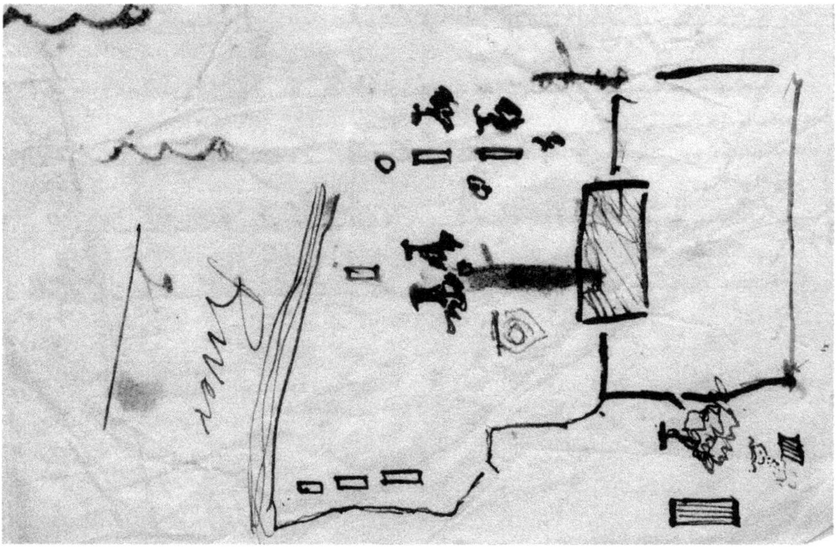

Figure 2.2 Newly digitized map in pen on the verso of an unpaginated page, on the manuscript of the "Author's Note" to *Almayer's Folly*, completed in 1895. The Rosenbach, Philadelphia.

reference to Almayer's house, which suggests that Conrad originally had planned for the "Author's Note" to comment on the house, or simply used the map as a springboard to jog his memory about the story.

There is also correspondence between the map and the text in the holograph of *An Outcast of the Islands* (Figure 2.3). Allan Simmons, the Cambridge editor of *An Outcast of the Islands*, reads the map to be of the courtyard, "showing the position of the river and part of the perimeter fence, and identifying by name the features 'omar's [*sic*] hut,' 'fire,' 'Tree,' and 'house'" (*OI* 305). Placed on the back of a manuscript page numbered 494, Conrad likely sketched the map as he was writing the page numbered 495, with the upside-down page next to him. If so, the map reflects Aissa's vision, whose "resolute eyes took in the courtyard in a circular glance" (277). However, half of the writing on page 495 is illegible and crossed out, which makes it difficult to make any determinate statements about the genealogy of the text and the map. Furthermore, the correspondence between map and text does not tell us whether the text preceded the map, or whether the map preceded the text. Or whether the map was intended to portray the text or vice versa. The map does therefore not necessarily function as a type of fact sheet to the text – as in the nature of

Figure 2.3 Newly digitized sketch of a map on the verso of a page numbered 494, from the manuscript of *An Outcast of the Islands*, completed in 1895. The Rosenbach, Philadelphia.

the Gilbert or Linati schema for James Joyce's *Ulysses* (1922). It is possible that Conrad used the map in the reverse order – rather than constructing a map to represent reality, he created a map from which he copied reality.

There are cases where it is apparent that the map was created after the text. Let us go back to the map on the verso of the "Author's Note" of *Almayer's Folly.* Since it is on the "Author's Note" that contains no reference to the depicted map and since the "Author's Note" was produced after the novel, it is clear that the text preceded the map. In the holograph of "The Secret Sharer" there is a sketch of the Captain's cabin and a sketch of the officers' quarters. In these studies every symbol on the map has a representative description in the text, so that the couch, desk, bookcase, lockers, the three doors and their placements are clearly visible in the sketch of the captain's cabin, which takes the form of an L-shape described in the story. The Cambridge Edition classifies these as "retrospective sketches" (221), presumably since they are done on a paper imprinted "OSWALDS, BISHOPSBOURNE, KENT"; Conrad moved to Oswalds in October 1919 – almost a decade after he had finished "The Secret Sharer." In the right-hand corner there is writing in French that dates the sketches to March 24, and attributes them to Conrad.

The handwriting is likely Jean-Aubry's, who translated "The Secret Sharer" into French. As with the map in the "Author's Note" of *Almayer's Folly*, the close correspondence between text and map is made possible by the fact that the map was produced after the text had been completed, so that the text could serve as copy-text for the map.

Navigating Fiction

It is noteworthy that when Conrad writes in private, for himself, he partly relies on sketches to complement the writing, or to tell a story more quickly than he can do with words. The "Up-river Book" documents how Conrad – who was to become one of the most celebrated writers in the modern era – resorts to drawing and visual expression for description. And, later on as an established writer, he appears to have used nonverbal symbols to think through a scene that was ultimately going to be displayed in verbal format – as if a hastily sketched picture offered something to his creative process that words could not provide.

In *Victory, Nostromo* and *An Outcast of the Islands*, the map is produced with the same ink and nib as the manuscript text and precedes a passage that describes the geography. Here the map functions as a preliminary stage in the writing process. Not as a complete and factual record, but as a draft open to changes: a draft from which to create a world. Conrad's process is similar to how many writers used notebooks or made detailed plans before writing – like Rousseau's notes on playing cards taken during walks; Thomas Hardy's eclectic thoughts in his multiple literary notebooks; the minute plans of Sylvia Plath's *The Bell Jar* (1963), Henry Miller's *Tropic of Capricorn* (1939) and William Faulkner's *A Fable* (1954). However, the notes Conrad made for himself were visual rather than verbal. There are no keywords in the margins of Conrad's manuscripts, but sketched maps. Would there be a way to verify that Conrad used maps as a part of his creative process? Could we consult the maps for visual evidence of this theory?

Although overlap in information between the visual map and written text demonstrates that they are connected, the similarity tells us little about how Conrad used the map when writing. Indeed, there is limited interest in a one-to-one correspondence between the map and the text: a mimetic relationship is just a duplication of facts (Borges engages with this possibility in the anthology of essays *A Universal History of Infamy* (1935), theorizing "a map of the empire that was of the same scale as the empire and that coincided with it point for point"[26]). The more intriguing possibility is whether the map tells us anything that is not apparent in

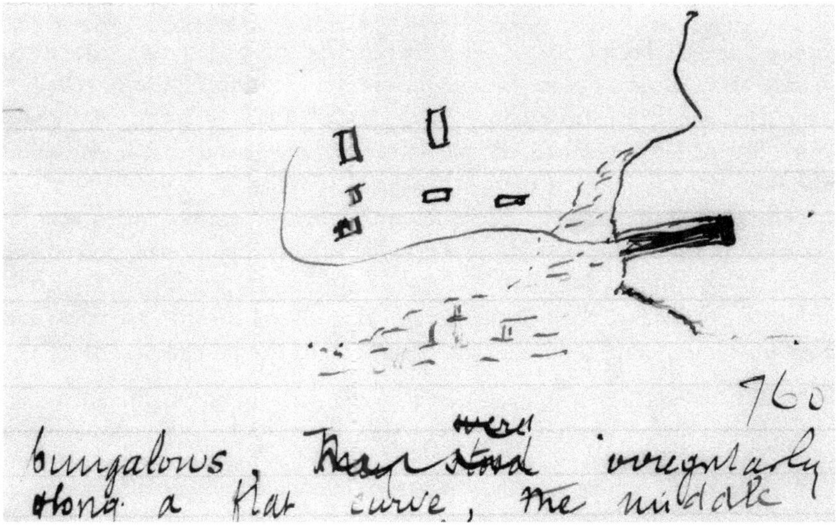

Figure 2.4 Newly digitized map in the handwritten manuscript of *Victory*, page numbered 760. Harry Ransom Center, University of Texas at Austin. The manuscript is dated to June 27, 1914 “That black jetty sticking out of the jungle into the empty sea, these roofridges of deserted houses peeping dismally above the long grass!” (*V* 48) describes Heyst’s compound and some of the elements in this sketch.

the written text. In *Victory*, for instance, the text is obviously not trying to directly describe the simple and small sketch of a map in the margin of its manuscript (Figure 2.4). The landscape described in the text – Heyst’s compound on Samburan – is much more complicated than this map. If you were to delete the text, it would not be sufficient to reproduce the map next to it. Similarly, the map cannot be reconstructed by looking at the text alone. So while the map invites interaction and imagination, it is not at a one-to-one relationship with the text. Indeed, unlike the text, the map in *Victory* appears crude, half-finished, barely noteworthy – no secondary source has noted its existence until now.

At first sight, *five* boxes on the map appear to illustrate the spatial relationship among the *three* bungalows described in the text. However, the paragraph immediately following the map in the original holograph manuscript (and reproduced from the Cambridge text below) provides a clear explanation for the other rectangular shapes in the map: “By protruding his head a little he commanded through the foliage of a festooning creeper a view of all three bungalows, irregularly disposed along a flat curve; the middle one in retreat on the two others, shuttered closely and unmasking imperfectly the angles and slopes of the corrugated iron store-houses at the back" (241). The manuscript map describes the three bungalows (Heyst's house, Wang's hut and a counting-house), as well as "the corrugated iron store-houses at the back." There also appears to be a dock (a coal-jetty) symbolized by a larger black segment that leads out to the sea: "Black Diamond Bay" (*V* 243).

The dashed markings could represent Wang's vegetable garden or "the space of burnt grass" (*V* 243–44), in which the company had cleared the ground. A third possibility is that the dashed markings represent the topographical decline of the ground that allows Ricardo to slip to the foot of the jetty and then take the path back to the bungalows, unseen:

> His proceedings were made easier by the declivity of the ground, which sloped sharply down to the water's edge. There, his feet feeling the warmth of the island's rocky foundation already heated by the sun, through the thin soles of his straw slippers he was, as it were, sunk out of sight of the houses. A short scramble of some twenty feet brought him up again to the upper level, at the place where the jetty had its root in the shore. (245)

The exercise of reducing paragraphs in *Victory* to the coordinates of a doodled map is difficult, if not impossible, to do. The existence of a map, or lack thereof, provides plenty of room for speculation but little room for conclusive statements – as the many interpretations (above) of the map in *Victory* demonstrate. Nevertheless, it is tempting to think that a map, or lack thereof, can be used as conclusive evidence for explaining identifying qualities of geographic, written descriptions. Indeed, due to arguable inconsistencies in the geography of *Nostromo*, Ben Kimpel and Duncan Eaves declare: "Conrad had no map of Costaguana, even in his own mind," he lacked "a detailed mental outline of the map of Costaguana."[27] As it happens, however, Conrad actually had sketched a relief map of Higuerota and a geographical description of Costaguana (Figure 2.5).

Even with a plan or map it is still possible to lose one's way. In fact, even though Conrad twice sketched Nelson's bungalow in "Freya of the Seven Isles," he managed to lose the direction of its immediate geography, resulting in a rare factual mistake. The Cambridge Edition of "'Twixt Land and Sea" notes the oversight: "to the left An error, found in all texts, for 'to the right'. See Fig. 22, Conrad's two sketches of Nelson's bungalow. This kind of mistake is rare in Conrad's fiction" (521). The same is arguably the case for *Victory* and the description of Heyst's compound. In a little-known article, John Derrick attempts to draw a map of Samburan only to find that cumulative information about the location of the Alfuro village, the jetty, the volcano, the central ridge and

Figure 2.5 Newly digitized map, in ink, on the verso of the first page of the holograph manuscript of *Nostromo*, part second, *the Isabels*, numbered 425. The Rosenbach, Philadelphia. The map takes up the entire page. On the recto, dated August 24, one can see the map through the quasitransparent page. The map is likely from 1902, the year Conrad started working on the short story which later became the novel *Nostromo*. *The Isabels*, part second of the published book, starts with a geographical description of Costaguana: the Campo, the San Tomé mine and Higuerota, and how they are interconnected geographically.

the setting of the sun produces insuperable "geographic problems." Reproducing three drawn maps, where each consecutive map is an attempt to redraft the original map according to subsequent information in later chapters in *Victory*, Derrick demonstrates that "there is no way we can redraft or rotate the island to fit this new picture with those previously accumulated."[28]

If Derrick and others are correct in their inferences, three of Conrad's rare factual mistakes (located in *Nostromo*, "Freya of the Seven Isles" and *Victory*) are associated with passages he also attempted to describe with visual sketches. This does not necessarily mean that by sketching the scene

Conrad lost control over it. The more likely explanation is that Conrad himself recognized the geographical complexity and thereby explored its coordinates in a sketch before he placed buildings, animals and characters within these coordinates. However, since maps are used to navigate the unknown it is almost a paradox that Conrad both created and used them. The maps would serve no use if he knew the area, and unless he knew the area he could not have produced the maps. On one level, however, it is no less sensible that a writer would do a preliminary sketch than an architect; both are builders of space.

As we have seen, maps are a type of text. On the most basic level, the visual, compressed format of maps elicits abbreviations and the opportunity for the writer to see whether his or her ideas can be written in pictorial form. Conrad's case, however, demonstrates that a writer can use maps in many more complicated ways. His maps occupy a liminal space between private imagination and public discourse; they serve to generate new ideas, to focus the imagination, to navigate complex geographies, and as an instrument by which to reflect on a prior work. Even when the doodled map precedes the text, the map is far from an instruction manual, fact sheet or litmus test of accuracy. Although three maps are linked to passages in Conrad's fiction that contain factual mistakes, it is unclear whether the maps led Conrad astray or whether he produced the maps because of the complicated geography. As we have seen, although maps are determinate in nature, Conrad's hand-drawn manuscript maps pose as many questions as they answer. Yet, tracing the history of the texts back to a few traced lines – an outline of a map – is to take a step forward in understanding the texts as living documents. The maps present a humbling picture of the writer at work, occasionally losing his way among his own created maps, in his successful attempt at creating literary masterpieces.

CHAPTER 3

Drawings and The Sisters

> he had locked something valuable in the drawer of a large writing desk . . .
>
> *Nostromo*

> there, in that writing-desk, the drawer on the left. It's not locked. You can pull it right out. There is a recess, and the board at the back pivots: a very simple hiding-place, when you know the way to it.
>
> *Victory*

> I had been struck by the wild hope of finding a trace of Rita's passage, a sign or something. I pulled out all the drawers violently, thinking that perhaps she had hidden there a scrap of paper, a note.
>
> *The Arrow of Gold*

Unsurprisingly, the locked drawers we meet in Conrad's imaginative literature are repositories of secrets. These drawers are enveloped by the sense of privacy *The Secret Agent*'s Professor bestows on the explosive content in his padlocked cupboard. In *The Shadow-Line*, in his captain's drawer, Mr Burns discovers "positive evidence" (48) for his conjecture about a love affair: a photograph of a woman. In "The Informer," Horne forces open the drawers of Mr Sevrin's desk and finds "a record of the most damnatory kind" (100). Just as Razumov in *Under Western Eyes* keeps his written confession in a locked drawer, Conrad himself kept certain documents out of public sight, in study drawers. According to Ford Madox Ford, Conrad thought of the manuscripts of *The Sisters* and *The Return* "as something slightly obscene at which one could only peep in secret. They shared the quality of things kept in a locked drawer."[1] While Conrad treated *The Sisters*, an unfinished novel intended to be about a painter, like a thing kept in a locked drawer, his drawings were literally locked in his drawers. Jessie Conrad's first memoir recounts how her husband took efforts to clean out her collection of his drawings/doodles from her "P. P. B. (Precious Property Bag)": "As I spent the first six months after my return home [from the hospital] upstairs in my room. I did not miss my treasures for a long time. My inquiries met with a somewhat curt reply that 'all that was of any value amongst that rubbish was locked in study drawers'."[2]

While the chapters on doodles and drawn maps introduce us to some aspects of Conrad's visual art, this chapter will examine Conrad's attitude to his own draftsmanship. Yet his successful efforts to keep his drawings in locked drawers, as if they were shady wares acquired from Mr Verloc's shop on Brett Street, suggest a need for privacy. We can presume that Conrad's close friends and acquaintances were largely unaware of Conrad's drawings, because there is no evidence of any record where they comment on them. This silence is reflected in Conrad's official life story: when biographers speak about his leisure activities, they do not mention his draftsmanship. John Stape's biography finds that Conrad had two leisure activities, "reading and chess"; Jeffrey Meyers's biography notes: "Though Conrad had no hobbies, he liked to play chess."[3]

Like Heidegger's poetry or Picasso's poems and plays, Conrad's drawings are generally considered to be autonomous entities, divorced from his main work. I have tried to counter this view with a chapter that identifies a link between Conrad's doodles and the theme of stagnation in *The Shadow-Line*, a chapter on doodled maps, and a published article that connects Conrad's impressionistic drawings with his verbal impressionism.[4] However, the idea that there are links between Conrad's visual and verbal art is far from an established view. Even Conrad's story about an amateur painter – *The Sisters* – remains unconnected to his interest in drawing. Without demonstrating an awareness of Conrad's drawings, Zdzisław Najder maintains that *The Sisters* was partly fated to fail because of its intention to approach an area of knowledge Conrad could not fathom, the first-person perspective of a painter. In a chapter titled "The Sisters: A Grandiose Failure," Najder primarily attributes the weaknesses of the story to Conrad's aim to write about a painter and a painter's aspirations, "an unfortunate decision because Conrad was consequently compelled to discuss – in vague and unconvincing terms – issues with which he was not familiar."[5] But, if we unlock the metaphorical drawers where Conrad's drawings have resided, and consider two recently discovered Conrad drawings from around 1895, it becomes clear that *The Sisters* (1895–96) was intended to be written on a calling Conrad pursued as an amateur. As I will discuss, if *The Sisters* is unconvincing as a story, it may be because an amateur and habitual draftsman may fail to write convincingly about his hobby. There are also many elements in *The Sisters* that are not autobiographical: it is rather a cautionary tale in its portrayal of Stephen's sacrifices and misguided artistic pilgrimage. For Stephen, to be an artist is not to practice art but to have access to a higher intellectual realm; this is a modern conception of art and the artist that was drastically different from Conrad's, who saw himself as a craftsman (a definition of the artist similar to the etymological Greek root of art, as *technē*: mastery of a craft).[6] *The Sisters*, then, is not so much a self-indulgent autobiography as a historical document and reflection on the modern artist – written during the advent of modernism in visual art.

I will further argue that *The Sisters*, rather than largely being a discussion of the act of painting, is more, in the spirit of Henry James's *The Tragic Muse* (1889–90), an elaboration of the shame associated with artistic drawing: a meditation on the need to keep this interest in a locked drawer. Although the debate about *The Sisters* may seem a topic of little import, corresponding in significance to the meager length of the manuscript, its 8,000 words relate to Conrad's original inspiration as a writer: *The Sisters* would have been his third novel. As noted by Donald Yelton, *The Sisters* is also Conrad's only explicit attempt to "dramatize the artist's consciousness."[7]

The Unfinished Manuscript

With twenty-eight pages of autograph manuscript, reproduced in 1928 in *The Bookman* on fifteen pages, the first four chapters of *The Sisters* introduce us to Stephen, a spectator of art and aspiring painter. As a young man supported by a wealthy family, Stephen leaves his birthplace, Ruthenia, to wander through Berlin, Bohemia, Cologne, Dresden, Munich, Paris, Rome, Vienna and the "cities of Italy" (481). His peregrinations take him to what he considers to be repositories of beauty – museums, galleries, cathedrals and the sublime constellations of nature. Stephen is in search of a creed: "He believed that among so many forms of created beauty there could be found the secret of genius. All those brains that had produced so many masterpieces had left amongst them, hidden from the crowd, but visible to the elect, the expression of their creed" (482). He fails. The masterpieces of nature and of plastic and visual art are mute and indifferent. Leaving Stephen in this dejected state, the remaining three chapters construct a parallel story that introduces the sisters Dolores and Rita, with the expectation that Rita and Stephen are to meet and fall in love (a situation reminiscent of the love triangle in *Nostromo* between Giovanni Battista Fidanza and the sisters Giselle and Linda Viola).

The unfinished manuscript ends, then, rather abruptly and leaves plenty of room for speculation and discussion. Although one could argue that the meaning and merit of a work of art is independent of its creator's intentions, the discussion about *The Sisters* pivots on the extent to which it is an autobiographical text: whether "artist" and "painter" are code-words for "writer." Bernard Meyer contends that the "autobiographical allusions in this fragment of a story of the 'wandering Slav' are self-evident."[8] Frederick Karl judges that *The Sisters* is more autobiographical than *Almayer's Folly* and "An Outpost of Progress."[9] Ian Watt classifies Stephen as an "autobiographical hero" and Susan Jones comments that Stephen "could easily be identified with Conrad himself."[10]

There are reasons, however, for thinking that the fictional fragment is lacking in autobiographical content. Najder explains that *The Sisters* is a lesser work since it is a step away from the autobiographical terrain.[11] In this, he follows the opinion of Thomas Moser's and Jocelyn Baines's writings from 1957 and 1959, respectively. Unlike Moser and Baines, Najder presents a precise hypothesis on how the theme of *The Sisters* diverges from Conrad's experiences. He suggests that Conrad consciously "made his hero a painter because as a painter searching for visual beauty Stephen did not force Conrad to deal with literary matters." This produced a predictable result: "the entirely non-painterlike sensitivity which this 'painter' exhibits; and the absence of any references to contemporary or past art all serve to render Stephen an indistinct, papier-mâché protagonist."[12]

In theory, a writer need not share the attributes of his characters to flesh them out successfully and there is the possibility that Conrad had the imaginative power to fabricate what he did not know intimately (like the contemporary painter Henri Rousseau who painted jungles without ever leaving France). That said, it seems unlikely that Conrad could have written *The Secret Agent* unless he had walked the streets of London; *Under Western Eyes* without having been personally afflicted by turbulent politics; *The Nigger of the 'Narcissus'* and *The Mirror of the Sea* if he had never sailed. Just as studies that compare Conrad and Marlow have expanded our understanding of *Heart of Darkness*, a comparison between Conrad and Stephen could be fruitful, if there is sufficient overlap between the author and the character.

Although there is justification for an autobiographical reading, then, this type of reading needs to be very careful. For instance, Najder's conclusion that the absence of specific references to painters in *The Sisters* is due to Conrad's unawareness of artists does not factor in that Conrad elsewhere mentions the painters Alice Kinkead, Augustus John, Botticelli, Corot, El Greco, Dante Gabriel Rossetti, Ford Madox Brown, Francis Petrus Paulus, Georg Sauter, Herbart Bernard, Jean Antoine Watteau, John Everett, John Lavery, Rembrandt, Rodin, Velasquez, Walter Ernest Tittle, Whistler, William Nicholson, William Rothenstein; the illustrators A. C. Michael, Claude Shepperson, David B. Waters, Dudley Hardy, William Hyde, Henry Hyde, Maurice Grieffenhagen and Glyn Philpot; the art historians Charles Waldstein and Sidney Colvin. Of course, most of these references were made after Conrad had written *The Sisters*, but the sheer number of them suggests that Conrad had an interest and understanding of visual art throughout his life.

Furthermore, if Conrad were unfamiliar with visual art and therefore unable to write well on the subject, as the critical consensus suggests, this cause-and-effect relationship would affect more of Conrad's characters than Stephen; Stephen is merely one of many amateur artists Conrad wrote about. Although no other Conrad character displays an equally prominent interest in visual art, one should not overlook the decorative flower paintings by Mrs Whalley in "The End of the Tether," Kurtz's painting of a draped and blindfolded woman in *Heart of Darkness*, Flora de Barral's attempts at draftsmanship in *Chance*, Henry Allègre's paintings in *The Arrow of Gold*, and in *Nostromo* Emilia Gould's sketch of Don José Avellanos and her watercolor painting of a waterfall. Moreover, Jenkins and Mr Churchill in *The Inheritors* are both painters; Kayerts and Carlier's predecessor in "An Outpost of Progress" (1897) had been "an unsuccessful painter" (77); Horne of "The Informer" "was an engraver and etcher of genius" (135); an early manuscript version of *Victory* constructs Axel Heyst as a watercolorist;[13] and Lord Jim of the eponymous story is partly based on the experiences of the painter Louis Garneray.[14] If Stephen appears to be "an indistinct, papier-mâché protagonist,"[15] his role as an amateur painter is therefore not a viable explanation any more than his taciturn nature would explain his singularity (Falk, MacWhirr, Whalley, Razumov, Renouard, Singleton and Axel Heyst are also taciturn). Stephen's indistinct nature may instead relate to the fact that *The Sisters* is an unfinished novel, a fragment reproduced in *The Bookman* on a mere fifteen pages – of which only nine pages are about him. My view, as will be discussed, is also that the portrayal of Stephen as one-dimensional is not *faute de mieux*, but a conscious choice on Conrad's behalf to construct Stephen as a dreamer, anti-hero, and failed artist.

Conrad was, of course, more concerned with the activity of writing than that of drawing and his decision to write about a painter seems, at first, as inexplicable as Stephen's decision to become a painter. Whereas the writer Richard Curle asserts that Conrad had no marked interest in visual art ("it cannot be said that either music or painting was in any degree essential to him . . . and in all his conversations to me I have no recollection of his talking, save casually, about pictures"), the painter William Rothenstein declares that Conrad "was curious about the painter's outlook on life."[16] Conrad had certainly been to the Musée du Louvre (mentioned by name in *The Arrow of Gold*), but there is no indication that he, like Stephen in *The Sisters*, or like Il Conde in the eponymous story, spent his days visiting art museums.[17] That said, he proposed to Jessie on the steps of London's National Gallery in 1896,[18] the year he started writing *The Sisters* – and he was a reader of the magazines in which his and others' stories were accompanied by illustrations. For example, his letters comment on the work of eight illustrators, and in *The Pall Mall Magazine* of 1902, *Typhoon* appeared alongside nine individualized drawings by Maurice Grieffenhagen, for whom Conrad expressed admiration. In uncharacteristically direct language, the "Author's Note" to *Typhoon* applauds Grieffenhagen for his knowledge of "how to combine in his illustrations the effect of his own most distinguished personal vision with an absolute fidelity to the inspiration of the writer" (ix). This is in contrast to Dudley Hardy's fanciful illustrations for *The Rescue* that feature a starry sky ("of unpardonable ugliness") and a bearded Lingard with a fur hat in the tropics ("What is it – a joke?" *CL* VI.328).

In addition to the exposure to visual art the literary magazines provided, Conrad also engaged this art form in a direct way: while most of his drawings were likely "burned at the end of the day" (*PR* 92), sixteen preserved drawings document his interest in visual art. Conrad was, like many of the writers he read avidly, a skilled amateur draftsman. Many of his sketches are drawn in the painterly technique, a technique that is conceptually difficult and defines visual impressionism.[19] Two examples of this technique are given by Conrad's two undated drawings of Doña Rita, a character in *The Sisters*. But, given that Doña Rita also makes an appearance in two of Conrad's later works, *The Mirror of the Sea* and *The Arrow of Gold*, it is uncertain whether these drawings originated while Conrad was writing *The Sisters*.

Conrad produced at least two drawings in 1895, a year during which he spent some time in Paris and began writing his story about a painter in Paris. He spent some time in Passy, the section of Paris Stephen visits. Whereas Passy is where Stephen "found rest . . . after his long wanderings" (490) – "an almost ideal retreat" (489) – Conrad was more of an occasional visitor, spending time there with the expressed wish to listen to "une douzaine des chapitres" (*CL* 1.215) of a Marguerite Poradowska novel. This activity coincided with the courting of his future wife, Jessie Conrad, whom he married on March 24, 1896. But the visit to Poradowska was not a veiled attempt to rekindle a complicated romantic interest during a moment of indecision, as if to hedge his bets; Conrad was professionally interested in Poradowska's novel *Pour Noemi*: *The Sisters* recalls "its principal plot," as Susan Jones has carefully demonstrated.[20]

Conrad also made several business trips to Paris in 1896 in aid of a friend's (John Rorke's) misplaced investments in the Roodeport gold reef: "I have been extremely busy and half the time in Paris. I have crossed the Channel six times (three trips) in a fortnight" (*CL* 1.215), he writes to E. L. Sanderson. A recently discovered drawing of a flower-seller (Figure 3.1) testifies to Conrad's time in Paris in 1895. Our limited information about this drawing is given by Jessie's note on its margin: "This flower seller Conrad saw in Paris sometime in early 1895. [*sic*] and was sketched by him." The picture is exclusively composed of saturated and monochromatic black and the flower-seller is somewhat buxom, beautifully detailed and accidentally disproportionate. For instance, although the viewer expects her arms to be – subject to perspective – of similar size, the one grasping the basket is smaller. This disproportion testifies more to the fact that the drawing was produced *al primo*, without preparatory work with a pencil, rather than to Conrad's level of skill as a draftsman. Indeed, the style of this drawing largely corresponds to the painterly technique of Conrad's other drawings. This is evident in the dissolution of form and the primacy of color over line in the basket; the top of the basket features lines that extend and move across different objects, in this way disrupting traditional forms. Jessie's note that this drawing was done in Paris is supported by the fact that in the Belle Époque flower-sellers were a familiar sight in Paris and were often depicted by painters. Certain contemporary French painters, such as Louis Marie de Schryver (1862–1942), made the portrayal of flower-sellers their signature work.

Whereas *The Sisters* is partly a story about a painter who does not paint (see page 60 on this aspect of Stephen's life), Conrad was doodling and drawing when at his writing table. On the verso of a newly discovered drawing (Figure 3.2), which can be dated to 1895, the year he started writing *The Sisters*, Jessie's penciled note reads: "To Richard Curle With much affection from his friend Jessie Conrad. This little sketch hear [*sic*] made by Joseph Conrad during writing hours, some thirty two years ago. It came into my possession after our marriage and required even greater

Figure 3.1 Conrad's ink sketch of a flower-seller. 1895, Paris. The Henry W. and Albert A. Berg Collection of English and American Literature, New York Public Library.

> He sought news of me from . . . the flower-girl at the door of the fashionable restaurant where I had my table. That young woman, whose business name was Irma, had come on duty about mid-day.
>
> *The Arrow of Gold*

> On the rich, stamped paper of the walls hung sketches, water-colours, engravings. His tastes were distinctly artistic . . . A pathetically lean girl flattened against a blank wall, turned up expiring eyes and tendered a flower for sale.
>
> *The Return*

care, than those early M.S. to preserve it from destruction by its author." Since Jessie's note is undated, "thirty two years ago" gives us unclear guidance to date the drawing. However, when Christie's auctioned the drawing in 1994, they dated it to the 1890s, and, indeed, it features a fashionable lady who sports enormous sleeves, which go under the names

Figure 3.2 Conrad's ink sketch of a lady. 1895, Paris. The Lilly Library, Indiana University, Bloomington.

A lady appeared suddenly. A real lady, in a black dress and with a parasol. She looked extremely elegant.

The Nigger of the 'Narcissus'

I saw her once – silk dress, pretty boots, all feathers and scent, pink face.

The Partner

She went very pale under the roses of her big straw hat, gloved, swinging a clear sunshade.

Nostromo

Her walk was not that hybrid and uncertain gliding affected by some women, but a frank, strong, healthy movement forward.

Under Western Eyes

of leg-of-mutton, balloon and gigot sleeves; these "were highly fashionable between 1894 and 1896 when women adopted them for all types of activities and occasions."[21] Although this style first bloomed in the 1830s (twenty-seven years before Conrad was born), it had a renaissance in the 1890s – "growing to their fullest proportions around the middle of the decade."[22]

The sketched lady's distinctive and dominant neckwear typifies the style of the 1890s, when fashionable women characteristically decorated their necks with "the long stole or boa of ruffled chiffon, or of ostrich feathers sometimes costing as much as ten guineas."[23] (A sailor on the *Judea* or the *Narcissus* would have needed to work five months at "two poun' ten a month," *NN* 100, to earn ten guineas.) This fashionable apparel was used partly to cover up the neck and partly to counter the flat shoulders of dresses popular at the time and visible in the drawing. For instance, *The Arrow of Gold*, a novel that builds on material from *The Sisters*, portrays the "initiated Paris" (36) – "the ultra-fashionable world" (31); "the world that rides in the morning in the Bois" (41) – and confirms a couple's apparent wealth by noting that "even his wife had never been seen in a low-necked dress" (72).

For a nineteenth-century European, 'fashionable' and 'Parisian' were intertwined concepts.[24] Seemingly resting on this equation between the fashionable and the Parisian (as clear in the Conrad lexicon as the equation between upper-class and silk hat – see Chapter 8), the Christie's auction catalogue describes the lady with a parasol as "a fashionable Parisian lady." If this placement is correct, Conrad produced at least two drawings in Paris or of Paris around 1895, when he was writing *The Sisters*, about a foreign painter in Paris. It might just be a coincidence but there are no extant drawings after 1896, the year Conrad stopped writing *The Sisters*: Jessie dates a pen-and-ink sketch of three ballet girls to 1896, the drawing of a lady in a bustle-dress to 1896, the portrayal of a couple on a couch to 1895, a drawing of a seated lady being serenaded to 1893, the sketch of a lady reaching with her hands toward the sky to 1891, the picture of a woman with a snake between the years 1892 and 94. A drawing of a girl wearing a tutu and holding a net is dated to 1893 in Conrad's own hand. In 1894, Conrad also posted a letter with a sketch of a lady (*CL* IX.11). (Stephen's bourgeois brother, who urged him to paint women, would have applauded Conrad's predominant motif.)

If the extant drawings are a guide to Conrad's overall activity, *The Sisters* was composed during his richest decade as a draftsman. *The Sisters* therefore coincided with and could have been inspired by this habitual activity or the drawings could have been done in an effort to understand his subject: Stephen.

Conrad and Stephen

Although Conrad's many attempts at drawing may give some credibility to William Rothenstein's exclamation that "Conrad seemed to understand what I too was aiming at in my [approach to] painting,"[25] it is clear that Conrad was neither a professional painter nor a professional draftsman. His drawings are good, but he lacked personal insight into the inner life of a professional painter. However, just as Conrad's long-standing interest in chess gives him license to write convincingly about Marlow losing at chess in *Chance*, Conrad had the requisite knowledge to write about a struggling painter (if there is, indeed, such a thing as requisite knowledge on which Najder and others insist).[26] *The Sisters* is very much, to borrow the words in *The Inheritors* to describe a journalistic piece, "a study of a broken-down painter" (28). Indeed, Conrad's Stephen is introduced neither as an artistic genius nor as a person of extraordinary painting talent; his artistic flower never blooms, and the reader is not led to believe that there is any seed of greatness in him: "he had no talent" (482); "At times he mourned over his own want of intelligence" (482); "He had paid an enormous price for the privilege of hopeless strife!" (487); "where he set up his easel, the hand of man seemed to raise an unscalable wall between him and his Maker" (488); "the illimitable had a reserve and a limit for him" (488). In his intended move from amateur to professional, Stephen is burdened with self-doubts and wonders whether he is one of the fortunate to be an artist ("Am I unworthy?" 487). Conrad, staying in the artistic hub that was Paris in 1895, could certainly sympathize with this sense of being an amateur draftsman – or with the sense of struggling to fulfill an aspiration, to which the aborted novel testifies. And, perhaps it was in Paris that Conrad took drawing lessons for "months and months" (*CL* IV.11). This possibility concurs with Edward Garnett's recollection that 1895 was "a leisurely year" (1) for Conrad.

Regarding *The Sisters* and its autobiographical ingredients, the question about whether Conrad liked, practiced and understood painting should, perhaps, not be overemphasized: the four chapters of *The Sisters* that introduce Stephen are not about the process of painting any more than *A Portrait of the Artist as a Young Man* (1916) gives us Stephen Dedalus composing poetry, apart from a villanelle. Whereas Stevie in *The Secret Agent* draws concentric and eccentric circles, Stephen in *The Sisters* is never depicted painting. We know, however, that the former Stephen's circles fall under the category of "mad art attempting the inconceivable" (*SA* 40) and that many classify Stephen in *The Sisters* as a "Madman" (482) and call his paintings "impossible" (482). Instead of giving us Stephen painting, the chapters on him primarily deal with his exile, sacrifice, depression, family, aspiration, guilt and "agonizing self-reproach" (486). He travels extensively, wanders in galleries, rests on the sofa of his studio, writes letters to his family, meets casual companions, climbs "lofty summits" (487) to look at sunrises, stares out of "the windows of commodious hotels" (487), and meditates, "standing motionless amongst canvasses" (487). Stephen, a "Dreamer" (482), does not paint any more than Jim in *Lord Jim* – with thoughts "full of valorous deeds ... and the success of his imaginary achievements" (18) – performs heroic deeds at sea. Along with Almayer in *Almayer's Folly* and Willems in *An Outcast of the Islands*, Stephen – like Lord Jim – is one of Conrad's dreamers.[27]

Conrad himself was a dreamer. His own difficulties with writing, and moments of staring at an empty sheet of paper, may have inspired him to write about a painter who is hardly painting. Indeed, Stephen allows Conrad to explore the equivalent of a writer's block for painting (an idea that cannot be found in books on visual art he read, like *The Premier and the Painter*, 1896, *Fort comme la mort*, 1889, and *L'œuvre*, 1886). This places Stephen alongside characters that struggle with writing, ranging from Conrad himself in numerous letters, Cosmo in *Suspense*, the old language teacher in *Under Western Eyes*, and the first-person narrator of *The Inheritors*: "forever sitting with uplifted pen" (35).

Another explanation for why Stephen is concerned with people's preconceptions and his own aspirations, rather than with painting, can be found in Conrad's attitude to his own drawings and need for privacy. He left his drawings unsigned and unframed and kept them in locked drawers. But he may also have been proud of his draftsmanship. Jessie's comments on certain drawings suggest that they were painted for her. As we have seen in Chapters 1 and 2, there are many doodles or small sketches in Conrad's holographic manuscripts; instead of covering them with ink, he has left them visible. This, despite or because of his knowledge that others would see the manuscripts, during, and after the production process. There is a Conrad drawing of Peyrol painted on the outside of an envelope addressed to his family. A letter of 1894 from Conrad to his former shipmate Walter Banks features a sketch of a young lady. The sketch in the top right-hand corner is unconnected to the content of the letter and the postscript reads: "excuse girl on paper. Can't find another sheet just now awful hurry" (*CL* IX.11). There is a humorous discrepancy between the current state of hurry in which the letter was apparently composed and its conspicuous mark of leisure or indulgence – a carefully sketched lady that testifies to a segment of unhurried time. It is also noteworthy that instead of erasing this sketch, or scribbling over it, Conrad has left it undisturbed and without comment. A possible explanation for the inclusion of the drawing is that Conrad wanted Banks to see it and/or that drawing was a habitual activity for Conrad.

That said, many factors indicate that Conrad was aware of the view that drawing is an unflattering and unproductive pursuit for an adult man. Conrad was an avid reader of Henry James, whose *The Tragic Muse* (1889–90) pivots on the commonly perceived contrast between painting and respectability. In the story, a statesman seeks to quit his job to pursue his dream of being a portrait painter. James, himself a competent painter, explains in the Preface to the story that he sought to articulate the tension between the ambition of fully devoting oneself to art and fulfilling the expectations of others. James contrasts the status of a member of parliament to that of a portrait painter, as if these occupations were at the opposite ends on a continuum of respectability; the artist is like an irresponsible child, like Mr Skimpole in Dickens's *Bleak House* (1853). Indeed, not only is painting at odds with material interests, it is frequently also perceived, as Virginia Woolf's Jacob explains in *Jacob's Room* (1922), to be "the least respectable of the arts."[28] Conrad articulates many of these views in *The Sisters* from the perspective of Stephen's father – a rich peasant who entertains dreams about his eldest son becoming a general. With disbelief or ignorance, the father asks: "Paint! Why paint? Paint what? Where? What's the good of it? Generals don't paint; nor do Councillors – even the writers in chancelleries don't paint. As to the General-Governors they would not even speak to a painter" (484). Indeed, Stephen's father classifies his son's ambition to paint as "an incomprehensible form of madness" (484). Also Stephen's brother holds painting in low regard, ascribing people's fascination with an exhibition of paintings in Petersburg to a general state of madness: "There's many mad folks in our country" (486). As in James's *The Tragic Muse*, the section on Stephen explores negative reactions to painting at greater length than it explores Stephen's own reasons for wanting to paint. The story therefore provides many reasons for keeping one's interest in visual art in a locked drawer.

However, *The Sisters* and Conrad's drawings are not autonomous artistic productions that can easily be ignored by Conrad scholars, as if they were still lying locked up in study drawers. They relate in time, space and shape to his other works. For instance, with a background of drawing and attempting to write his novel about a painter in 1896, Conrad published *Lord Jim* in 1899–1900, where Marlow is "trying to interpret for you into slow speech the instantaneous effect of visual impressions" (*LJ* 42). Marlow expresses a mimetic ideal between the visual and the verbal that is reminiscent of a painter's premodern attempt of copying reality (rather than questioning or redefining reality, or concerning him- or herself with the non-figurative): "'Imitation'," as the art historian/philosopher Arthur Danto explains, "was the standard philosophical answer to the question of what [visual] art is from Aristotle and down into the nineteenth century, and well into the twentieth."[29] Similar to Marlow's mimetic ideal, the celebrated American Preface to *The Nigger of the 'Narcissus'* (published in 1897, a year after he had abandoned *The Sisters*) speaks about how "art itself may be defined as a single-minded attempt to render the highest kind of justice to the visible universe" (vii) and how the artist's aim "is, before all, to make you *see*" (x).

The Preface is frequently treated as a manifesto for verbal impressionism. The clearest connection to *The Sisters*, however, is not about impressionism – verbal or visual – but in the way the Preface responds to Stephen's query about what constitutes the hidden meaning of art. In vain, Stephen has sought an answer, from Dresden to Munich, on sea horizons and in art museums, "where immortal masterpieces kept their secret" (487). He "looked for the magic sign" (482), "that message" (482), "an unveiled religion" (481), "the secret of genius" (482), "the secrets of the trade" (485). His assumption seems to be that all great artists have access to a secret code, which effortlessly unlocks superb artistic creations and instantaneous greatness, along with the title of artist. Unsurprisingly, this secret is difficult to find and neither "the dead nor the living would speak intelligibly to him" (482). From this perspective the Preface is written for Stephen and those like him; it offers "an answer" to those who look "for immediate profit, demand specifically to be edified, consoled, amused" (482). Rather than placating Stephen in his disappointment that no "angel's voice spoke from above to him" (481), the Preface opposes the notion of the existence of a secret of art, or epiphany. The Conrad of the Preface does not attribute his success to the visitation of an angel of art, or veiled message unearthed from an old masterpiece; instead we find a writer abandoned to "the stammerings of his conscience and to the outspoken consciousness of the difficulties of his work" (xi). And, whereas Stephen in *The Sisters* seeks "the last word" (481) – "the one, the final, the appeasing" (482), "the word that would fling open the doors of beyond" (486) – Conrad in the Preface explains that the aim of art is "not in the clear logic of a triumphant conclusion" (x).

Historical Context: The Advent of Modernism

The difference between Stephen's view on art and those expressed by Conrad are striking and highlight Conrad's complex relationship to modernism. If Stephen's life is supposed to be contemporary with the production of *The Sisters*, he lives during the advent of modernism in visual art – and the advent of the modern artist. "Had he been more fully described," Najder explains, Stephen "would have been the earliest novelistic presentation of one of the long row of either talented, or merely ambitious, artists from Eastern Europe who about the turn of the century wandered to Germany and France: from Constantin Brancusi to Marc Chagall, Jules Pascin or Chaim Soutine."[30] All three of the painters Najder mentions are modern painters: on the front line of a dramatic shift in the history of visual art that started in France around the beginning of the twentieth century – where we have located Stephen in *The Sisters*. As Danto explains in his unapologetic generalization of art history: "Early in the twentieth century, beginning in France, the visual arts were revolutionized. Up until that point, they ... had been dedicated to copying visual appearances in various media."[31] While Clement Greenberg agrees on how dramatic this change in the history of visual art was, he dates its beginning to the 1860s: "as an unmistakable, full-fledged fact, as a phenomenon that declared itself as radically new, modernism began only in Manet's paintings of the early 1860s."[32] To get a sense of "the historical rupture that modernism implied,"[33] it is useful to consider how stable the definition of visual art was before the advent of modernism. This background will help us locate *The Sisters* as a historical document written in the midst of this pivotal change, with Stephen as an emblematic modern artist.

With postmodernism and modernism, the definition of visual art seems to be ever changing, as if it is within the eternal nature of visual art to question its own boundaries (think about the concept of avant-garde, for instance). The only static definition of art seems to lie in its essential heterogeneity, an idea exemplified by Wittgenstein's argument that since not all works of art share a single property, the distinct elements classified as art at best share a family resemblance.[34] Yet art has not always been defined along the lines of multiplicity and dynamic change – nor has it always been seen as difficult or even meaningful to define. The master narrative of visual art is not the history of unstable foundations: even the idea of painting in a specific style (rather than skill) is a fairly modern invention that was first properly conceptualized by Johann Joachim

Winckelmann (1717–68) and, later, Georg Hegel (1770–1831). Indeed, while other arts might be said to be episodic, discontinuous and devoid of a unidirectional and developmental history, Giorgio Vasari, Heinrich Wölfflin, E. H. Gombrich, Arthur Danto, Clement Greenberg and other art historians describe the history of visual art as a teleological history of visual representation: "concerned with copying visual appearances in various media."[35] This view of history deserves lengthy explanation since it provides essential background information for *The Sisters*, yet it has become an increasingly controversial position (the revolution has been so successful that we no longer perceive it as one – to repurpose one of Nietzsche's sayings on religion). Indeed, the conception of a uniform and progressive history is drastically at odds with modern views of art, particularly the notion that a work of art is autonomous, absolute and sui generis. In this reading, a work of art cannot be reduced to a link in the chain of evolution, where paintings are ranked as relatively more advanced than others. In the progressive view of art history, artists knowingly pursue the same goal of visual representation, seeking "to do a given thing better and better"[36] as if art were a competition that has been going on since prehistory.

In *The End of the History of Art?* (1987) Hans Belting points out that there "have always been skeptics who deny outright that one could ever trace the history of an abstraction such as 'art,' as well as pious worshipers of art who adduce the proverbially timeless beauty of the museum-bound masterpiece as evidence for the independence of art from history." Belting also cautions against attempts at reducing "the entire problem of artistic form to an act of imitation. Imitation is only measurable where art imitates *nature*. But when art imitates *reality* – social, religious, personal – the constants against which the result of the imitation are to be measured fall away."[37] These objections aside, the teleological and unidirectional theory offers extraordinary explanatory potential. Today the theory has been used extensively to identify and attribute works of art to different time periods. Apart from this empirical evidence, this seemingly simplistic theory accounts for changes in technique across time and orders art works along a conceptual line that overlaps with a temporal line. In other words, in a scenario where no dates or prior information were given about paintings, where we had forgotten all history and context about all paintings, the morphology of the paintings would be sufficient to arrange them in a temporal sequence. While problematic, the key supplied by the conception of art history as a set of evolutions along the progress of time, then, unlocks a coherent, theoretical perspective that succeeds in accounting for most paintings in history – and their place in history.

Think about the visual and plastic art produced in the beginning of the twentieth century: Dadaism, Fauvism, Futurism, Suprematism and Geometric Abstraction – all produced in Conrad's later years, in his forties, fifties and sixties. Works like Kandinsky's *Improvisation 27* (1912), Kazimir Malevich's *Black Square* (1915) and Duchamp's *Fountain* (1917) are so divorced from representational art that they could not have been made before the advent of modernism ("not everything is possible in every period"[38]). These artworks represent the crystallization of a new movement in art history that started around the time Conrad was writing *The Sisters.* From a historical perspective, it is easy to understand Conrad's interest in visual art in this era when it underwent tumultuous change: a new direction from the stable past of visual representation. Turning a porcelain urinal upside down, naming it *Fountain*, signing it "R. Mutt" and displaying it in a museum, like Duchamp did in 1917, was a reaction to the static past of art history: not a reflection of its ever-changing nature.

My point is that *The Sisters'* portrayal of Stephen is of a visual artist who does not fit the model of art and the artist as described by the unidirectional theory of art history. Stephen's exception is instead typical of his time and place: France around the beginning of the twentieth century, where this paradigmatic shift in art history originated. Indeed, *The Sisters* was written in the midst of this paradigm shift, where visual art became, to an unprecedented extent, concerned with making art out of questioning art. With a provoking but tempting generalization, Arthur Danto classifies modernism as "the Age of Manifestos."[39] It is first with modernism and the advent of the camera, Danto argues, that visual art moves away from imitation to idea (which also means that the visual art still concerned with representation suddenly becomes a style – a choice – rather than a default mode). Thus, as "the truly revolutionary invention in the history of representational technology in modern times," "The camera made Modernism happen."[40]

This makes *The Sisters* a historical document that stands between the history of visual art and "the end of art": the end of a history of art. As Danto maintains, modernism is not the fulfillment or goal of art history, but a completely new direction: "If everyone goes off in different directions, there is no longer a direction toward which a narrative can point. It is a wholesale case of living happily ever after. And that, I have claimed, is the state of the art world after the end of art."[41] In this narrative, premodern art never strived toward abstraction; although abstract art follows premodern art on a temporal sequence, they are not part of the same conceptual chain. It is difficult to say whether *The Sisters* was part of this paradigm shift or, as I think is more likely, written in reaction – maybe even in protest. First, *The Sisters* does certainly not further the aim of modernism in the manner a manifesto would: Stephen's role as a modern artist is not a positive one. Instead, Stephen's impassivity, unproductivity and frustration are, in this reading, symptomatic of an era where the role of the artist was uncertain; in Stephen's time, there was no clear answer to what to paint and why. The history of art, in general, had offered a clear-cut definition of art and the goal the artist was supposed to strive toward. With modernism, the visual artist faced an existential challenge. My view is that *The Sisters* documents Conrad's hesitation about this drastic change.

While Conrad's attitude to modern visual art is complicated, his distaste for photography, enthusiasm for mimetic art (as seen in the aforementioned quotation from *Lord Jim* and the Preface to *The Nigger of the 'Narcissus'*), his tendency to classify himself as a craftsman, and to rely on anachronistic concepts for interpreting his art (the ideas he "suggests for interpreting his novels are 'honor' and 'fidelity' – hardly the stuff of current fashion"[42]) oppose the emblematic driving forces of modern visual art. Conrad's ideal of craftsmanship, for instance, is at odds with Stephen's view on what it means to be an artist, which is more a question of attitude, inspiration and way of life than a commitment to manual labor. Stephen is so concerned with ideas that he does not start painting – a type of impasse that would not be a valid excuse for a craftsman qua craftsman. For Stephen, living in an era when "the end of art" was marked by visual art becoming philosophical and self-conscious, to be an artist was not to be a craftsman but a philosopher. Stephen should therefore be seen as Conrad's own exploration of what it means to be an artist: a question that – as we have seen – was introduced, to an unprecedented extent, during the advent of modernism that introduced a plurality of definitions.

The Sisters: Beyond Chapter Seven

It is difficult to speak of Stephen as a fully formed character for the obvious reason that *The Sisters* is "a true fragment" (*CL* v.255), as Conrad writes in a letter to John Quinn, who in the 1920s owned one of the world's largest collections of modern paintings. Given Conrad's negative appraisal of Stephen's artistic outlook, however, *The Sisters* is far from a self-indulgent autobiography. There is instead the possibility that the fictional fragment we identify with *The Sisters* is the beginning of a Bildungsroman, where Stephen's original position is similar to that of the young captain in *The Shadow-Line*.[43] The captain's original tendency to feel himself misunderstood and misdirected is later rectified by a more mature view that fits the facts better, where the world is not dull, uninspiring and unoriginal. Had *The Sisters* continued beyond its seven chapters, Stephen might have changed his unproductive views about art to align more with those of the Preface to *The Nigger of the 'Narcissus'*. "His work," after all, "lay yet in the future" (*Sisters* 487). It is therefore tempting to think that the planned continuation of *The Sisters* would change Stephen's naïve perceptions and gloomy outlook, perhaps even the stilted indirect voice used to portray him. Indeed, the sections that are not focalized through Stephen (chapters 2, 5, 6 and 7) are written in a different, more ironic tone. In contrast, Stephen's discouragement and irritation are patent in the texture of the prose, as when he classifies a museum as a "sham temple" (487), a mountain as "a disorderly mob of peaks" (487), and the whole of nature "as a super-civilized actress personating a gypsy, with the scent of manufactured perfumes lingering under the dainty and picturesque rags" (488). In addition, Stephen's overall narrative about himself seems like it is consciously constructed around clichés, such as the idea of the bourgeoisie and uneducated as unable to understand and appreciate art, the conservative father speaking out against his son pursuing an artistic path, the artist as a misunderstood and unique individual, the artist not as a craftsman but as an intellectual, and so on.

Without seeing how the sections on Stephen might function in a larger context beyond the first chapters, it is easy to classify Stephen's prose as negative, repetitive and stilted. *The Sisters*, according to Jocelyn Baines, "reads like a compulsory exercise in the art of beautiful writing."[44] Of course, not all of Conrad's completed stories are of uncontested literary value, but given Conrad's experiments with writing one text in more than one style, one should be cautious about reading and evaluating one isolated section as if it sets the tone for the final product.[45] There are multiple possibilities for why the opening pages of *The Sisters* were not a *faute de mieux*, then, but were written to work in a larger context. For instance, if Stephen, beyond chapter 7, were to have reached the success of the painter Henry Allègre in *The Arrow of Gold*, his youthful complaints would have formed an interesting contrast.

To conclude, *The Sisters* is a much more complicated fragment than hitherto acknowledged. It is not an anomalous product to be placed on the margins of Conrad scholarship. The text relates to contemporary debates, Conrad's life and many of his works, both visual and verbal. While the critical consensus critiques *The Sisters* for dealing with a subject matter Conrad was not intimately familiar with, Stephen's role as a painter aligns with the author's interests: Conrad pursued drawing as a pastime, took drawing lessons for several months, sketched one of *The Sisters'* characters (Doña Rita), continued to mention visual art and painters in his books, and produced multiple drawings the year he started the unfinished story. Written during the advent of modern visual art, *The Sisters* is of further interest in its portrayal of Stephen as a modern artist. The metaphors on painting Conrad used in the Preface to *The Nigger of the 'Narcissus'* relate to this discussion: they contextualize and oppose Stephen's thoughts about what it means to be an artist, and delimit the extent to which Conrad embraced all notions of modernity and the so-called end of art.

PART II

Published Texts
Working Method and Philosophy

CHAPTER 4

Decoding and Heart of Darkness

> I do not want you to think about the piece of chalk I am holding, but of what you see when you look at the chalk.
>
> Bertrand Russell, *The Philosophy of Logical Atomism* (1919)

> The purpose of art is to impart the sensation of things as they are perceived and not as they are known.
>
> Viktor Shklovsky, *Art as Technique* (1917)

Why did one of the most well-known philosophers of language of all time name two of his sons after Conrad, although he had only met him on a few occasions? While secondary literature has explored Conrad and Bertrand Russell's social relationship – where and how they met, the romantic undertones and the reverential attitudes[1] – this chapter will explore the relationship from the standpoint that they were two of the most innovative thinkers on language and writing of their generation. This gap in the research is the primary motivation for this chapter on Conrad and Bertrand Russell, a founder of analytic philosophy, who played a fundamental part in the so-called linguistic turn in philosophy. Similar to the ideas of visual impressionism developed in the preceding chapter, Russell found truth in minute, detailed, atomic, sensory experience – a philosophic vision that merged logic and empiricism, and agreed with the science at the time. His philosophy of logical atomism, although never intended to be a work of aesthetics, can be seen as providing a philosophical justification to much art and literature. While the previous chapters use evidence from preprint documents to discuss Conrad's working method and structure of his texts, this chapter on decoding explores a philosophical justification for Conrad's authorship. The chapter identifies strong links between analytic philosophy and Conrad's delayed decoding: a method commonly associated with verbal impressionism. This chapter is therefore intended as a continuation of the uncompleted discussion on Conrad's working method from the three previous chapters. Transitioning from a discussion of doodles and drawings to an abstract discussion of philosophy, the monograph's aim is to gain a layered and comprehensive understanding of Conrad's commitment to the marginal, and to provide a major argument for the importance of the minor details of Conrad's prose. My argument is that the topic of margins and details (as defined in this monograph) is of such substance for Conrad's writing that it manifests itself inside and outside of the text. If many of the other chapters in this monograph can be read as manifestations or examples of an attitude to writing (and what counts as important and true in writing), this chapter is a fairly explicit philosophical articulation of that attitude. By exploring the philosophical presuppositions of Conrad's literary impressionism the chapter follows Peters's *Conrad and Impressionism*, in its wide assumption that while there are certainly specific techniques associated with literary impressionism, the techniques are generally grounded in and symptomatic of a specific, philosophical worldview. The discussion here aims to complement *Conrad and Impressionism*, which – if not explicitly following any philosophical system – is influenced by the continental philosophers Edmund Husserl and Maurice Merleau-Ponty ("catalysts for my own views on literary impressionism"[2]). By discussing the analytic philosophy of Bertrand Russell, the picture of Conrad's writing and his impressionism is more explicitly tied to sensory detail than in *Conrad and Impressionism*, where its expansive discussion of literary impressionism includes "the gamut of objects of consciousness: physical objects, human subjects, events, ideas, space, and time."[3]

In *Portraits from Memory and Other Essays* (1956), Russell tells how his first meeting with Conrad inspired a feeling of "passionate love," as if he had found his soul mate:

> At our very first meeting, we talked with continually increasing intimacy. We seemed to sink through layer after layer of what was superficial, till we gradually both reached the central fire. It was an experience unlike any other I have ever known. We looked into each other's eyes, half appalled and half intoxicated to find ourselves in such a region. The emotion was as intense as passionate love, and at the same time all-embracing. I came away bewildered, and hardly able to find my way among ordinary affairs.[4]

Conrad expressed in writing equal passion for this encounter; he felt "a deep admiring affection, which, if you were never to see me again and forgot my existence to-morrow, will be unalterably yours usque ad finem" (*CL* II.318).

Russell cemented the bond by making Conrad godfather to his first child, John Conrad, and naming his second child Conrad Sebastian Robert. In "something very fundamental we were extraordinarily at one,"[5] Russell opined about his and Conrad's relationship. Despite being innovative and prominent thinkers on language, no study has yet appeared that connects Conrad's and Russell's interest in language. This is surprising as Conrad and Russell, who exchanged letters, manuscripts and books, also – if we are to trust Russell's comment – mirrored each other at the core.

This chapter explores connections between Russell's analytic philosophy and Conrad's delayed decoding, while also explaining and defining these innovative approaches to communication. Specifically, the first section of this chapter argues that delayed decoding and logical atomism both require that their executors be "privately" acquainted (on a sense-data level) with what they hope to communicate; intend to break concepts or situations down into easily understandable parts (or more precisely: never advance to conceptualization but meditate on immediate sense-impressions); and seek to enable successful communication of important experiences or opinions. In short, what Russell's logical atomism sought to do for philosophy, Conrad's delayed decoding attempted to do in literature.

Both Russell and Conrad thought that verbal natural language (from now on: language) often failed in precision. Russell puts the problem succinctly: "When one person uses a word, he does not mean by it the same thing as another person means by it."[6] Or, as Conrad says in one of his characteristic, sweeping expressions on the unreliability of language: "Half the words we use have no meaning whatever and of the other half each man understands each word after the fashion of his own folly and conceit" (*CL* II.17).[7] On the shoulders of his idol Maupassant and from his disillusioned view of colonialism, Conrad emphasizes the limits of language in remembered conversations, private letters, public texts; with narrators, personifications, plots, sketches; ironically, factually and logically. Russell is as acutely aware of the treacherousness of language as Conrad and asks us, who aspire to do philosophy, to question our unbounded faith in language: "This influence of language on philosophy has, I believe, been profound and almost unrecognized. If we are not to be misled by this influence, it is necessary to become conscious of it, and to ask ourselves deliberately how far it is legitimate."[8] In direct agreement with the German mathematician Gottlob Frege and his *Begriffsschrift* (1879), Russell maintains that ordinary language is convenient for ordinary occasions, but not on occasions that demand complete accuracy. A view which can also be ascribed to Conrad: "Words which are the common property of mankind are but fit for common occasions" (*CL* III.328), he writes in a letter from 1906.[9]

Russell holds what Foucault classifies as the classical theory of language, which centers on symbols and the symbolized. Here words are interpreted as – more or less successful – designators, signs, representations and metaphors. For Russell, words are not self-subsisting, mind-independent universals that instantiate the visual world; Russell, like Conrad and the dominant strands of modern and analytic philosophy, rejects Platonism.[10] In particular, Russell's logical atomism rejects the Platonic view that words stand for abstract concepts that, analogous to cookie-cutters, instantiate imperfect replicas of themselves in physical things. Russell therefore tries to work against the unconscious and unfortunate habit in philosophy of analyzing the symbols as the symbolized, as tangible entities. He holds that proper names – like Conrad, colonialism, *Nostromo*, Poland, table, leaf and apple – are "complex systems bound together into some kind of unity, that sort of a unity that leads to the bestowal of a single appellation."[11] The "apple" in your hand could be more accurately described as a round and cold patch of red; the "leaf" on the path may be a sinewy, brownish, asymmetrical thing, and so on. In other words, these complex systems, in Russell's opinion, can be broken down into more reliable components that one can sense, see or smell.

Siding with G. E. Moore rather than with German Idealism, Russell is the philosopher of common sense, and the atomic constituents of his language are meant to correspond to the layman's conception of the external world, of physical reality – "from absolutely undeniable data," "so obvious that it is actually laughable to mention them," based "upon direct acquaintance with the objects which are the meaning of certain simple symbols."[12]

Russell believed that a philosophically clear language, a "logically perfect language,"[13] would eliminate many of the disagreements that constitute the non-teleological history of Western philosophy. In what has come to be known as the linguistic turn in philosophy, Russell stressed that some "of the notions that have been thought absolutely fundamental in philosophy have arisen, I believe, entirely through mistakes as to symbolism," "bad grammar."[14] He sought to identify the smallest (i.e., the least abstract) components of language: the linguistic atoms of immediate experience that, like Descartes's conception of God, gain their indisputability by being clear and lucid to the apprehending subject. These linguistic atoms are defined as "things immediately known in sensation: such things as colours, sounds, smells, hardnesses, roughnesses, and so on."[15] According to Russell's extreme empiricism, the user of his language needs to be personally acquainted with all the sense-data that the linguistic atoms represent. Borrowing an argument from David Hume and G. E. Moore, Russell maintains that one cannot explain what red looks like to someone who has never seen the color.

This identification of truth with atomic particulars implies a way of communicating experience, of presenting a chain of sense-impressions – linguistic atoms – rather than the object or event they putatively instantiate. This method links delayed decoding with logical atomism. Ian Watt famously explains that delayed decoding is the process of giving the sense-impression before its consequent naming: presenting the raw, uninterpreted, immediate sense-impressions before the abstraction, the blunt word, and the holistic picture ("It was a trickle, dark, swift, thin ... Blood!" *SA* 107). Similar to the scientific spirit of analytic philosophy, Conrad generally aspires to leave events uninterpreted, to show but not tell, to compose texts disinterestedly, objectively and diplomatically. His essays in *Notes on Life and Letters* voice an ambition to write in a "sober," "impartial," "detached," "manly," "serious" and "faithful" language.[16] Likewise, in "Stephen Crane," Conrad praises Crane's detached writing and "imaginative grasp of facts" (*NLL* 43). He also applauds John Galsworthy, in an essay bearing his friend's name, for his impartiality, a method "meant for a humanity which has outgrown the stage of fairy-tales" (*Last Essays*, 126). Perhaps Russell is correct in his judgment that "All great literature requires the rare and all but impossible combination of fiery emotion with an intellect capable of viewing it impersonally."[17]

Conrad looked unfavorably upon authors who subjugated their works to a personal opinion rather than to the truth of craftsmanship. He considered Rousseau's *Émile* (1762) to be the intoxicated outburst of the author's provincial morality. It is fair to say that Conrad had as much faith in Rousseau as he did in the narrator's commitment in *The Inheritors* "to that kind of emotional, lyrical outburst that one dislikes so much on re-reading" (101). In "Legends," Conrad explains why a writer should avoid emotional attachment to his fictional characters: "love is uncritical. It is an enthusiastic state seeing romance in what may be not true to the spirit of its subject, so to speak. And thus the false which is often fatuous also creeps into a worthy or even noble story" (44).[18]

Far from an expression of personal opinion or subjective judgment, delayed decoding attempts to give the reader undigested sense-impressions, unclothed in metaphor, uncolored by feelings and unperturbed by reason. Delayed decoding gradually describes the quasi-atomic ingredients of a sensory experience rather than trying to distill the sensory experience, in its final rationalized shape, with one word or sentence. To this extent, delayed decoding feeds into the conception of Conrad as the literary equivalent of a visual impressionist: he is concerned with pictorial, private and phenomenological reality – not with conceptualized, symbolic and figurative reality.

Conrad's delayed decoding is illustrated in "The Secret Sharer," when the unnamed captain, in the middle of the sea, encounters a "mystery floating alongside [his ship]" (178). By piecemeal descriptions, which accord with the captain's immediate experience, the object slowly takes shape before the reader's eyes:

> With a gasp I saw revealed to my stare a pair of feet, the long legs, a broad livid back immersed right up to the neck in a greenish cadaverous glow. One hand, awash, clutched the bottom rung of the ladder. He was complete but for the head. A headless corpse! . . . I suppose he raised up his face, a dimly pale oval in the shadow of the ship's side. (178)

If the captain had retold the experience as "then I discovered a person next to the boat," the subtleties of his experience would have been erased and misrepresented. In fact, literally the last thing the captain experienced was a person.

Delayed decoding works similarly in *Heart of Darkness* (the story that, according to Russell, best expresses Conrad's "philosophy of life"[19]) when Marlow gradually discovers that his helmsman has been speared:

> Something big appeared in the air before the shutter, the rifle went overboard, and the man stepped back swiftly, looked at me over his shoulder in an extraordinary, profound, familiar manner, and fell upon my feet. The side of his head hit the wheel twice, and the end of what appeared a long cane clattered round and knocked over a little camp-stool . . . The man had rolled on his back and stared straight up at me; both his hands clutched that cane. It was the shaft of a spear that, either thrown or lunged through the opening, had caught him in the side just below the ribs; the blade had gone in out of sight, after making a frightful gash; my shoes were full; a pool of blood lay very still, gleaming dark-red under the wheel; his eyes shone with an amazing lustre. (90–91)

Again, it would be inadequate of Marlow, the narrator, to condense this experience into "then a spear killed my helmsman," since this was not what he experienced.

Both delayed decoding and logical atomism deal, then, with raw sense-impressions; they construct a truth hierarchy where the particular is above the abstract. Delayed decoding and logical atomism therefore differ from stream of consciousness by, inter alia, deeming experience to be constituted by discrete and discontinuous impressions (if you will, atomic particulars); stream of consciousness is, in opposition, treating experience as one continuum. This, at least, is the Bergsonian touch that William James gives to stream of consciousness in his *The Principles of Psychology* (1890): "Most books [on psychology or philosophy] start with sensations, as the simplest mental facts ... But this is abandoning the empirical method of investigation. No one ever had a simple sensation by itself."[20] In short, what Russell takes as axiomatic truth, atomic particulars, James views as figments of the imagination. Thus, whereas Russell's logical atomism and Conrad's delayed decoding treat experience as a chain of isolated links, stream of consciousness treats it as something unified, elongated, singular and indivisible. Another way of putting this is that Russell and Conrad first think they see and sense a red, round and cold patch before naming it "apple," while James first sees an apple, before deconstructing its elements into red, round and cold.

For Russell, however, there is one great advantage with his complicated language constructed on simples: analogous to how the axioms of mathematics can be trusted – but not always the derived proofs – the sensory atoms (the simple particulars) can be trusted, but not always the bundled molecular-form. The need to generalize or abstract, Russell argues, erases the subtle uniqueness of the taste of the individual sense-data. This is analogous to the process of someone with several photographs who seeks out the common denominator by erasing everything that is not common in the photographs. This element of Russell's argument has an illustrious history; Hume, Locke and Nietzsche contend that abstract concepts bundle incompatible particulars. (These ideas are similar to those on the habit of perception, made many years later, by the literary scholar Viktor Shklovsky in "Art as Technique," without acknowledging/recognizing a history of philosophical precedents).

Russell maintains that "table" is an entangled, compounded construct of sense-data – the mixture of immediate sensory experience into a muddy soup (more concretely: "table" represents a class – an abstraction that promises to contain all tables – "a logical fiction"[21]). Instead of using the complicated concept "table," one could, to unbundle the sensory experience, say: "brown, here, hard, now." This rests, of course, on the supposition that the subject experiences the details before the whole: that the immediate experience is "brown, here, hard, now" rather than "table." This corresponds, then, to a fundamental assumption about the advantage of Conrad's delayed decoding: the apprehending subject never immediately experiences an event in concrete shape, but constructs one post hoc from a flush of details and impressions. The realistic portrayal of ongoing reality therefore requires sumptuous detail, not sweeping abstractions in the shape of blunt, overused words.

As mentioned in the introduction of the monograph, a more concrete example of a blunt word than "table" which constantly fails to explain a particular feeling or situation is "love." Nietzsche's *Morgenröte* (1881) explains that the word "love" (*Liebe*) is actually a superlative and that our misunderstanding of it derives from excessive usage. Nevertheless, the word "love," for all its mystery, deserves explanation and it would certainly be extraordinary if this elusive, multifaceted and superlative word could be reduced to its linguistic atoms – assuming, of course, that it encapsulates a bundled experience.

We often take the rational approach, when trying to understand a confusing reality, of reducing the concept, question, object or situation into its smaller parts. To understand a sentence, we learn what the individual words mean. To understand a molecule, we learn what atoms constitute it. To understand a melody, we learn it tone by tone (unless we are Henri Bergson, Christian von Ehrenfels or one of their followers). Could delayed decoding be used to understand the melody of love? To find the clear and lucid ingredients (the "simple particulars") of an important experience, like love, and serve them on a platter for fresh consumption, is what Conrad sought to achieve when employing delayed decoding. This conception nicely links up with his ambition as a writer, namely, faithfully to depict the truth of his sensations.[22] Just as Russell's language of philosophical atomism rests on the prerequisite that the speaker is personally acquainted with the object that every word denotes, Conrad intended to write about his phenomenological reality.

Cecil Roberts, the English journalist and novelist, attributes the absence of the word "love" in Conrad's romantic *The Rescue* to a conscious effort by Conrad to go beyond the world of blunt words: "His human creatures, in love or anger, never sought words for expression. In that saga of a woman's heart, *The Rescue*, the word 'love' is never mentioned in its four hundred pages, despite the theme."[23] Indeed, in a letter written during the composition of *The Rescue*, Conrad explains that he has consciously avoided the word "love" in the story: "Attempting to tell romantically a love story in which the word love is not to be pronounced, seems to be courting disaster deliberately" (*CL* II.122). Since the readers of *The Rescue* are left to create their own vision of "love" – rather than let the blunt word flatten and discolor the unique narrative – this can be seen as an example of delayed decoding: a large-scale example where the delay may be indefinite.

To make the recreated experience as vivid and flavorful to our tastebuds as the original experience may have been the object of Conrad's attempt to unbundle experience through delayed decoding. (Conrad shared perhaps Nabokov's outlook: "As an artist and scholar I prefer the specific detail to the generalization, images to ideas, obscure facts to clear symbols, and the discovered wild fruit to the synthetic jam."[24]) Those who, for example, have tasted nothing but a muddy, difficult soup when reading *Heart of Darkness* are, if this is the case, likely to have escaped Conrad's intention.

Russell never praises logical atomism above conventional language, but demarcates their respective usage areas. He advises against the use of logical atomism for conventional communication; logical atomism is "intolerably prolix"[25] and inordinately tasks the users' time and imagination for everyday communication. In atomic language there are no shortcuts or abbreviations: every molecular experience is painfully spelled out in atomic form. This implies that the receiver will herself need to bundle the atomic particulars into molecular form. Delayed decoding, when it showers the reader with details, similarly demands that the reader does the work of bundling the multiple sensory impressions into one holistic picture. A passive reader who only scans the text, without interpreting it, will miss the big picture. Both delayed decoding and logical atomism tax, then, the imagination of the recipient – the decoder of the sender's message.

Given the taxing nature of logical atomism and "because the needs of logic are so extraordinarily different from the needs of daily life,"[26] Russell assigned different roles to logical atomism and conventional language. Analogously, Conrad does not employ delayed decoding throughout his texts, but leaves this narrative method, in its fullest form, for pivotal and/or harrowing events – such as the experience of encountering a denuded man in the middle of the ocean ("The Secret Sharer") or seeing death pick, by the act of chance and the instrument of a spear, not you but the person next to you (*Heart of Darkness*). It is therefore unsurprising that Conrad, who was aware of both the necessity of invoking the reader's imagination to compromise with the inadequacy of language as well as the reader's preference for passiveness,[27] would employ delayed decoding sparingly.

Delayed decoding and logical atomism share a basic skeletal structure and were developed for similar reasons, yet they are far from being synonymous terms. Russell argued for the necessity of neologisms to verbalize all immediate experiences into linguistic atoms: "atomic facts."[28] Although Conrad certainly sculpts nouns with many adjectives, he does not invent new words – he reinvents old ones. One can understand the titles of Conrad's novels *Chance* and *Victory* as neologisms. The words 'chance' and 'victory' gain their own life from the novels: every page of the novels respectively shapes these words and the words later stand as signposts for these respective reading experiences. In *Under Western Eyes*, the teacher of languages similarly explains his narrative goal, namely, the rendering

> of the moral conditions ruling over a large portion of this earth's surface; conditions not easily to be understood, much less discovered in the limits of a story, till some key-word is found; a word that could stand at the back of all the words covering the pages; a word which, if not truth itself, may perchance hold truth enough to help the moral discovery which should be the object of every tale. (58)

Conrad feared that prospective readers would misjudge the content of *Victory*, based on its title, which, he thought, hinted at the war then underway. Anyone who has read the book, however, connects the title word "Victory" to the cadence-induced "sting" at the unexpected ending – and to manly folly, womanly strength, sacrifice, beauty and love (vague, outdated terms themselves in need of specificity!). "Victory" serves as the "key-word" that singlehandedly unlocks the story/sketch to readers who have finished the novel: "a word that could stand at the back of all the words covering the pages."

Although Conrad and Russell agree with each other in their aims to make intersubjective communication of experience more accurate, they disagree somewhat on why "accuracy" is important and how to define it. Russell was an empiricist who trusted his senses, and to him logical atomism rests on the supposition of the reality of the empirical world's mind-independent existence: "We think of matter as having existed long before there were any minds, and it is hard to think of it as a mere product of mental activity."[29] Conrad had no such philosophical prejudice; there is no conclusive evidence that he favored empiricism over rationalism, or vice versa. Conrad merely wanted accurately to portray reality ("truth") and, therefore, depicted the one he had intimate access to: his own. Whereas Russell thought that language had an insidious influence on our philosophical worldview (such as inspiring beliefs in Platonism[30]), this was not an area that Conrad, who rejected Platonism but often employed Platonic metaphor, explored. Building on these findings, the next section will complicate the discussion on delayed decoding further by introducing the idea of delayed miscoding – a further step toward understanding Conrad's impressionistic prose. By discussing an example from *Heart of Darkness* at length, the next section will show the example's agreement with the main ideas developed in this first section.

Delayed Miscoding

While navigating the snake-shaped river in the foggy landscape of *Heart of Darkness*, Marlow observes objects whizzing and swarming around his sluggish, beetle-like steamer. He struggles to name these puzzling objects. At subsequent points, he labels and relabels these phenomena as belonging to the same family of objects: "Sticks" (89), "little sticks" (89), "these things" (89), "Arrows" (89). No surprises here: this hesitancy and re-evaluation are typical of his meandering narrative method.

While Marlow hesitates, one of Conrad's most perceptive critics confidently labels and categorizes these observations. Ian Watt's "delayed decoding" divides sections of Marlow's "inconclusive experiences" (*HD* 47) into categories of correct and incorrect; the objects Marlow labels and relabels are arrows, not sticks. His hesitant labeling, Watt argues, exemplifies Marlow's delayed understanding and is therefore an aspect of delayed decoding, a time-lag between the registration of "sensory impressions" and an understanding of their meaning: delayed decoding "combines the forward temporal progression of the mind, as it receives messages from the outside world, with the much slower reflexive process of making out their meaning."[31]

As was discussed in the previous section, delayed decoding has proved to be an efficient way to communicate an element of Conrad's detail-rich narrative technique and attempt to unbundle sensory experience. But the technical concept contains overlooked difficulties, which is one reason why the preceding section was on Conrad's use of delayed decoding rather than on Watt's theory and understanding of delayed decoding. Regarding the arrow/stick episode in *Heart of Darkness* – the most quoted example used to illustrate this hallmark of Conrad scholarship – Watt's delayed decoding comes across as logocentric and inconsistent: misguided in its ambition, to borrow a phrase from an aspiring writer in *The Inheritors*, "to get back to tangible ideas – ideas that one could name and date and label" (127).

In its forty-year lifetime, delayed decoding has received one serious challenge – that, in the event, fell short. Bruce Johnson famously and elegantly criticizes many of Watt's examples of delayed decoding in his 1985 essay. Yet, Watt's primary example – where Marlow suddenly re-evaluates his initial understanding of the "little sticks": "Arrows by Jove! We were being shot at" (89) – is not fully undermined by Johnson's analysis. As will be discussed, this is one explanation for why Johnson's analysis, despite its strengths, has not changed how most subsequent criticism understands Watt's theory. To address this blind spot in

Conrad criticism and the snag in Johnson's hypothesis, this chapter will argue that in *Heart of Darkness* the label "arrows" is not an upgraded understanding of the label "sticks," and that Marlow, Watt, Johnson and subsequent criticism's post hoc judgments are mistaken on this point.

The novella's celebrated indeterminacy and inconclusiveness should not be compromised by delayed decoding's attempt to monopolize this event's interpretation, or delayed decoding's reliance on binary-reading and bivalent logic – its judgment that one reading is correct and another incorrect. Watt himself emphasizes that the novella "embodies more thoroughly than any previous fiction the posture of uncertainty and doubt; one of Marlow's functions is to represent how much a man cannot know; and he assumes that reality is essentially private and individual."[32] Yet such a posture seems irreconcilable with delayed decoding's attempt to map assertions of the text onto a true/false model.[33]

Marlow's narrative about the stick episode is better understood as a tripartite transition than as a two-step equation. In common with equations for which one expects a conclusion (that could be timely or delayed), the two-step process of delayed decoding has a sense of finality, telos, inevitability and progress. A teleological process, however, is at odds with the possibility that *Heart of Darkness* is a stagnant journey. In agreement with the text's aesthetics and Conrad's idiolect, a transitional process of numerous steps can comfortably fit into an endless chain of nonhierarchical observations. This is an approach that Johnson does not explore when re-evaluating delayed decoding.

A Hierarchy of Knowledge

Watt speaks about how the narrator, experiencing "delayed decoding," transitions from minimally interpreted sense-data to more conceptualized data. For him, the narrator progresses from ignorance to "meaning" and with this, "understanding."[34] As if the novella had a clear criterion for what constitutes truth, or could be read as if it had one, Watt makes no explicit attempt to qualify the words "understanding" and "meaning."

Johnson's essay views Watt's word-use – "meaning"/"understanding" – as severely misguided; it emphasizes how Watt has imposed on Conrad a hierarchy of knowledge by attributing understanding simpliciter to conceptualization – rather than to more immediate, minimally interpreted sensory experience. In *Heart of Darkness,* Johnson explains, "traditional meanings and traditional names no longer function." Truth has an expiration date: "the impress upon the mind of immediate sensual impulses, lies closer to the origin of meaning than the operation of subsequent thought"; "The only thing we can rely on in this devolution of abstract, traditional language and categories are the utterly fresh, sensory impressions."[35]

The dominant academic discussion, however, still views "delayed decoding" as "a form of deferred explanation,"[36] a transition from ignorance to a heightened sense of knowledge: to unqualified "understanding," "meaning," "comprehensibility" and "unmasking."[37] In these situations of decoding, a narrator can suddenly "comprehend," "grasp," "realize" or "recognize" what his initial sense-impressions mean.[38] In direct opposition to Johnson, the dominant view of secondary literature therefore understands delayed decoding as delayed understanding. By dissecting the pivotal example Johnson himself hesitated on, the analysis here of the arrow/stick episode challenges this majority view.

Whereas Johnson's essay stresses that "attack" is an inaccurate decoding of the flying-sticks event, it regards the "little sticks" as "arrows": the "arrows seem at first to be little sticks."[39] On this point he agrees with Watt. Johnson's *Conrad's Models of Mind* (1971) explicitly states that the little sticks are arrows – a belief he shares with many. Yet, if the sense-impression "little sticks" is shown to have different rather than inferior epistemic content to "arrows," this would undermine the notion that the decoding is delayed: that the move from deictically immediate sensory perception to mediated concepts equates to the move from ignorance to understanding. It would also (partly) dispute the claim that *Heart of Darkness* assumes that there is such a thing as "the truth" or absolute meaning in the form of unqualified "understanding," "comprehension" or "realization."

Names and Objects

Marlow's revised opinion that the sticks are arrows singlehandedly allows him to understand the flying-sticks episode as an attack. The syllogism is explicit, a premise in the shape of an empirical observation followed by a conclusion: "Arrows by Jove! We were being shot at" (89). It is tempting to believe that "by Jove!" here signifies a realization of a rational kind. But, in other instances and texts where Conrad employs this exclamation, it signifies extraordinary surprise – such as one experiences when faced with the irrational: "By Jove! I've never seen anything so unreal in my life" (39); "The smell of mud, of primeval mud, by Jove!" (46); "For her he had died only yesterday. And, by Jove! the impression was so powerful that for me too he seemed to have died only yesterday – nay, this very minute" (122).

The realization "Arrows" is also at odds with empirical reality: here defined as the landscape assumed to be seen from Marlow's eyes. In particular, the crew is never under "attack": "What we afterwards alluded to as an attack was really an attempt at repulse" (88), Marlow explains. Since the interpretation "arrows" is what leads Marlow *falsely* to characterize the event as an attack, the "little flying sticks" interpretation likely represents a clearer understanding than the arrow interpretation. Flying little sticks better fit the description of the action, an action that "was very far from being aggressive; it was not even defensive, in the usual sense; it was undertaken under the stress of desperation, and in its essence was purely protective" (122). This was therefore a type of action undertaken with subdued ferocity, as in *Under Western Eyes*, where we find Razumov using a stable fork (a potentially deadly object capable of piercing cloth and skin) as a stick, to rain blows of frustration on the prostrate and drunk Ziemianitch. In *Heart of Darkness*, is calling the sticks arrows another example of an abstraction that simplifies the true nature of the original observation, such as calling the attempt at repulse "an attack" (78), the forest-dwellers "enemies" (45), the European opportunists "pilgrims" (56), Kurtz's victims "rebels" (95), the voice/shadow (Kurtz) "an emissary of pity" (57)? Are the sticks arrows due to their innate function or due to an epistemological imperialism?

The disjunction between names and objects is illustrated when Marlow refers to Kurtz and insists on a dichotomy between sign and signified, name and man: "the name of the man" (59); "the name of Kurtz" (66); "I did not see the man in the name any more than you do" (70). According to Johnson, only when Marlow goes beyond everyday concepts and equates "Kurtz" with an individual and immediate sense-impression ("the voice"/"shadow") does the reader encounter a truth among numerous rumors and second-hand impressions. This Conradian truth hierarchy functions by the ease with which Conrad, like Decoud in *Nostromo*, can be constructed as "the man with no faith in anything except the truth of his own sensations" (229). It is consequently unlikely that Conrad would equate the move from an immediate sense-impression ("little sticks") to an easily communicable expression ("arrows") with the move from unqualified ignorance to unqualified understanding. In this way, delayed decoding's logocentric nature is diametrically opposed to the self-conscious narrative of *Heart of Darkness* that continuously reflects on language's ability to falsify experience: its tendency to express private, individual experience with "common everyday words" (113).[40]

Binary Observations

Watt finds that Marlow's predisposed mind blinds him from immediately interpreting the sticks as arrows. Marlow's putative miscoding would here be somewhat similar to how the native people incorrectly see the steamer as a river-demon (according to Marlow's imagination). Or, how in *Nostromo* Father Roman conceives of Europe as "a country of saints and miracles" (103); we all interpret facts according to preconceptions. Since Marlow is unacquainted with arrows he has forced them into a conventional channel of interpretation that has skewed their actual significance: "our interpretations of impressions are normally distorted by habitual expectations – Marlow perceives the unfamiliar arrows as familiar sticks," Watt argues.[41] He believes, then, in the accuracy of Marlow's sense-impressions, but maintains that Marlow's decoding of these impressions is delayed.

This presumed relation between words and sense-impressions illustrates how delayed decoding is inextricably entangled in assumptions. Only on the basis that there exists a mind-independent reality can the labels "arrows"/"sticks" be classified as correct or incorrect; the labels are correct when they correspond to the novella's empirical/external reality, otherwise they are incorrect. If there is an arrow in empirical reality, the perception of an arrow is correct. Yet it is far from certain that the novella portrays an external and internal reality or maintains that these realities are different.

Watt accepts that the original observation "little sticks" is correct: the arrows must, he insists, have appeared in this way. In this manner, "little sticks" are not opposed to "arrows," any more than a swarm of "naked breasts, arms, legs, glaring eyes . . . human limbs in movement, glistening, of bronze colour" (89) is opposed to the existence of people in the forest; "round carved balls" (96) are incompatible with heads on sticks; "squirting lead" (90, 112) is at odds with flying bullets. Watt's reasoning runs thus: in the same way that someone reports that he heard barking, felt fur and saw paws, but is unable to understand that the sense-impressions indicate the presence of a dog, Marlow initially fails to *decode* that these sticks are arrows. He fails to solve the mental puzzle, like Jukes, in *Typhoon*, who initially fails to puzzle together "a face, an oilskin coat, somebody's boots . . . a pair of stout arms" (42) into one whole: Captain MacWhirr.

Yet the rational conclusion of what the swarm of little sticks "means" (to borrow Watt's word), is not unquestionably arrows: it is not the only solution to the equation – if we are, indeed, dealing with an equation.

Without knowledge of the people hiding in the forest, several alternative rationalizations are more plausible than arrows to account for the sense-impressions of these sticks. First, Marlow is on a river in what to him appears to be a foreign world: "an earth that wore the aspect of an unknown planet" (79). Flying sticks might have surprised him when sailing up the Thames, but not in this deadly, primeval and snake-shaped river, where "mighty splashes and snorts" (73) conjure up an ichthyosaurus in his imagination. On this river, before the attack, he felt as though he "had been buried miles deep in a heap of cotton-wool . . . choking, warm, stifling" (87). Short sticks flying around in this opaque and thick atmosphere seem compatible with that environment – as if they were just another ingredient of its stifling atmosphere, not a conspicuous aberration of its construct in the form of a human-made product: arrows. Indeed, like insects these little sticks fly in "swarms," and although they do not buzz, they "whizz." Marlow explains how these little sticks "were whizzing before my nose, dropping below me, striking behind me against my pilot house" (89). This is reminiscent of a passage in *An Outcast of the Islands* where "over him, under him, through him . . . the endless and minute throng of insects would swarm in streams" (332).

Up to the point when the arrow/stick episode occurs, the wilderness has largely been envisioned as a nonhuman landscape, unsuccessfully invaded by man-made stations of progress ("of change, of conquest, of trade, of massacres, of blessings," 116). In an earlier passage when the sound of human screaming occurs, it is therefore unsurprising that Marlow attributes this human scream to the mist: "A complaining clamour, modulated in savage discords, filled our ears . . . to me it seemed as though the mist itself had screamed" (83). His perception works similarly when he observes that the "bush began to howl" (90), in response to the squirted lead, produced by the Winchesters. Given Marlow's present understanding of the wilderness as a phenomenon devoid of innate, human life, the perceptions that the mist had screamed and the bush howled are rational: in accord with his previous experience and available information. And, if the mist can scream it can certainly produce flying sticks. If you instead see the sticks as arrows you have to engage, at this point, with the somewhat irrational assumption that human beings are hiding in the wilderness; the existence of a literal swarm of arrows requires the presence of a copious number of people to launch them.

As Johnson notes, before the flying sticks swarm around the steamer, there is information speaking against the occurrence of an attack. Marlow explains: "what made the idea of an attack inconceivable to me was the nature of the noise – of the cries we had heard. They had not the fierce character boding of immediate hostile intention" (87). "Unexpected, wild, and violent as they had been," he continues, "they had given me an irresistible impression of sorrow. The glimpse of the steamboat had for some reason filled those savages with unrestrained grief . . . extreme grief may ultimately vent itself in violence – but more generally takes the form of apathy" (87). Francis Ford Coppola's 1979 film *Apocalypse Now* – contemporary with Watt's publications on delayed decoding – is sensitive to the position that the attack was an attempt at scaring, not injuring: the attack on the gunboat initially takes the form of harmless sticks. Yet, the litmus test of whether the little sticks can be decoded as arrows is given by whether rational agents interpret the passage, roughly up to the point where Marlow says "Arrows!," as indicating that arrows are being fired at the steamer.

Without revealing where the passage came from, I introduced it to people unfamiliar with Conrad's writings and asked what they thought it described. They explained that the event Marlow described was that of a dream without an objective explanation; a burgeoning hurricane or tornado ("I seem to remember that right before a hurricane/tornado hits, everything goes quiet/still, just like what is described at the very end"); a latent sea creature; an insect manifestation; or the outcome of the boat having struck a tree that suddenly lets little sticks fly into the air. One person offered a second, and, in her opinion, less probable explanation: "They are being attacked and the sticks are arrows. 'Snag in the fairway' is a block in the river set up by the attackers." That this interpretation accords with the subsequent passage does not prove that the passage harbors this truth and that it lies open for decoding. She offered this as but one of many guesses, not as the sole, rational conclusion from the information available.

The current academic consensus seems to be, in the words of John G. Peters, that we "as readers are just as much in the dark about what is occurring as is the character Marlow."[42] Several critics state in passing that Marlow and the (astute) reader are puzzled about the meaning of this display of sensory impressions. This indicates that an arrow-attack is not an updated and upgraded understanding of the original observation of thickly flying sticks; rather than being synonymous descriptive terms, these descriptions decode different epistemic contents. They convey alternative (and non-competing?) interpretations of a puzzling event and an array of ambiguous signs.

If, like Watt, one assumes that Marlow's delayed decoding explains the transition from ignorance qua ignorance to understanding qua understanding, one limits the fundamental inconclusiveness of Marlow's experience. This also negates the possibility that *Heart of Darkness* fully engages with ideas of perspectivism and the existence of competing epistemic fields, where there is no clear truth hierarchy between rational and irrational, sensory and conceptual. As such, Watt's promotion of the idea of the existence of unqualified understanding, or his very notion that this is a useful concept in Conradian theory, is not an uncontroversial move. Indeed, indeterminacy and ambiguity are keynotes of Conrad's imaginative literature, where affirmations are frequently followed by qualifications ("as simple as a village maid – a glorified village maid," *S* 148; "An idiot. A one-ideaed creature. Only the idea was complex," *AG* 310; "Verloc, steady like a rock – a soft kind of rock," *SA* 17; "A little behind them, on the stairway, there was a space. Perhaps I was mistaken; perhaps there was no space – I do not know," *I* 106).

The "courageous recognition of all irreconcilable antagonisms" (*CL* II.348) "is central to Conrad's work and to any appreciation of its power, ambivalence, and appeal."[43] As Harkness observes in his introduction to *The Secret Agent*, Conrad "became the apostle, not of the Everlasting Yea or Everlasting Nay, but of the Eternal Why."[44] "Art for me is an end in itself. Conclusions are not for it" (*CL* V.237), Conrad writes in a letter. If we apply this generalization to *Heart of Darkness*, we should take Marlow seriously when he states that outsiders "can only see the mere show – and can never tell what it really means" (72): this quotation should be read as a fact, not as a challenge.

Andrew Michael Roberts's reading of delayed decoding exemplifies how much later criticism seems to have ignored Johnson's espousal of epistemological relativism within *Heart of Darkness*. For Roberts, delayed decoding assumes a universal reality with a *bivalent* logic: the effect of delayed decoding "tends to be to reassure us of the existence of a shared (non-private) reality, since it presents us with a false reading of the situation followed by a correct one. Delayed decoding is a sort of ambush for the reader, in which a momentary puzzle is followed by a discovery of reality."[45] Watt's delayed decoding is bivalent in the sense that it separates and opposes impression with understanding, false with correct, sensory with conceptual, unintelligible with communicable, subjective with objective, coded with decoded.

The assumption of bivalence in delayed decoding is, however, neither obvious nor unambiguous. If we look at the stick/arrow example, we can easily construct a tripartite transition, where Marlow moves from a primary, to a secondary, to a tertiary perception/verbalization: (1) "little sticks," (2), "these things," (3) "Arrows": "Sticks, little sticks, were flying about ... I could only hear ... the patter of these things ... Arrows by Jove!" (89). "These things" is a distinct, separate observation that is synonymous with neither sticks nor arrows. "These things" is also a description of less specificity than either little sticks or arrows; "little sticks" and "Arrows" are attempts to name a visual observation, whereas "these things" could be an example of what Roger Fowler calls under-lexicalization – the recognition that one lacks a specific word, or set of words, to describe an event.[46] In these circumstances, one instead refers to the event with overly unspecific words such as a "thingy" or "wotsit." When Marlow draws attention to the inadequacy of his expressions by saying "these things," he may signal that his experience falls outside of his Western language – a language not relevant to his present experience: "the overwhelming realities of this strange world of plants and water and silence" (77). This might, then, be an example of what Hawthorn classifies as an occasion "where Conrad wants us to look at words, rather than to experience sensations through them."[47] So, a tripartite transition ("sticks," "things," "Arrows") better accounts for Marlow's recounted experience – and the relationship between his perception, verbalization and understanding – than the bivalent version offered by delayed decoding.

Watt finds another example of delayed decoding in the passage where Marlow on successive occasions calls the same object a cane and a spear. But Marlow's observations are not necessarily binary. He ascribes more than two names to his observations of the same object: "Something big appeared," "a long cane," "that thing," "that cane," "a spear" (84). It is therefore arbitrary to speak of a bivalent rather than trivalent, or tetravalent, judgment.

There are further difficulties with delayed decoding. Watt finds that "it is only when Marlow has finished attending to his duty as captain, and negotiated the next snag, that his understanding can finally decode the little sticks."[48] Yet, a reader who is neither captaining a boat nor avoiding snags, but singularly focused on the passage (the chronological observations/sensations therein depicted), would not rationally conclude that Marlow's crew is under an arrow-attack. As Johnson stresses, an analysis of Conrad's delayed decoding shows that the "explanations" are not "encoded in the original sensation."[49] To review Watt's argument in detail, let us look at the passage closely and see what evidence we can find that the sticks are arrows.

A traditional arrow is a deadly weapon and has certain characteristics that allow it to fly aerodynamically, straight, forcefully and predictably;

this is also the case for darts fired by blowpipe: "the boat went as straight as a bushman's dart when it leaves the end of the *sumpitan*" ("The Lagoon," 163). The little sticks Marlow describes exhibit few of these characteristics. Whereas traditional arrows range in length from 18 in. to 5 ft. (45–150 cm), these objects were short: "little sticks" (89). Traditional arrows have a ferocious look that accords with their function: cutting flesh. These sticks, Marlow states later, "looked as though they wouldn't kill a cat" (90). Traditional arrows are straight. There is a reason why the expression "straight as an arrow" exists – a simile used in *Almayer's Folly, Nostromo, The Rescue, The Rover* and *Under Western Eyes*. Little sticks may well be bent or crooked.

If fired at a wooden plank, traditional arrows penetrate the surface and leave an accompanying sound (perhaps a "thunk"?) that accords with this quick and hard clash. In contrast, when these sticks hit the steamer's light planks and teak-wood they created a light sound, such as when the rain hits a surface: "the patter of these things" (89). The onomatopoeic word "patter" has a clearly demarcated meaning. The word commonly describes a light, soft and repetitive sound ("a light swift pattering," *UWE* 55), such as when it rains. Based on usage, Conrad understood the word similarly: rain patters in *Almayer's Folly, An Outcast of the Islands, The Nigger of the 'Narcissus'* and *Lord Jim*. The word "patter" is similar in construct to "chatter"; the connection with patter and chatter is consistent (on a somewhat fanciful level) with the possibility that the stick-attack is an act of communication: an attempt to frighten Marlow and his crew.

In Victorian literature, traditional arrows were commonly understood to have three essential components: a head, a shaft and fins/fletches – respectively constructed out of three materials: metal/stone/skeleton, wood and feathers. Classical (and controversial) anthropological publications describe arrows in this way. Yes, *Heart of Darkness* is more readily classified as a work of fiction than history (for instance, the alligators in the novella are not native to its presumed setting, the Congo); however, the word "arrow" is not defined exclusively by the boundaries of the novella, but also by extra-fictional demarcations, such as anthropological accounts. In *Hunting and Hunted in the Belgian Congo* (1914), Reginald Davey Cooper contends that the native Congolese "are extremely clever in iron work, and the decoration of their weapons of war. I have by me a number of cleverly fashioned arrow-heads ... all are extremely ingenious in design and fashioning."[50] In *The Pygmies* (1895), Armand de Quatrefages de Breau reports that the pygmies used bamboo, fishbone and shell for arrowheads. Marlow does not report that the wooden sticks had three parts, were constructed out of more than one material, or were equipped with handcrafted components. If a wooden shaft lacks both arrowhead and fins, it fulfills the definition of a stick better than an arrow.

Traditional arrows tend to make a distinct sound when released from the bow and string: a pomph, thunk or twang ("the twang of the bow," *LJ* 86). Later on, Marlow arguably discovers that the little sticks were shot from the nearby shore: "I saw a face amongst the leaves on the level with my own, looking at me very fierce and steady, and then suddenly, as though a veil had been removed from my eyes I made out, deep in the tangled gloom, naked breasts, arms, legs, glaring eyes – the bush was swarming with human limbs in movement" (89). Since swarms of arrows demand a copious number of bows or blowpipes, it is natural to ask: "Were there any sounds coming from the shore that suggested that arrows were being fired?" Before Marlow opines that the little sticks were arrows, he observed: "All this time [as the little sticks showered the steamer] the river, the shore, the woods, were very quiet – perfectly quiet. I could only hear the heavy splashy thump of the stern-wheel, and the patter of these things" (89).

Traditional arrows make a whoosh or swoosh sound as they cut the air; these sticks whizz. Whizz sounds closer to buzz than whoosh or swoosh. In Conradian lingo, whizz is a word closely connected with non-teleological flying trajectories, such as the aimless buzzing of insects. In "The Return," the narrator mentions "a certain thought that was whizzing about loose in his [Alan Hervey's] head" (109). In *Almayer's Folly*, the house-keys whizz as Almayer throws them in the river. In *An Outcast of the Islands*, a kriss, an asymmetrical dagger with a wavy blade, makes a whizzing sound as it is suddenly abandoned by its bearer and thrown at the ground. A kriss and a set of keys are, unlike arrows, not constructed to be lunged into the air and gain a smooth, predictable and teleological flying trajectory. Since Conrad was a devotee of *le mot juste*, it is likely that his tendency to describe non-teleological flying trajectories with a whizzing sound was meditated, not haphazard. Whereas one expects an arrow to cut the wind fiercely – "a cry arose whose shrillness pierced the still air like a sharp arrow" (105) – whizzing is a less threatening sound, related to that of an airborne stick more than an airborne arrow.

There is certainly a metaphysical possibility that "arrow" is not an intrinsic property, but the product of the context – such that a stick by virtue of being fired by a bow gains the ontological status "arrow" during its flight trajectory, before getting redefined as "stick" when it hits the ground. A contextual argument of this sort is, however, difficult to make for *Heart of Darkness*. Not one of Marlow's crew-members were reported to have been hurt or even hit by the sticks. In contrast to sticks, traditional arrows can be fired with devastating accuracy.

Without denying the text's poetic nature, one can draw from controversial, "anthropological" accounts to show that this is how arrows were understood to work. These reports are often self-serving and of uncertain value on how the native people lived in Conrad's Congo, but the accounts are invaluable for grasping how others understood arrows. Reginald Davey Cooper explains: "Seeing is believing, this and other exhibitions of skill I have witnessed, prove that a bow and arrow in the hands of the average warrior in the Congo is worthy of respect."[51] Armand de Quatrefages de Breau writes in *The Pygmies* that the forest-dwellers "use with ease bows which the strongest English sailors could not even string"[52] and that their arrows can easily penetrate the clothing and flesh of a person 50 meters away. "They were wonderfully quick with their weapons," *The Autobiography of Sir Henry Morton Stanley* (1909) explains, "and wounded to death several of my followers. The custom in the forest is to shoot at sight, and their craft, quick sight, correct aim, and general expertness, added to the fatal character of the poison of their arrows, made them no despicable antagonists."[53] In short, on the basis of decoding that covers textual analysis and historical context (to illustrate how arrows were perceived), it is difficult to see how the sticks could be arrows.

The Unbridgeable Gap

In one way, delayed decoding is an attempt to translate the impressionistic quality of Conrad's prose into the binary language of true and false. To some extent, then, delayed decoding is the verbal equivalent of analyzing a Monet painting by erasing its hazy, foggy atmosphere in the hope of revealing what the painting "really" depicts. Yet, impressionism seeks to depict surface reality, with all its haziness. Approaching a Monet painting with the aim of finding its redeeming realist features is to miss the point.

The arrow/stick episode is not an equation any more than a Monet painting. It is better to view the episode as part of an inconclusive chain. The episode is not reducible to a two-step process that goes from ignorance to understanding; it is, rather, a tripartite transition from one observation to the next. This transition does not come with a realization or telos, but is part of a larger chain of endless attempts at naming. This view is consistent with the possibility that Marlow's narrative does not progress on the truth axis, but questions the very idea of existence of such an axis.

Unlike what Johnson, Watt and others have maintained, the arrow/stick episode could hint at the possibility of genuine ambiguity that cannot be decoded, or that Marlow's mind is unbalanced so that, when asked to rationalize, it simplifies – or falsifies – events. For this reason, updated experience is not necessarily upgraded experience. Just as Ossipon, in *The Secret Agent*, was incapable "of judging what could be true, possible, or even probable in this astounding universe" (216), Marlow is equally at a loss to conceptualize his conflicting reality.

This is not to say that Watt's delayed decoding as such should be discarded. However, at times it is helpful to emphasize that its binary structure and bivalent logic are limited ways for analyzing a text that is paradigmatically ambiguous. Delayed decoding can certainly be part of an explanation, but should not exclude other explanations. Can delayed decoding exist without the assumption about unqualified understanding? Or the assumption that there is such a thing as a correct and an incorrect reading? In Watt's first discussion of this issue in 1975, he hints that Conrad developed delayed decoding out of "an urgent sense that there was a more absolute disjunction between the interior experience of the individual and all the accepted assumptions of the world outside as they were normally expressed in language and literature". In the same discussion, he perceptively writes about how delayed decoding echoes the "ultimately unbridgeable gap between private perception and public meaning."[54] This early intuitive explanation may be closer to the truth than its subsequent decoded form in *Conrad in the Nineteenth Century* (1979).

CHAPTER 5

Distraction and Heart of Darkness, Lord Jim, The Secret Agent *and* Under Western Eyes

> Method is digression [*Umweg*].
>
> Walter Benjamin, *The Origin of German Tragic Drama*

> By indirections find directions out . . .
>
> Shakespeare, *Hamlet*

> I'm long because my thought is always multiple – but it is to the point anyhow.
>
> Conrad, letter to Edward Garnett

Twirling of thumbs, wringing of fat hands, doodling of squares and triangles, drumming with finger tips, chain smoking of cigarettes, nibbling at quill pens, playing with cards and fire embers – all of these exemplify the theme of distraction in Conrad's fiction, a state of between whiles: where persons, plots and animals diverge from a set and straight path – along with Conrad and his imagination. Here, the plot-oriented reader's assumptions about what is key, fundamental and important are challenged by Razumov in *Under Western Eyes*, endlessly scraping his nail with a penknife, by Mrs Fyne in *Chance* thoughtfully toying with a teaspoon, and by an old man in *Nostromo* who "fell silent, chewing his white moustache" (394). Whereas there is tolerance and even praise for Conrad's "philosophic indulgence" (108), to borrow a phrase from *Lord Jim*, there is less critical interest in these sideshows. There is no critical paper, for instance, dedicated to the act of the old man chewing his moustache in *Nostromo.* Indeed, such a research paper would seem to go against everything that is relevant – even in the field of literary studies, itself often classified as oblivious to the demands of the real world. The problem is that at the heart of "everyday realism,"[1] if we are to trust the structure of Conrad's fiction, we frequently find someone who gives "himself up to the critical examination of his toes" (*LJ* 36), or, is not listening, but "evidently thinking of something else the while" (*HD* 52), like "a dry leaf imprisoned in an eddy of wind" (*LJ* 141).

The previous chapter attempts to show that Conrad's prose took the fleeting sense-impression seriously, which partly explains its focus on detail. The focus on detail is, in turn, partly a product of delayed decoding and partly the product of the very opposite of a formulaic, mechanical technique: distraction. This distraction, I argue, is characteristic of Conrad's atypical writing method: he eloquently wrote about his inability to write; admitted to his difficulties in finding the right word (I "rang the bell violently, or perhaps I should say resolutely, or perhaps I should say eagerly, I do not know," *PR* 70); he stuttered his way through his texts with nonlexical grunts, snarls, howls, murmurs, gurgles, snorts and hems; and he sought to stay true to "the stammerings of his conscience" (xliii), a working method alluded to in the Preface to *The Nigger of the 'Narcissus'*. As has already been indicated in the chapter on doodles, Conrad used uncertainty, truancy, hesitation and disbelief in part as fuel for his writing.[2] I argue that distraction – usually a writer's enemy – is another of these unexpected features that Conrad used to propel his writing. Indeed, by allowing distraction, inattentiveness and absentmindedness to become part of his fiction Conrad was able to stay productive, steal the reader's attention and add a level of everyday realism to his texts. By looking more closely at instances of distraction in Conrad's text, I will suggest that distraction was a fundamental and serious part of Conrad's literary enterprise. I will also develop a model of Conradian distraction as stolen attention (rather than lost or diminished attention) and show that he systematically pays attention to those who do not pay attention.[3]

To argue this is by no means self-evident. Distraction is usually associated with the trivial or unproductive, thereby unworthy of anyone's attention – even the critic's.[4] It is also counterintuitive to write a focused essay on "distraction" and it is problematic to assume that "distraction" is a topic rather than the avoidance of a topic: an absence rather than presence. Paul North, in *The Problem of Distraction* (2012), notes that distraction is often defined negatively, as if there "is no distraction, only an attention to the zero degree."[5] If distraction and attention are different concepts, attention has nevertheless been the main focus of scholarly investigation. Yet the notion of attention came to the foreground when it became a problem: when something else took its place. This happened in the so-called modern world; a view of cultural history often attributed to the writings of Walter Benjamin and Siegfried Kracauer, who "identified distraction with modernity and technical reproduction."[6] Whilst two recent books, *Loiterature* (1999) by Ross Chambers and *Veering* (2011) by Nicholas Royle, do not see distraction as a defining element of modernism, Conrad's scattered references to distraction correspond to an interest developing in the 1870s, when "there was an explosion of research and debate on this topic. It was a major issue in the influential work of Gustav Fechner, Wilhelm Wundt, Titchener, Theodor Lipps, Carl Stumpf, Oswald Külpe, Ernst Mach, William James, and many others."[7] Conrad's texts, authored in this modern period, were not only reproduced in periodicals with distracting advertisements printed alongside the text, but were themselves filled with distracted narratives, characters and sounds: "the distracting clatter of the bell" (*SA* 214); "The noise, he remarked, had been distracting" (*LJ* 70); "the great, distracting, hissing noise" (*LJ* 89); "distracted by the dull roar of the busy street" (*NN* 170); "Suddenly, behind my back some ass blew his nose" ("Falk," 186). Conrad, however, rejects the possibility that his work was itself the product of distraction; in the "Author's Note" to *The Rescue* he rejects idleness as an explanation for why its production was delayed: "I dropped 'The Rescue' not to give myself up to idleness, regrets, or dreaming, but to begin 'The Nigger of the 'Narcissus'" (xi). So, why the urgency to study distraction now? And why at this point of the monograph?

The previous chapter on decoding explains how an element of Conrad's fiction equated truth with immediate sense-experience. Delayed decoding, the technique Conrad developed, sought to record immediate, private, individual experience. Conrad's modernism, however, was far from an isolated exercise in extreme empiricism and logical positivism. It was primarily a focus on the particularities of individual experience – including what can wrongfully be labeled as trivialities. Indeed, as a starting point for determining what is interesting and important for a writer and his prose, one can look at what he tends to write about most. In Conrad's fiction, distraction is ever-present as theme: Stephen in *The Sisters* stands "motionless amongst canvasses" (487) and spends his time complaining about why he cannot paint (rather than painting); Lord Jim daydreams about heroic acts and thus misses opportunities to be a hero; Willems is easily distracted from work by contemplations of his own greatness; Almayer dreams about wealth and a prosperous future for his daughter, Nina, meanwhile failing to see how his daughter is being taken away from him. What is interesting about Conrad is how the theme of distraction becomes a narrative technique and strategy; he writes about distraction while being distracted, or with the aid of distraction. Whereas content is not often classified as technique, it is not impossible for it to play this role. Consider Mrs Fyne's "handbook for women with grievances" (*C* 65), as Marlow calls it; the writing, I dare say, is itself a grievance: an extended speech act.

And regarding *The Secret Agent*, we have to ask: is it just Stevie who gives in to the "attractions of stray cats and dogs, which he followed down narrow alleys into unsavoury courts" (13)? Or is it also Conrad? Is it because Conrad gave in to these imaginary distractions of cats and dogs that Stevie had to follow them?

Sending Stevie into unsavory courts after cats and dogs extends the narrative, which was intended to be a short story but became a novel: "Verloc" became *The Secret Agent.* As is well known, when Conrad's stated task was to write a short story, he often failed. He seems to have been distracted by parallel and tangential narratives. He could not resist sending Stevie after cats and dogs, although this would extend the planned story, seemingly moving it away from its main theme of anarchism. "Conrad would tell himself that he was writing a short story," Batchelor observes, "and that short story would then grow into a substantial novel: *Lord Jim, The Secret Agent, Under Western Eyes, Chance, Victory*, and *The Rover* were all written this way."[8] Batchelor finds the cause-and-effect pattern to be one of positive procrastination: Conrad stayed productive by doing what he was not supposed to do – through a constant awareness of a looming task. One more explanation for why the short stories extend into novels is that distraction as a theme is unsuitable for focused narratives. The oblique, inconclusive, indirect and plotless texts we associate with Conrad do not closely follow a theme, but give in to side stories – as if their many narrators could not help being distracted: "But all this is beside the point" (*AG* 177); "This has nothing to do with Jim, directly" (*LJ* 39); "all that is to no purpose" (*HD* 62). Or formulated as an excuse: "But this is a digression indeed . . ." (*UWE* 86); "[Language Teacher:] I must apologise for the digression" (*UWE* 58); "I mention this because it has some bearing on what is to follow" (*SS* 83). And, in Conrad's own voice, regarding the production of "An Outpost of Progress": "I remember perfectly well the inflexible and solemn resolve not to be led astray by my subject" (285). The narrators and Conrad display a lack of interest in telos; or demonstrate how the telos itself can be an organic narrative, which moves beyond the default mode of dividing a story into main and side, center and periphery.

Modernism itself can be conceived of as a plotless segment of literary history. Gregory Ulmer argues convincingly, in "The Object of Post-Criticism" (1983), that the criticism of modernism has only belatedly become modern; it is still concerned with categories, labels and structures rather than with collage and montage. On the whole, Conrad criticism is no exception.[9] In Chapter 6 I engage with the possibility that critics too readily accept the questions offered by the texts as key to the texts (rather than directives for how Conrad wants us to read a specific text). To revisit and repeat an observation from the Introduction, focused questions often asked by readers ("Is Lord Jim 'one of us'?" "Is Jimmy Wait an impostor?" "Who is Kurtz?") are meaningful but may be at odds with the stated aim of Conrad's primary investigations. In a somewhat defensive letter in response to an "attack" on *Heart of Darkness*, Conrad explains that the novella is "mainly a vehicle for conveying a batch of personal impressions" (*CL* II.460). If so, Kurtz, although he appears central to the story, is not its focus – he is used as glue to hold impressions together; this is the "Apologia pro Vita Kurtzii" (*CL* II.460). While Conrad's response can be explained as a gracious misrepresentation of his method to appease the addressee of his letter (Elise Hueffer), Conrad expresses himself similarly – in other contexts and to other people – about a few of his other so-called major characters. For instance, in the "Author's Note" to *Typhoon and Other Stories*, the existence of Captain MacWhirr is explained as a convenient narrative solution rather than as a person of independent interest; he is "needed" to add structure to a "mere anecdote" and "a bit of sea yarn": "I felt that to bring out its deeper significance which was quite apparent to me, something other, something more was required; a leading motive that would harmonize all these violent noises, and a point of view that would put all that elemental fury into its proper place" (viii); Captain MacWhirr "was the man for the situation" (viii). In the "Author's Note" to *The Nigger of the 'Narcissus'*, Conrad stresses that the crew is the protagonist – not Jimmy Wait, the title character. Like Kurtz and Captain MacWhirr, Jimmy is the vehicle of the story: "he is nothing; he is merely the centre of the ship's collective psychology and the pivot of the action" (xi), the book is "written round him" (vii). It might be argued that neither is the title character of *Lord Jim* the focus of the novel; while Lord Jim is certainly viewed from many angles and perspectives, Greaney suggests that "*Lord Jim* is a portrait not of its eponymous hero but of Brierly, Jones, the French Lieutenant, Bob Stanton, Chester, Old Robinson, and all other members of the narratorial ensemble – a portrait, in short, of 'us'."[10] In addition, Conrad admits to Hugh Clifford that "the whole story" of *Lord Jim* "is made up of such side shows just because the main show is not particularly interesting – or engaging I should rather say" (*CL* II.226).

While secondary literature is not always keen on these investigations, one can identify sideshows like those in *Lord Jim* across Conrad's writings.[11] For instance, even a seemingly insignificant object, like the hat, is displayed with a surprising amount of variety. Although the narratives are not concerned with hat history, there are more than twenty-five types of hat in Conrad's fiction (explored in more depth in Chapter 8). In Chapter 9 of this monograph, I have counted more than 150 different species of animal in Conrad's texts. Another such sideshow can be constructed from the texts' attention to facial hair: ranging in color from gold, blond, auburn, brown, inky, reddish, jet-black to snow- or silver-white; styled like Lord Dundreary's whiskers, "Capuchin's beard" ("Falk," 201), the "beard of Father Neptune" ("To-Morrow," 253), and placed at the forefront of the narrative gaze: "At first I saw nothing of him but his whiskers: they were black and cut somewhat in the shape of a shark's fin and so very fine that the least breath of air animated them into a sort of playful restlessness" (*AG* 264). Whether the aforementioned should be classified as a descriptive or a distracted narrative is difficult to say – particularly as a distracted narrative may also be a descriptive one (whiskers animated into playful restlessness fit both categories). Theoretically, one need not have access to an author's intentions to classify his or her prose as "distracted." Like "descriptive," "distracted" is simply an adjective that describes the appearance, intention or form of a text. The importance of distraction as a guiding principle for Conrad's work can be illustrated with case studies of distraction by taking a closer look at *Lord Jim, The Secret Agent, Under Western Eyes* and *Heart of Darkness.*

Between Whiles: *Lord Jim* and Distracted Narration

In *Conrad the Novelist* (1958), Albert Guerard classifies *Lord Jim* as "an art novel, a novelist's novel, a critic's novel – perhaps the first important one in England after *Tristram Shandy.*"[12] It is interesting that Guerard links *Tristram Shandy* (1759–67) with *Lord Jim,* as both novels meditate on distraction and digression; the first is "a parody of a novel"[13] or anti-novel, the other – using similar narrative digressions – is written in a serious and subtle tone. *Lord Jim,* "a free and wandering tale" (5), "is but one yarn with interruptions affording some measure of relief" (5), Conrad explains in the "Author's Note." The story concerns "the development of one situation" (*CL* II.282) over forty-five chapters, of which thirty chapters are primarily in the form of a monologue; Marlow only momentarily breaks off from the telling. To maintain a sense of unity, Conrad argued against dividing the story into chapters; he particularly opposed the idea of titling every new section with the modifier "chapter" (the roman numerals are intended to mark pauses rather than chapters, *CL* II.282). If *Lord Jim* is conceived as one monologue running over several hundreds of pages, all of its "interruptions" ("Author's Note," 5) are welcoming resting places for one's imagination. These distractions are not to be pruned out in the search for a linear narrative, exemplum or allegory; the novel should be read as if it were more than a *roman à thèse* or giant puzzle.[14] To open the text further, here I recognize the distractions as integral aspects of the novel.

Regarding interruptions, the idea that one could easily get distracted or bored when reading in general ("I was smoking pipe after pipe over a confoundedly bad French novel that I found in the book-shelves," *I* 26) and when reading Conrad in particular is countered by narrators and narratives that are also easily distracted. For this we need not only consider *Lord Jim*: Almayer daydreams about the fate of a drifting tree; Kurtz about how kings will meet him at railway stations; Jimmy Wait in *The Nigger of the 'Narcissus'* daydreams about a Canton Street girl, and his shipmate, Mr Creighton, daydreams about "a girl in a light dress, smiling under a sunshade" (22). These distractions not only signal the characters' humanity but also serve as escapes and pauses, embedded within the text. When a character takes a pause from the dominant narrative in this manner, the reader follows. As Ian Watt notes with respect to the drifting tree in *Almayer's Folly*: "our attention, along with Almayer's, is captured by the mute appeal of the denuded branch."[15]

In his "Author's Note" to *Lord Jim* Conrad explains that certain interruptions to Marlow's narrative are not reported, but assumed: "though I have kept strictly all such insignificant details out of the tale – we may presume that there must have been refreshments on that night, a glass of mineral water of some sort to help the narrator on" (5). Although *Lord Jim* does not report on Marlow drinking mineral water, the reader and Marlow are distracted from the main events in the narrative when "Marlow paused to put new life into his expiring cheroot, seemed to forget all about the story, and abruptly began again" (75); start of episode XXI: "'I don't suppose any of you have ever heard of Patusan?' Marlow resumed, after a silence occupied in the careful lighting of a cigar" (166). In *Heart of Darkness*, the reader is distracted from Marlow's story in similar ways: "Good Lord! mustn't a man ever – Here, give me some tobacco' ... he took vigorous draws at his pipe" (92). Marlow, like Mr Powell in *Chance* or the boatswain on the *Narcissus*, tells stories "between the whiffs of his pipe" (*NN* 32). To read the stories we have to tolerate Marlow's intermittent smoking, nonchalant requests ("Pass the bottle," in "Youth," 16, 18, 20, 24, 26), and – in both *Heart of Darkness* and *Lord Jim* – occasional jabs at his listeners' cognitive abilities.

Although Ian Watt finds that the lack of information about Marlow's birthplace, home, school and significant others make him "difficult to believe in as a fictional character,"[16] I think Marlow's occasional smoke breaks are telling signs of his humanity (rather than say the information that he has an aunt in Brussels, as we are told in *Heart of Darkness*, or that he is forty-two years old, as we are told in "Youth"). Like Razumov in *Under Western Eyes*, Marlow would certainly deny being a character in a novel – and what better evidence than to refer to his temptations and distractions? As a human being Marlow is subject to temptations, like the characters in Conrad's stories that consume English, Virginian or "native tobacco" (*OP* 82); smoke a cheroot, a Turkish chibouk or a black briar-root pipe; chew betel or tobacco ("as big as a baby's fist," *V* 138); swallow opium pills; drink palm wine, brandy, gin, whiskey, schnapps, cognac, punch, curaçao and "vermuth" (*HD* 52).

Generalizing about the Marlows across Conrad's stories, Virginia Woolf judges that Marlow cannot be reduced to a full-time chain-smoking narrator, noting that many other distractions interrupt his narratives: "Nor did Marlow live entirely wreathed in the smoke of his own cigars. He had a habit of opening his eyes suddenly and looking – at a rubbish heap, at a port, at a shop counter."[17] Indeed, Conradian distraction frequently takes the form of a character or narrator focusing his gaze on an object – such as a clock, sock, stone, foot, banjo, carpet, banana, drifting tree, a yellow cur, "the broad back of a policeman" (*SA* 24), or "the stripes of the grey fur of the cat" (*UWE* 171). This distraction has direction and preference, in particular for ladies' shoes and heels. Indeed, like Jacobus in "A Smile of Fortune," Conrad's narrator is at times lost "deep in the interior of that shoe" (67) or at least the exterior: "All that appertained to her haunted me . . . the very shape, feel, and warmth of her high-heeled slipper" (*AG* 164); "Her admirable little foot, marvellously shod in a black shoe" (*AG* 176); "I couldn't see her face, but I remember looking at the high French heel of her little shoe" (*N* 234); "the heels of her feet were round and polished like shells of eggs" ("Karain," 34).

Out of context, these quotes suggest foot fetishism, but this distracted narrative gaze extends – if I may revisit a paragraph from the Introduction – to the spirit of Razumov in *Under Western Eyes* who, when lectured on the horrors of Russian feudalism, "went on studying the stripes of the grey fur of the cat" (171); like Adolf Verloc, who in *The Secret Agent*, when lectured on the philosophy of bomb throwing, focuses his mind on the material and color of a sock – "Mr Vladimir's hand clasped the ankle reposing on his knee. The sock was of dark blue silk" (22); like Marlow in *Heart of Darkness*, who in haste toward the Company's station, finds his attention drawn to a bit of white worsted tied round a native's neck: "Where did he get it? Was it a badge – an ornament – a charm – a propitiatory act? Was there any idea at all connected with it? It looked startling round his black neck, this bit of white thread from beyond the seas" (58–59); or like Conrad who in the midst of attempting to finish an autobiographical text cannot seem to help stating how, regarding his writing desk, his eye "was attracted by the good form of the same drawer's brass handles" (*PR* 37). These distractions are intimate, private, endearing, embarrassing – and uncensored: the readers seemingly follow the narrator and his thoughts everywhere (with the exception of the toilet, where no Conrad character goes).

If Nabokov and others introduce us to unreliable narrators, Conrad introduces us to unprofessional narrators. The narrators get tired, need a drink or a smoke break, and are easily distracted (a far cry from the quasi-divine narrator of other oral narratives: a muse assists with telling *Paradise Lost, The Odyssey, The Aeneid* and other epics). A story is not told for its inherent interest but simply for lack of better alternatives. The story about Jim is told by Marlow because he and his listeners are too tired to play whist; in *Heart of Darkness* Marlow retells his experiences on a snake-shaped river when the crew of the *Nellie* is too tired to begin a game of dominoes. We are not given a well-rehearsed speech and the setting of the story is not a speaker's podium. From the context, it is likely that many of the narrators are tipsy: in "Falk" a story is told as an after-dinner conversation over wine; in "The Brute" (1906), the main narrator is in a bar at the Three Crows; in "The Partner" (1911) the text unfolds as a conversation with "an imposing old ruffian" (77) drinking beer in a smoking room; in "Youth" Marlow tells a story leaning on his elbows drinking claret; in *Chance*, Marlow tells a story in a riverside inn. In *Lord Jim*, Marlow constructs a large part of the story from a dinner conversation, with Jim leaning "over the table with his knuckles propped amongst coffee-cups, liqueur-glasses, cigar-ends" (90–91); Conrad himself admits to being deeply "buried in cigarette-ends" (*CL* II.331) when writing *Lord Jim*, a manuscript with multiple cigarette stains. In this context of a *tête-à-tête* with a tipsy listener, outside of the courtroom narrative of yeses and noes – a narrative construct Jim finds limiting – there is an allowance for the tangential: for cigar smoke, yellow curs, rattan chairs and sleeping suits. Marlow is not the most focused narrator and, for this reason, he is able to tell Jim's story in all its detail, complete with digressions and distractions – he makes it into something more than a journey from the ship *Patna* to a lifeboat. Less imaginative characters, like Captain Brierly or Jim's father, the preacher, would have given us a less complicated picture of Jim and his guilt: a picture as straightforward as their ideas about conduct and morality, plotted along a line of simpleminded certainties – "with perhaps a platitude or two thrown in on occasion not from a desire to dazzle, but from honest conviction" (*SL* 17).

Despite the fact that Jim's story contains elements of digression and distraction, the novel is also, as Conrad writes in a letter, "as near a story as I will ever get" (*CL* II.271). This prediction is not completely accurate, as many of the fifteen books he was to write after this statement – like *Chance, The Rescue* and *Victory* – are more plot-driven than *Lord Jim.* By "story" Conrad may refer to the second part of the novel: if we are introduced to Jim daydreaming in the first part (on the *Patna*), the second part deals with actual heroic and romantic events: a daydream lived out. Fredric Jameson calls the Patusan episode "a virtual paradigm of romance" (191). A fanciful way to account for the *Patna*/Patusan split is that it marks the transition from a daydreaming protagonist, Lord Jim, to a daydreaming author, Conrad. Similarly, in *Almayer's Folly*, "the fantasies which are mocked in Almayer are used uncritically in the treatment of Nina."[18] One possibility why readers have viewed the second half of *Lord Jim* as less compelling than the first is the lack of a daydreaming protagonist. When Lord Jim is living in the present, his story is less human – to maintain the reader's attention, distraction is necessary.

Stevie's Shuffling Feet: *The Secret Agent*

"The most remarkable feature of the structure of *The Secret Agent*," John Hagan explains in one of the most convincing readings of the novel, "is that it is made up of a series of interviews."[19] Verloc and Vladimir (chapter II), Verloc and Winnie (chapter III), Ossipon and the Professor (chapter IV), etc. – for a total of seventeen interviews. These interviews are not reported as mere verbal exchanges, but are told from a cinematic perspective. Set in London – a "town of marvels and mud" (203), "an immensity of greasy slime and damp plaster interspersed with lamps" (116) – starring Winnie and Mr Verloc (husband, double agent, "peripatetic philosopher," 174), this is a story of "scheming and insomnia" (195), "the luminous glory of oranges and lemons" (116), "drooping moustaches, the colour of ripe corn" (68), "walls nodding" (53), the Cheshire Cheese, Stevie's shuffling feet, and a horse "dancing mincingly on his toes with infinite patience" (121). These are significant elements of *The Secret Agent*, which collectively stress that this is not only a novel of interviews but a novel written by a collection of distracted interviewers/reporters. *The Secret*

Agent is, then, not only a spy-novel, tragicomedy, "domestic drama" (168), or as Conrad once called it, "Winnie Verloc's story" ("Author's Note," 8), but also a novel about distraction.

The Secret Agent was rewritten as a stage play by Conrad and performed in 1922. If the stage play is a visual and aural approximation of the novel, it is significant that here – when Conrad provides guidance on how the actors should interpret the text – he explains that multiple characters are frequently in a brown study: like the interview subjects and reporters in the novel. These reporters are repeatedly in the role of a distracted and unprofessional amanuensis, noting things such as: "Sir Ethelred opened a wide mouth, like a cavern, into which the hooked nose seemed anxious to peer; there came from it a subdued rolling sound, as from a distant organ with the scornful indignation stop" (107). This anxious nose is not tangential to the novel, but holds the reporter's attention, perhaps as much as the reader's.

How should one make sense of these textual elements that seem to diverge from an overarching narrative? Baines finds that the novel consists of "a succession of only superficially related scenes" and lacks "a unifying theme."[20] Guerard explains that these tangential narratives are subordinate to dominant themes: "The asides . . . furnish footnotes."[21] If the details that do not directly relate to a master narrative are footnotes, as Guerard seems to suggest, the novel consists mostly of footnotes. I therefore hesitate to divide the novel into center and aside in this way. (Actual asides, which Conrad places on the periphery of the narrative, are put into parentheses.[22]) In addition, a commitment to "asides" can coexist with a commitment to a unifying theme: there is no necessary subordination of one to the other.[23]

The majority of critics disagree with Baines's verdict that the novel is a collection of unrelated scenes. Indeed, although *The Secret Agent* contains so many moments of distraction, it is itself a unified whole: a work of "total control";[24] "a work of virtuosity";[25] "his richest work of art";[26] "perhaps the least problematic and the most perfectly crafted of Conrad's works,"[27] plotted like "a chain reaction."[28] The digressive details are part of the whole. As will be discussed in the next chapter, every detail in the novel can be accounted for and related to different aspects of the novel. For instance, at first sight it appears that the indoor pet cat that Mr Verloc caressed in chapter one of *The Secret Agent* changed residence, as if Conrad had forgotten that it was part of the household. After Mr Verloc's caress, the cat is never mentioned again in the novel. This is a surprising silence – the secret cat in *The Secret Agent* – as household pets are useful narrative components and important members of a household: Conrad showed this with the parrot in *Nostromo*, a monkey in *Almayer's Folly*, Captain Brierly's dog (Rover) in *Lord Jim*, the *dame de compagnie's* cat in *Under Western Eyes*, and the Fyne dog in *Chance*, which possibly prevented Flora de Barral from committing suicide. So, why is there no further reference to the Verlocs' cat? For instance, the cat might have been attracted to the blood-drenched hat on the floor, toward the end of the book, or found a companion in Stevie. If Stevie demonstrates such compassion for the cleaning lady Mrs Neale, the taxi driver and his "dancing horse" (122) – not to say the persons who figure in stories in the newspapers he reads or the stories he overhears – where does the cat figure in Stevie's sympathy? Why are we, as readers, not told about Stevie's interest in taking the cat to bed with him? ("To be taken into a bed of compassion was the supreme remedy, with the only one disadvantage of being difficult of application on a large scale," *SA* 129.) And whose cat is this? Was it taken in or purchased to keep Winnie's mother company? Is the ever-tired Mr Verloc a cat person, needing to share the household with a being whose very stereotyped identity is that of laziness? Is it, perhaps, Winnie's cat? When Winnie's mother moves out and decides to leave her best furniture to Winnie, why is there no reference to the cat?

Cats are said to be independent in nature and in the novel there is a reference to "the vagabond, lawless, and amorous soul of a cat" (*SA* 210): the street cat. Although no further reference is made to the Verlocs' cat, its existence would explain the mystery of why the outer door of the shop is left "suspiciously ajar in the obscure and narrow street" (148). The way the novel adds up in these ways partly explains, I think, why "*The Secret Agent* is unusually rewarding on re-reading."[29] Conrad is able to combine a distracted focus with a sustained attention to the novel as a holistic structure: he keeps track of the cat that stole Mr Verloc's attention and makes sure it has a way in and out of the house; it is reminiscent of how in *The Nigger of the 'Narcissus'* the cat Tom reappears in the narrative after being absent for several chapters. The difficulty in combining these two seemingly antagonistic approaches – distracted narrative and holistic consistency – highlights Conrad's skill and style. Indeed, although Stevie easily gets distracted and loses his way in London, Conrad does not forget about him. But there is an element of overlap between fictional and actual distraction. In addition to launching bread-pellets from his dinner table ("I have seen them fly into the soup-plates and glasses of our guests"[30]), Conrad lets Lord Jim, when sitting silent, play "thoughtfully with the bread-crumbs on the cloth" (178). Instead of merely doodling in his manuscripts, he writes about how Blunt, Razumov and Stevie doodle. And, in addition to playfully admitting that he enjoys chasing wild geese ("Quelle est votre plus grande distraction? Chasing wild geese"[31]), he lets Stevie give in to the attractions of stray cats and dogs – without losing sight of Stevie.

Conrad systematically pays attention to the ones who do not pay attention. For instance, as a minor character with occasional appearances, Wamibo is easily overlooked on a reading of *The Nigger of the 'Narcissus'*; in discussion, an eminent Conradian admitted that he had forgotten about Wamibo's presence in the novel. Only when puzzling together Wamibo's occasional appearances – scattered in sentences across the novel – does a unified image of a character appear. In his everyday work as a sailor, during the solemn moment of Jimmy Wait's funeral, and – twice – when confronted by a bellicose Donkin, "Wamibo dreamed" (106, 159, 168). His bodily presence is sailing from Bombay to London, but Wamibo is on his own journey – contemplating an object, daydreaming, and failing to understand multiple situations. His introspectiveness and distance from the crew can partly be explained by his inability to understand spoken English, like Yanko Goorall in "Amy Foster." But even when his interpreter, Archie, conveys a situation Wamibo fails to understand. Wamibo is instead occupied by "long periods of staring dreaminess" (*NN* 42). A holistic understanding of *The Nigger of the 'Narcissus'* does not require a unified understanding of Wamibo. Conrad, however, has made sure that Wamibo participates in many activities and situations – although Wamibo is persistently absentminded and although we, as readers, may not have the attention to take him in.

"There goes my silver medal!": *Under Western Eyes*

Four years after the publication of *The Secret Agent* in book form, Conrad publishes another major landmark: *Under Western Eyes* (1911), which continues the theme of distraction and digression. *Under Western Eyes* has been productively studied for its potent political and psychological themes; in this way, it is at odds with the treatment of these themes in *The Secret Agent*. The latter work aimed to sustain a note of irony, as Conrad's correspondence explains and many critics have discussed ("we don't look for the secrets of Conrad's soul in *The Secret Agent*," F. R. Leavis remarks[32]). How, then, does *Under Western Eyes*, this searching political novel, engage with distraction and digression? "It is obvious," Guerard explains about *Under Western Eyes*, "that Conrad made a conscious effort to chasten and simplify style, to subdue temperamental evasiveness and control digressive fantasy."[33] I find Guerard's observation surprising. Conrad may not have been distracted, but Razumov in *Under Western Eyes* embodies digressive fantasy, and is indeed one of Conrad's most distracted characters, in thought and act. In fact, Razumov's distraction is such a pervasive and obvious character trait that it is also surprising that no one has discussed Razumov under this label previously. Given that *Under Western Eyes* is primarily based on Razumov's dated journal entries, I will argue that the novel is a superb meditation on digression and distraction – rather than an evasion of these qualities. To explain the artistic merit of *Under Western Eyes* as being its repression of digressive fantasy is to misrepresent a core idea of the novel, which, like *The Brothers Karamazov* (1880), indulges in digressions.

In a tumultuous political climate, Kirylo Sidorovitch Razumov is "a man of studious and retired habits" (5), preferring the peaceful light of his reading lamp to the heated revolutionary debates among his peers. As a third-year student of philosophy at St Petersburg University, he is at work on trying to win a silver medal – a key to distinction, acknowledgment and an administrative appointment; a step on the ladder toward becoming a celebrated old Professor ("one of the glories of Russia – nothing more!" 19). All this changes as Victor Haldin (a "political saint," 54 / "sanguinary fanatic," 34) unexpectedly interrupts Razumov's solitary existence: "It was I who removed de P – this morning" (20). Under the logic of autocracy, Razumov is no longer a promising student but a subversive, guilty by association. The sudden appearance of Haldin has uprooted his life plan and taken over his thoughts.

After locking up Haldin in his room Razumov goes to set up a meeting with the town peasant Ziemianitch, but finds himself oblivious to his immediate surroundings: he fails to hear "the crash of two colliding sledges close to the curb" (30), walks in "the wrong direction" (31) until he finds himself stopped with his legs firmly planted in an obstinate snowdrift. After this snowy walk on which he encountered Ziemianitch, Prince K— and a hallucination, he is back in his room. Here he doodles, drops a watch on the floor, attempts to write and imagines that there is a police agent outside, smelling of "raw onions and spirits" (56). After a night of distracted sleeping, he spends the day yawning, walking around the table in his room, "drumming on the window with his finger-tips quietly" (59), and drinking "large quantities of tea" (59). Although he repeatedly tells himself that "it is done" (56), Razumov cannot move on but is haunted to distraction by the specter of Haldin: "And all this was Haldin, always

Haldin – nothing but Haldin – everywhere Haldin" (230). Distracted, he lives post-Haldin in "a state of peculiar irresolution" (66). He suffers from post-traumatic stress, like Dr Monygham in *Nostromo* after being tortured, Captain Hagberd in "To-morrow" after the death of his wife, Ossipon in *The Secret Agent* after deceiving Winnie, Marlow in *Heart of Darkness* after returning to London from his journey to Kurtz's station, and to some extent Lord Jim after the *Patna* incident.

Like *The Secret Agent, Under Western Eyes* can be constructed as a set of interviews: part first: Razumov–Haldin; Razumov–Prince K—; Razumov–Madcap Kostia; Razumov–Councillor Mikulin. Razumov, the interviewee, is in part a case study in distraction: "I don't think that in his distraction he is ever monstrous" (6), Conrad writes in the "Author's Note" and identifies a cause-and-effect relationship between Razumov's environment and distraction. Conrad also identifies a link between monstrousness and distraction. Distraction seems like an everyday, harmless act – how can it be conceived of as monstrous? Conrad uses the word 'monstrous' to explain the appearance of London in *Heart of Darkness*, a pair of fat cheeks in *Nostromo*, a blank page and a pair of thick boots in *Under Western Eyes*. But there is certainly the possibility of being monstrous in one's distraction. If Razumov's post-Haldin state is defined by distraction, his post-Haldin acts should be evaluated in this light. It is tempting to classify a few of Razumov's cynical thoughts about Nathalia Haldin – and his plan to marry her on the basis of deception – as monstrous. Equally, when Razumov attacks the impoverished, inebriated and unconscious sledge-driver Ziemianitch with a stable fork, he is acting illogically and distractedly. Conrad is not condoning Razumov's behavior in saying that his acts are not monstrous: he merely sees him as a human being. Distraction is a human trait – not a monstrous one. The novel's Ur-text, Razumov's journal, was itself produced as a means of distraction from his role as a secret agent. With its peculiar details, such as how Razumov finds himself "attracted by a stone of a peculiar shape" (217) on a small steamboat pier, the story – retold by a digressive old teacher of languages – takes distraction seriously. Indeed, the fact that Razumov decides to write down the moments of distraction in his secret journal and that the teacher of languages decides to retell them (meanwhile distracted by his love for Nathalia Haldin), mean that distraction controls the novel.

"The criminality of inefficiency": *Heart of Darkness*

Heart of Darkness is more than a meditation on language, colonialism and its cruelty: it is also a study of senseless waiting, dead time, inefficiency, distraction and delay. When the story is first mentioned, "colonialism" (the elephant in the room?) is not directly mentioned: "The criminality of inefficiency and pure selfishness when tackling the civilizing work in Africa is a justifiable idea [for a work of fiction]" (*CL* 1.139–40), Conrad writes in a letter from 1898 to his Scottish publisher William Blackwood, a conservative who believed in the "civilizing" work of colonialism. Critics have explored the doublespeak and hypocritical nature of colonialism extensively, but the notion of "criminality of inefficiency" is underexplored. Like its precursor "An Outpost of Progress", which features the "stupidity and laziness" (81) of two colonial agents, *Heart of Darkness* has a sustained focus on the misallocation of resources: a topic of importance not only for the "dismal science of economics," to rely on Thomas Carlyle's description,[34] but also for literature. It is not merely a question of the sham trading of brass wire and "calico, cotton prints, beads" (65) for ivory, which is "collected, bartered, swindled, or stolen" (92). It is also a question of the misallocation of human resources, reminiscent of Adam Smith's argument against slavery due to its economic inefficiency: the overall economy is best served with a free labor market.

An ink-stained, unshaven, "vermuth"-drinking doctor – occupied in measuring Marlow's head with callipers and speaking disconnectedly – is emblematic of this journey of inefficiency and distraction. So is the rhythmically clicking chain-gang employed at building a railway. A cliff that "was not in the way of anything" (56) is being blasted away. A vast, unmarked, dug-out hole – "the purpose of which I find it impossible to divine. It wasn't a quarry or a sandpit anyhow. It was just a hole" (57) – is the product of previous labor. Marlow learns that the steamer he is supposed to be in charge of is sunk and that his predecessor died in a quarrel over two black hens (in "An Outpost of Progress" Carlier dies in a quarrel over a few lumps of sugar; in *Lord Jim*, Marlow explains that Dutch and English adventurers used to "cut each other's throats" for "a bag of pepper," 172). While waiting for several months at the Central Station for the arrival of rivets to repair the steamer, he finds the agents engaged in gossiping and quibbles; speaks with a boilermaker who "raved about pigeons" (72); hears about how a grass shed "burst into blaze" (65); learns that a hippo is routinely (and unsuccessfully) fired at; and observes the pyjama-wearing dress code of the so-called pilgrims. The accumulated evidence seems to say: this is Western civilization, efficiency and colonialism at full display.

Within this environment of cruelty, inefficiency and pyjama-wearing, there is also an immaculately turned out accountant – a scented "hairdresser's dummy" (59) – with parted and oiled hair, "a high, starched collar, white cuffs, a light alpaca jacket, snowy trousers, a clear silk necktie and varnished boots" (59). The attention to his outer appearance is, on the one hand, proof of rare, undivided focus and, on the other, the very opposite: the senseless cruelty and mismanagement of the colonial operation passes him by. Perhaps he has willingly decided to keep himself distracted with his shirt cuffs and starched collar, as he sits in his decrepit, half-built office and sums up Kurtz's work as "very satisfactory" (61). Cedric Watts explains that the accountant "is like an ostrich with its head in the sand: surrounded by the vile and horrific, he can be seen as taking refuge in myopic devotion to his books and clothing."[35] There is, indeed, an interesting contrast between the order of accounting and the disorder of the colonial enterprise. In "An Outpost of Progress," the accountant Makola, or Henry Price, creatively overlooks the exchange of ten men for ivory: "No trade, no entry in books; all correct" (42). When he discovers that Kayerts has killed Carlier, he tells Kayerts: "He died of fever" (65).

While the accountant in *Heart of Darkness* keeps his books in apple-pie order, "Everything else in the station was in muddle – heads, things, buildings" (60). The literary school of deconstruction has found disunity between the moral and linguistic orders of the novella[36] – but not in the everyday work-life atmosphere of the novella itself, which I see as a meditation on disorder: a nightmare of inefficiency, suitable as an example of bad practice for a management textbook. Marlow is a helpless observer, finding the inefficiency beyond his "power of meddling" (82) and lives in "an infernal mess of rust, filings, nuts, bolts, spanners, hammers, ratchet-drills" (116). The story he is in, *Heart of Darkness*, is a stagnant, directionless journey of inconclusive experiences and interminable distractions.

"Or – or – perhaps": Exceptions and Compromises

In contrast to the distracted narrative outlook stand Conrad's unimaginative characters, like Captain Mitchell in *Nostromo*, Captain Brierly in *Lord Jim*,[37] Captain Hagberd in "To-morrow," Captain MacWhirr in *Typhoon*, and (maybe) Captain Allistoun in *The Nigger of the 'Narcissus'* (that all these characters happen to be captains speaks to an unrealistic view of the requirements for this professional title, which Conrad was only to hold briefly). The literal-minded Captain MacWhirr does not possess the mental toolset for fancy: "It was, in truth, as impossible for him to take a flight of fancy as it would be for a watchmaker to put together a chronometer with nothing except a two-pound hammer and a whip-saw in the way of tools" (*T* 5). His lack of imagination makes him a poor reader: when reading about typhoons he fails to connect the writing to the foul weather surrounding the ship; instead, he becomes angry at the text "with such a lot of words and with so much advice, all head-work and supposition, without a glimmer of certitude" (33). His steadfast outlook seems to have placed blinders on his imagination, and in "his unseeing, unimaginative way" (34), he cannot deal with exceptions – he sends the ship straight into the typhoon, despite the signs supplied by the weather, Mr. Jukes and the ship's instruments.

Captain Habgerd, Captain Mitchell, Captain Brierly and Captain MacWhirr – none would do well as writers of imaginative literature. They would more aptly be employed in writing Notices to Mariners, a type of writing Conrad expressed admiration for in "Outside Literature" (1922). These notices were not only written with the utmost exactness, but also without digressions: as if limiting digressions meant being *outside literature*. Yet, Conrad admired this type of writing – in the same way that he admired unimaginative characters, like Singleton in *The Nigger of the 'Narcissus'*. Being literal minded is not necessarily the product of a lack of intelligence; it can also be a commitment to one perspective, and a necessity for work and action.

In his commitment to fidelity, duty, loyalty and service, Conrad even brought the British Merchant Mariner's moral codex to his writing table. A Protestant work ethic or what Marlow in *Lord Jim* calls "the service of the Red Rag" (39), both aided and hindered his creative process as it chained him to his work – he rarely took breaks from work, but he frequently had breakdowns. As we discussed in the chapter on doodles, this constant effort may not always have served Conrad in his artistic goals. The anecdote about Conrad playing chess with his son is telling here: John reports how Conrad would play a couple of moves, then write a few words, as if taking a break to play chess helped him to realign his thoughts. The key to Conrad's productivity may have been to make distraction not different from work, but part of work. Indeed, the intriguing thing about Conrad is how the craftsman and the artist work together: forming *les mot justes* about distractions and digressions. Conrad's rambling digressions are part of a quest for verbal precision. Relying on the work ethic of a Captain MacWhirr to exploit the imagination of an artist and enable his focus, the homo-duplex is the perfect artist. Marlow, "the imaginative sea captain,"[38] embodies the success of Conrad's endeavor.

In Medias Distractionis: Conrad's Working Method

A workaholic is more susceptible to distraction than others: he or she has a clearly defined goal (like winning a silver medal), and constant pursuit of that goal renders distraction inevitable. There are two detailed examples in *A Personal Record* of Conrad's distraction. Onboard a steamer, he finds his work on *Almayer's Folly* interrupted by a friendly third officer and his question, "What are you always scribbling there, if it's fair to ask?" (*PR* 20). His work on *Nostromo* is thwarted by a general's daughter's sudden presence and question, "How do you do?" (*PR* 91). In the latter case, Conrad describes the sense of being physically uprooted from one space and time – "a fall, let us say, from the highest of the clouds" (*PR* 90) – and deposited onto a writer's desk, facing a general's daughter. As explained in various letters, Conrad was also distracted and hindered by gout, headache, toothache, bronchitis, sciatica, depression, exhaustion, finances, doubts, hallucinations, world events (World War One and the Anglo-Boer war), and by family members. A servant girl was fired for being distracted: "Our girl's temperament was to[o] artistic. She would wander off and disappear for hours at a time. What she found to dream about on country roads in the mud and after dark I can't imagine" (*CL* II.120). The Conrads would likely have done better with a less imaginative servant – someone with the steadfast temperament of Captain Hagberd, Captain MacWhirr or Captain Brierly. Unlike his artistic servant girl, Conrad could afford to combine dreaming with his occupational demands and turn distraction itself into a working method. As we have seen – distracted characters, distracted texts, distracted reading and distracted writing, overlap in complicated ways in Conrad's fiction.

Rather than suppress the reader's need for distraction, Conrad's keen insight was to speak directly to this need. A common misconception is to define distraction as the opposite of attention, or as attention "to the lowest degree."[39] But there are, as we have seen, multiple examples in Conrad's texts of distraction as intense focus. When someone is distracted in Conrad's texts, focus is redirected rather than lost. Distraction steals attention despite the wishes of the person concerned. If, as a writer, you can control the direction of distraction – you have a powerful tool for holding the reader's attention: "the control of the public's (audience, readers) attention is in a sense the beginning and end of artistic method" (*CL* IV.422). This is one explanation for why *Lord Jim, An Outcast of the Islands* and *Almayer's Folly* start with Jim, Willems and Almayer daydreaming; they start *in medias distractionis* rather than *in medias res.*

If the sole aim of an opening was to hook a reader, *Almayer's Folly* could have started with the young Nina Almayer being sent away to Singapore as her mother desperately swims after her in the river, or an episode from the secret love affair of Nina and the Malayan Prince Dain Maroola, or Almayer burning up his house, or a native corpse floating down the river. Yet, in the first chapter of Conrad's first book, an action-packed adventure of pirates and gun-running, Almayer is distracted from daydreaming by a drifting tree.

Almayer first sees the tree on its way downstream; registers how it hisses and foams; speculates that its denuded branch is "like a hand lifted in mute appeal to heaven against the river's brutal and unnecessary violence" (6); follows it down the river; ponders whether it will make it through a low point – and speculates about its future (How far out to sea would the tree drift? "Would the current carry it north or south?" 6). It is remarkable that Conrad decides to open the first chapter of his first novel with distraction and daydreaming – a moment when we expect the narrator to be fully focused and in clear view of where he is going: keen on making a good first impression. So, at the start of the book, when Conrad has the reader's full attention, he starts in a moment of idleness; he introduces Almayer who only pays attention to his distraction.

A "writer tends to be on his or her best behaviour at the beginning of Chapter 1," Terry Eagleton writes, "eager to impress, keen to catch the fickle reader's eye, and occasionally intent on pulling out all the stops."[40] Conrad, expected to be at his best behavior, introduces us to a distracted narrative as if his aim were to miss the target; we learn about the fate of a drifting tree rather than the title character, Almayer. Although the journey of the drifting tree helps us to understand Almayer and his surroundings, it is possible that the drifting tree is introduced on the basis of its own inherent interest. While it is tempting to distance oneself from Almayer's distracted mind and maintain that the drifting tree "is not particularly arresting in itself,"[41] Conrad may have calculated on the possibility that his readers, just like Almayer, would find the drifting tree interesting. Rather than sidetracking the narrative – hindering its process – distraction here becomes a self-generative narrative concept: a seed that flowers into further distraction: "Distracted from distraction by distraction" (T. S. Eliot).[42] Or, in Conrad's case: distracted from daydreaming by distraction.

If we are to believe Ford Madox Ford, he and Conrad – "more than most writers" – agreed on the importance of openings. The ideal novel "must begin either with a dramatic scene or with a note that should suggest the whole book."[43] The reason Conrad opens three novels with a daydreaming character is, I think, that for Conrad, distractions carry the story forward in a circular motion. Consider (again) *The Secret Agent*, a remarkably unified novel, where every detail fits as if in a large puzzle. For a novel that declares that science is the fetish of today[44] and meditates on the possibility of throwing a bomb into pure mathematics, it is tempting to describe the narrative structure with mathematical notation. If we want to use allegorical mathematics, we need a more flexible concept than "nonlinear narrative" or "fractured line narrative." "Nonlinear" is too general a term (everything except a line is nonlinear) and although the novel contains episodes of distraction, nonchronological chapters and events, it is not aptly described as a fractured line, which would suggest gaps and imperfections. Apart from the circular imagery (as when Stevie draws circles), the novel circles around certain events (like the bomb explosion in Greenwich – "The only positive action against the *status quo* in this story of stasis"[45]), without providing a first-hand account – an unmediated vision – in the same way that pivots of the action in other of Conrad's stories are withheld. For instance, we never get any clear view of Napoleon in *Suspense* or Kurtz in *Heart of Darkness*. The distracted perspectives, which occur with almost rigid regularity, carry the novel forward in a circular motion, however erratically, along the plot and time axis. Like a sine wave, the novel moves in a circle as it simultaneously progresses forward.[46]

Since it seems to be a fact of life that "the most pedestrian mind will sometimes take a flight from the office where it works . . . towards subjects of poetic fancy, its children, its lady-love, its glass of beer" ("Outside Literature," 31), Conrad's willingness to display these fancies in full is a testament to his fidelity to his craft, where imagination meets fact and distraction becomes a key to productivity. Here, a yellow cur, a stray cat, a drifting tree, an anxious nose and a Canton Street girl carry the plot forward in a circular motion – between the whiffs of the pipe. Conrad's method, developed at the historical moment when critics started to theorize distraction, was to fuse the production process with the theme and transform distraction into a self-generating narrative tool. Seeking to follow this method, the next chapter turns, *in medias distractionis*, to a completely different theme: details in *The Secret Agent*.

CHAPTER 6

Details and The Secret Agent

Having acquired "a kind of cult status as the classic of the post 9/11 age,"[1] *The Secret Agent* is one of the most widely referenced fictional books in discourses on terrorism. It is also one of Conrad's most frequently misread books, even by some of his most perceptive readers. All too often, unwarranted parallels are drawn between the main topic of *The Secret Agent* and its form – resulting in the amalgam "Anarchist Aesthetics," to borrow the subtitle of Daphna Erdinast-Vulcan's excellent essay on the novel.[2] Thus, many readers see strong connections between *The Secret Agent*'s nonchronological narration and its anarchistic theme. In an otherwise wonderful essay on time in *The Secret Agent*, R. W. Stallman explains that "the confused chronology," "effects a structure which is at one with the theme."[3] Allan Simmons states that the "novel's fractured chronology represents the destabilizing effect of anarchism upon both the form and substance of the tale."[4] John Stape maintains that "revolutionary time as a separate category inflects the novel"[5] and Ludwig Schnauder remarks that "time is 'exploded' on the discourse level through unchronological narration."[6] While these bite-size explanations are appealing, many of Conrad's texts display chapters in nonchronological order without anarchists in the story to destabilize time (like *Chance, Lord Jim* and *Under Western Eyes*). Apart from *The Nigger of the 'Narcissus', The Shadow-Line* and *Typhoon*, Conrad's novels disrupt linear time. And although "sixteen of Conrad's twenty-three short stories are characterized by inversion,"[7] his two short stories about anarchists, "The Informer" and "An Anarchist," are told in chronological time. Anarchism, then, is not a relevant variable for explaining a standard characteristic of Conrad's prose.

As I will argue, rather than invoking fragmentation, the nonchronological chapters in *The Secret Agent* allow for unity and consistency: a way to display control. The novel is knitted in an overlapping pattern of interweaving sequences and temporal criss-crossings; it has multiple "tentacular bonds" – to borrow Cedric Watts's phrase for the entangled structure of

Heart of Darkness (he compares interpreting the novella to wrestling with an octopus).[8] A hand-to-hand combat with a slippery eight-limbed mollusk is challenging, but I like to look upon the entangled structure of *The Secret Agent* positively: there are multiple links and connections across the chapters beyond the march of time.

Nonchronology alone, then, cannot be equated to disorder qua disorder. Similarly, chapters ordered chronologically can feel as if they were in disorder. *The Secret Agent,* if printed with its thirteen chapters in different permutations, would result in 6,227,020,800 distinct novels (if you take the factorial of thirteen). To say that the nonchronological order is synonymous with disorder is to say that more than 6 billion other permutations (6,227,020,800 – 1) are less ordered than the chronological order: which is a massive, unfounded assumption. In *The Secret Agent* there is instead order to nonchronology. The order and unity of the novel can be found in its scattered and eclectic details.

Unlike previous readings which have structured the novel around an overarching theme or argument (anarchism, terrorism, time, place and so on),[9] I see *The Secret Agent* as a manifesto of marginality or manifest marginality: a novel written in the margins – or, if you will, a novel with tentacles. This chapter will approach marginality, then, not just as a way to unify scattered discussions of doodles, sticks, arrows, cats, hats and bats (as in Chapters 1, 4, 8, 9), but as a way to explain the structure of a novel. *The Secret Agent,* in this reading, is a novel about anarchists but it is not an anarchist novel. The structure is at odds with the theme – somewhat like an abstract painting within a classic, ornate frame. (Or to take an example closer to the text: *The Secret Agent,* a work on impoverished revolutionaries, is now a classic work of literature, published in the most reputable form by an old and established university press, printed in hardback in a conservative black color and priced like a luxury good.) Conrad is, in short, very concerned with order for writing a novel about anarchists. By placing the disordered anarchists in an ordered creation, Conrad – in my reading – is a propagandist by deed.

At first sight *The Secret Agent* is a novel where content and form seamlessly overlap. The novel has persistently been accused of lacking an alternative moral perspective in relation to the "sordid surroundings" and "moral squalor" ("Author's Note," 3) it depicts. "What one misses in *The Secret Agent,*" Irving Howe explains, "is some dramatic principle of contradiction, some force of resistance; in a word, a moral positive to serve literary ends."[10] Daphna Erdinast-Vulcan, writing a few years after Howe, contends that "the glaring absence of any alternatives to this mode of existence within the world of the text, is extremely disturbing."[11] "The novel locates itself in an environment of such abject banality that one suspects Conrad shares the destructive fantasies of its more unbalanced inhabitants," Michael Greaney notes.[12] In *The Secret Agent*, "Conrad's voice and the voice of the darkness most nearly become one," according to J. Hillis Miller.[13]

Indeed, although the novel lampoons political revolutionaries, it is also a satire of the political system and the status quo: a society that protects the upper class and their "hygienic idleness" (15).[14] This narrative outlook is used less for the case of trying to complicate the question of right and wrong and more for the sake of creating an extended merciless parody – a stalemate of moral dialogue, where no side has the upper hand. The reaction of the Teacher of Languages to Razumov's journal in *Under Western Eyes* seems appropriate to this type of unsympathetic narrative voice: "I turn over for the hundredth time the leaves of Mr. Razumov's record, I lay it aside, I take up the pen – and the pen being ready for its office of setting down black on white I hesitate. For the word that persists in creeping under its point is no other word than Cynicism" (58).

There is admittedly much to say in favor of this notion of anarchist aesthetics, where "Everything exists in contradictions of itself, and nothing is but what it is not."[15] "The novel is unable to speak of its contradictions," Terry Eagleton explains in one of the more inventive readings of the novel, "it is, rather, precisely, its contradictions which speak."[16] Thus, among "strayed houses" and "topographical mysteries" (17), the characters in *The Secret Agent* voice the possibility that there "are several kinds of logic" (60), deal with Vladimir's fantasy about throwing a bomb into pure mathematics, explore an attempt at attacking the coordinates of space and time, and examine numerous incoherencies of thought. The many incongruities and contradictions within the novel are not resolved but seem, to use a quote from *Heart of Darkness*, to have "a right to exist" (94).

Thus, Michaelis is a Marxist, socialite and aspiring author: "first awakened by the offer of five hundred pounds from a publisher" (94). Like the brickmaker in *Heart of Darkness* who does not make bricks, Karl Yundt the so-called terrorist "had never in his life raised personally as much as his little finger against the social edifice" (42). The Professor, "the Perfect Anarchist," consumes beer after beer in the Silenus Restaurant while simultaneously praising his own work ethic and ascetic nature. Based on his "imperfect formula" (66) about how society is constructed, the Perfect Anarchist seeks to develop a perfect detonator. Reminiscent of Mr Kirilov in Dostoevsky's *The Devils* (1871–72), who "is in favour of the latest principle of general destruction for the sake of the ultimate good,"[17] the Professor calls "madness and despair to the regeneration of the world" (231) and rails against the exploitation of the strong by the weak (a position Nietzsche would not have deemed inherently contradictory). The Professor's political friend Alexander Ossipon believes in science in a world of patent medicine, invigorating electric belts and the writings of the Italian criminologist Cesare Lombroso.

Ossipon, Michaelis and Karl Yundt frequently congregate at Adolf Verloc's "respectable" home, which is "Ensconced cosily behind the shop of doubtful wares" (148). Adolf Verloc is a married, well-fed shop owner with a cleaning lady and professes to be an anarchist ("Anarchists, I suppose, have no families," "The Informer," 75).[18] He complains that Ossipon, Michaelis and Karl Yundt "had women to fall back upon; whereas he had a woman to provide for" (46). Yet as owner of a "pornography shop"[19] he also makes a living off women; to emphasize the odd fact that Verloc's wife and her childlike brother work at the shop, Ellen Burton Harrington calls it "the family pornography shop."[20] In addition, his loveless marriage to Winnie (who talks the "wifely talk," 139, performs "domestic duties," 145, and gets "into bed in a calm business-like manner," 48) fits well with his "instinctive leaning towards shady transactions" (46), although he believes that he is loved for himself (a humanizing detail in the context). Mr Verloc also *sells* the anti-capitalistic pamphlets handed out by his friends, in his shop. He has the appearance of a "reflective beast" (193) and is "steady like a rock – a soft kind of rock" (17). "The fellow was a secret agent to my certain knowledge" (101), Chief Inspector Heat tells the Assistant Commissioner.

The way the novel engages with disorder is perhaps seen most clearly at the macroscopic level; the book is ordered around a failed attempt at blowing up the Greenwich observatory. The aim of uprooting the political status quo leads to an uprooted tree; Stevie's bomb explodes prematurely when he stumbles on a tree branch.[21] A planned attack on science becomes an unintended attack on nature. At the heart of this event lies a paradox: Mr Verloc is asked to commit an anarchist outrage that should not be politically motivated. He is asked, in short, to make a giant fool of himself: instigate "the most alarming display of ferocious imbecility" (31). This is humorous because Mr Verloc is respectable and very much part of the bourgeoisie, reminiscent of a "respectable grocer" (57) or a sign-painter of "a superior sort" (81): "He looked uncommonly like a master plumber come to present his bill" (26); "his general get up was that of a well to do mechanic in business for himself. He might have been anything from a picture-frame maker to a locksmith; an employer of labour in a small way" (16). At a cursory glance, Mr Verloc represents "the very perfection of mediocrity" (159), to borrow a phrase from *Under Western Eyes.* He has brushed hair, polished shoes and a round hat; he is in his forties, married and the owner of a small shop – in outer appearance, a respectable family man and a productive member of society. On a closer look: a former convict, agent provocateur, double agent, and "a seller of shady wares" (11) – who is about to accidentally orchestrate his brother-in-law's death. The actual attack on time itself is, of course, a failure: solved within twelve hours. Time is instead measured out in the agent provocateur's blood. When Mr Verloc's time on earth ends time does not come to a stop, but seemingly picks up speed and becomes more noticeable: "Tic, tic, tic… Dark drops fell on the floorcloth one after another, with a sound of ticking growing fast and furious like the pulse of an insane clock" (198–99).[22]

The Secret Agent displays Conrad speaking, like the Assistant Commissioner, "with a studious fidelity to a parenthetical manner, into which every little fact – that is, every detail – fitted with delightful ease" (107). The contradictions are ideological rather than formal; no invisible taxis, for example, are needed to make sense of the space and time references, as in Virginia Woolf's fiction.[23] Thus, appropriate to the "passion for maps" (38) articulated in *Heart of Darkness*, "the [developed] taste of poring over maps" (12) elaborated in "Geography and Some Explorers" and explored in *A Personal Record* (and in the second chapter of this monograph), *The Secret Agent* can be mapped geographically. All major editions of the novel supply a map to guide the reader. Again, it is not merely interesting to explore the map – but also to explore the very fact that the London of *The Secret Agent* can be mapped and that editors have felt inclined to do so. It is a significant feat that there is this underlying, invisible order to the novel where characters get lost in the streets, are confused about space, time, events and display a completely subjective view of reality. There is room for a concrete map in this abstract landscape.

The Secret Agent is not characterized by disorder qua disorder but by its tentacular form, intelligent ideological paradoxes and unorthodox narrative proportions. Thus, the central event of the novel occurs within a paragraph break, the first-person narrator is a minor character that makes an appearance in a single inconspicuous paragraph ("I," 16), the entire first chapter is written as a parenthesis to Mr Verloc's walk, Ossipon's extraordinarily lengthy walk across London takes up less than half a page, and so on. The aforementioned needs more explanation and the best approach to the tentacular form of the novel is to patiently fondle its details; like

Marlow, in *Lord Jim*, who is "trying to interpret for you into slow speech the instantaneous effect of visual impressions" (42), or like Marlow in *Chance* who "has the habit, or, say, the fault, of defective mantelpiece clocks, of suddenly stopping in the very fullness of the tick" (285). Think about how *The Secret Agent* does *not* begin:

> Mr Verloc, going out in the morning, left his shop nominally in charge of his brother-in law. It was unusually early for him; his whole person exhaled the charm of almost dewy freshness; he wore his blue cloth overcoat unbuttoned; his boots were shiny; his cheeks, freshly shaven, had a sort of gloss; and even his heavy-lidded eyes, refreshed by a night of peaceful slumber, sent out glances of comparative alertness.

The first sentence is from the first sentence of the first chapter; the second, from the second chapter. The sentences are not meant to be read together. The above constructed paragraph exists nowhere else than in this chapter. Yet it is an almost seamless transition between these two sentences; as will be maintained, this is partly because the entire first chapter is written as a "digression" from Mr Verloc's walk. Mr Verloc – "a peripatetic philosopher" (174) – walks between chapters.

Let us start with a lengthy quotation from the actual opening of the text:

> Mr Verloc, going out in the morning, left his shop nominally in charge of his brother-in-law. It could be done, because there was very little business at any time, and practically none at all before the evening. Mr Verloc cared but little about his ostensible business. And, moreover, his wife was in charge of his brother-in-law.
>
> The shop was small, and so was the house. It was one of those grimy brick houses which existed in large quantities before the era of reconstruction dawned upon London. The shop was a square box of a place, with the front glazed in small panes. In the daytime the door remained closed; in the evening it stood discreetly but suspiciously ajar.
>
> The window contained photographs of more or less undressed dancing girls; nondescript packages in wrappers like patent medicines; closed yellow paper envelopes, very flimsy, and marked two and six in heavy black figures; a few numbers of ancient French comic publications hung across a string as if to dry; a dingy blue china bowl, a casket of black wood, bottles of marking ink, and rubber stamps; a few books, with titles hinting at impropriety; a few apparently old copies of obscure newspapers, badly printed, with titles like *The Torch, The Gong* – rousing titles. And the two gas jets inside the panes were always turned low, either for economy's sake or for the sake of the customers.
>
> These customers were either very young men, who hung about the window for a time before slipping in suddenly; or men of a more mature age, but looking generally as if they were not in funds. Some of that last

> kind had the collars of their overcoats turned right up to their moustaches, and traces of mud on the bottom of their nether garments, which had the appearance of being much worn and not very valuable. And the legs inside them did not, as a general rule, seem of much account either. With their hands plunged deep in the side pockets of their coats, they dodged in sideways, one shoulder first, as if afraid to start the bell going.
>
> The bell, hung on the door by means of a curved ribbon of steel, was difficult to circumvent. It was hopelessly cracked; but of an evening, at the slightest provocation, it clattered behind the customer with impudent virulence. (9–10)

From *Lord Jim* that starts with an image of Jim walking, to *The Nigger of the 'Narcissus'* whose first sentence describes Mr Baker's stride onto the quarter deck, to *An Outcast of the Islands* that begins with a metaphor about stepping off the path of honesty (away from the "safe stride of virtue," 3), *The Secret Agent* opens on a familiar kinetic theme. The first sentence starts with Adolf Verloc – alias Prozor, Secret Agent delta, Vice President of the Red Delegate Committee and the Future of the Proletariat – walking. "Mr Verloc, going out in the morning, left his shop nominally in charge of his brother-in-law" (9). Beginning from the next sentence, there follows an abrupt halt in the telling of Verloc's walk, an abruptness reminiscent of the "twenty pages of retrospective digression"[24] inserted in the midst of a conversation in chapter v. Indeed, Mr Verloc is only allowed to continue on his sunny walk to the Embassy in the next chapter, after the reader has been introduced to a descriptive chapter about "the house, the household, and the business Mr Verloc left behind him on his way westward at the hour of half past ten in the morning" (15) – as the first sentence of chapter II explains. While the interruption has the structure of a cliffhanger, going out for a walk is an ordinary, uneventful activity. The primary interest of the first chapter is neither Mr Verloc nor where he is going but what he leaves behind. So the first sentence starts with the title character getting out of sight so that the reader can spy on the secret agent's private life. "Verloc," as the first sheets of *The Secret Agent*'s holograph were originally titled, is, therefore, not really part of the first chapter (any more than the novel is a simple tale, despite what is stated in a subtitle, a letter, a dedication and a Preface).

The first sentence is abrupt for more reasons than that it reads like it was taken from the start of the second chapter. First, as Cedric Watts perceptively noted, the sentence appears to be a product of "awkwardly-translated French": "Correct phrasing would be: 'Mr Verloc, going out in the morning, left his brother-in-law nominally in charge of his shop'."[25] Second, the first sentence involves a particular *action* of the ongoing present ("going," 9) and the remaining chapter deals with generalizations and descriptions about the static past. Yet the first-time reader certainly does not register the abrupt change – during the reading of the first chapter, he or she never asks, "Why is Mr Verloc out for a walk?", "Where is Mr Verloc going?" The move from ongoing action to description of the past does not read like a digression, side note or parenthetical observation. Indeed, by the start of the second chapter, Conrad not only summarizes the first chapter but he also reminds the reader that Mr Verloc is out walking: "Such was the house, the household, and the business Mr Verloc left behind him on his way westward at the hour of half past ten in the morning" (15).

Questions then follow: what is the advantage of ordering the novel in this way? Why seemingly detach a sentence from the second chapter and place it at the start of the first? And why does the remaining chapter not read like a side note? Here lies a key to the structure of the novel that is reminiscent of an interruption Erich Auerbach highlighted in Homer's *Odyssey*. The washing of Odysseus's foot is interrupted (in the narrative) by more than seventy verses, before Euryclea lets "Odysseus's foot fall back into the basin." The aim of the side note is not "to keep the reader or hearer breathless." What happens to Odysseus's foot is not of more interest than the side story about the hunt. Indeed, "The broadly narrated, charming, and subtly fashioned story of the hunt, with all its elegance and self-sufficiency, its wealth of idyllic pictures, seeks to win the reader over wholly to itself as long as he is hearing it, to make him forget what had just taken place during the foot-washing." Put differently, the reader is not anxiously waiting to hear about the washing of Odysseus's foot, but is fully absorbed in the "side story." Thus, what Homer "narrates is for the time being the only present, and fills both the stage and the reader's mind completely."[26] In the end, it is ultimately senseless to divide the *Odyssey* into foreground/background, center/aside: it is arbitrary to speak of one element of the story as more interesting and important than another. There is no hierarchy: "the story of the wound becomes an independent and exclusive present."[27]

Had the digression not been pointed out, it would not have been understood as one. Similarly, the scarcity of criticism on this narrative crux in *The Secret Agent* implies that it is not an issue of great concern for Conrad connoisseurs either. Critics instead notice, "The disjunction between behaviour and motive,"[28] the many "conditional statements" in the opening paragraph,[29] "The [grammatical and idiomatic] awkwardness of the textual phrasing."[30] However, my chapter is not the first in identifying this digression; a sentence in an inconspicuous paragraph in R. W. Stallman's fine essay from 1959 declares that the "opening phrase of the novel – 'Mr Verloc, *going out in the morning*' – is misleading, inasmuch as Mr. Verloc does not go out of the shop until the scene of Chapter II, all of Chapter I being a cutback taking us *inside* the shop. It's rather like a film run backwards; in effect, time stands still."[31] As if his discovery is little more than a statement of an expected fact, Stallman does not comment on the implication of structuring the text in this highly idiosyncratic manner, and why it is symptomatic of Conrad's technique. However, as has been shown, this narrative crux frames the first chapter and connects it with the second chapter – meanwhile turning the first chapter into a digression. The importance of this element, then, extends to the style of the novel.

For instance, the charge that *The Secret Agent* is made of "interminable descriptions"[32] can certainly be supported by the first chapter where the de facto only action/event is that of Mr Verloc walking, which only concerns one sentence and is quickly interrupted. The novel, however, does not read like description: Conrad achieves a sense of narrated action. Although the novel changes perspective from the ongoing present of Mr Verloc's walk ("going," 9) to the static past, the narrator takes off from where Mr Verloc leaves: from just outside the shop, describing how it appears like "a square box of a place" (9), enumerating eleven different items in its window, and describing the appearance of the customers as they enter the shop. The reader is also informed that the bell that announces a new customer is difficult to circumvent. Then, just like a potential customer of shady wares, the reader enters the shop through the narrator's perspective. With apt timing on Conrad's part, as a reader you enter a description of the shop after a description of how the bell "clattered behind the customer with impudent virulence" (10), as if you as reader set the bell off. The reader then observes things of a nature that a potential customer would, like a typical transaction with Mrs Verloc for an overpriced bottle of marking ink. The past action happens to the reader in the present.

By giving the digressions central stage, Conrad challenges generic expectations. The title itself, *The Secret Agent*, is explanatory and clarifying insofar as it applies to anyone with secret agency in the novel (many of its characters have a secretive motive or a secret side), yet it also labels the first chapter as a digression: "The novel's first paragraphs are a decidedly inauspicious opening for a thriller with such a promising title," Greaney writes, stressing the way the novel differs from the conventional genre of spy-thrillers.[33] The stark disconnect between the whodunit title and the descriptive content should take the most astute reader unaware; unlike unreliable narrators, unreliable titles are not a recognized category. As unguarded readers, then, we expect the title to function like a label, as if you could add "This book is about" to the start of the title without changing its meaning. Labels are subservient to the content. If you were to change the label of a biscuit jar it would generally not change the content; in "The Informer" cans labeled *Stone's Dried Soup* contain anarchist literature despite the advertisement. Unlike the label of a biscuit jar, the title of a novel can drastically change the content. The critical reaction to *The Shadow-Line* as a novel bearing upon the supernatural was related to the title; if he had published the tale "under the title of *First Command*, no suggestion of the Supernatural would have been found in it by any impartial reader" ("Author's Note," 6), Conrad speculates. Analogously, if Conrad's text for *The Secret Agent* had been titled *The Transparent Agent*, or *Stevie's Life*, or *Mr Verloc's Ostensible Business*, or *Domestic Disputes and Dilemmas: A Complicated Tale*, it would have been a different novel.

All this is to say that the title is not a mere descriptive name but a significant part of the artwork. The title is the element of the artwork you have to mention every time you discuss it, as if the author had requested that you keep a few specific words in mind every time you discuss a text. The way the title works differently from a mere framing device can best be seen by reference to artworks that use their titles in unconventional ways, like *Landscape with the Fall of Icarus* (1560s), an oil painting by the Flemish artist Pieter Bruegel the Elder (1525–69). With awareness of the title, the first-time viewer is actively searching the painting, looking for Icarus who is seemingly nowhere to be seen. The viewer of the painting sees a *Weltlandschaft* with a stretching horizon and a sea view with ships, framed by a plowman on a hill. In the far-off distance, there is an idyllic city on the seaside. There are many characters: sailors, a shepherd, an angler, a plowman, a horse, a dog, a hawk; multiple sheep and birds. Icarus is nowhere to be seen.

In the right-hand corner, two legs stick up from the water. The epic event of Icarus's fall is depicted as it would have likely played out, as a mere splash in the water with others focused on their own lives: plowing ahead with a single-minded focus. A few feathers in the sky, a splash, and two legs mark a momentous event played out in the margins. While Bruegel's painting gives no account that his characters are aware of Icarus's fall, W. H. Auden's poem "Musée des Beaux Arts" (1938) reads the fact that they look the other way as proof of their limited empathy. (Yet different from Auden's poem is Ovid's account where Icarus's fall is watched by mesmerized side characters.)

The title, *Landscape with the Fall of Icarus*, tasks the viewer to explore the painting in a specific manner – as if it were a treasure hunt. This is similar not just to how the title and the text of *The Secret Agent* relate to one another, but also to one of Martin Handford's colorful drawings in his puzzle books for children; consider the difference of approaching his drawings, with or without the directive, *Where's Wally?* The viewer is tasked with locating Wally among numerous other characters, including many look-alikes, yet Wally is not so much the conclusion and answer to the painting, as a way for Handford to direct the viewer: a parallel, indeed, for how to read or not read *The Secret Agent.* Indeed, the titles of *Landscape with the Fall of Icarus*, a *Where's Wally?* painting and *The Secret Agent* all function similarly, suggesting that Icarus, Wally and the Secret Agent are central to the artwork. Searching for Icarus, Wally and the Secret Agent is the way Bruegel, Handford and Conrad want us to approach the visual or verbal text – but the meaning of the artwork is by no means equated to locating them. Our role as critics is not to centralize the detail – find Wally and applaud ourselves (or explain that the painting is disorganized since Wally is not in the middle). Wally himself is unimportant and uninteresting: there is little value to a profile photo of Wally with the title "There's Wally." It is more meaningful to discuss the mechanics of the artwork and the way the detail is embedded in the text. Arthur Danto, in a perceptive chapter on Bruegel, observes what should be obvious but is not: "To interpret Breugel's painting as simply about Icarus involves at best identifying the legs and the relationship between their owner and the sun, implying a narrative structure, a story a painting not so much tells as presupposes in order to integrate the elements."[34] Analogously, the title of *The Secret Agent* only tells us where to look; the function of the title is more like an intentionally misplaced traffic sign by an artistic traffic manager than a key to the central meaning. The meaning of the artwork, as with Bruegel's Icarus, lies in relationships and connections: in the margins.

On multiple levels *Where's Wally?* and *Landscape with the Fall of Icarus* are instructive for how to read *The Secret Agent* as a story of marginality. Despite Icarus's marginal position, Bruegel does not dislocate his attention from the boy. The painting is about his fall – in all its marginality. It is not about the plowman. The plowman is there in his relationship to Icarus and to make us think about our relationship to the external world. Icarus is in the center and the "plowman must be read together with the boy. It is hard to read the plowman together with the ship."[35] Without losing sight of Icarus, Bruegel allows the plowman to plow ahead – for the sake of telling a story about Icarus. In *The Secret Agent*, we are faced with a similar sense of subjectivity and marginality; a feature that seems to dominate the structure. Indeed, elements of the story may appear distinct and isolated, such as the novel's lengthy expositions on the act of people-watching in an Italian restaurant, a dancing horse of apocalyptic misery, the Professor's wallpaper of arsenical green, the *via dolorosa* of Mrs Neale's life, and the figure on Sir Ethelred's desk, "a little bronze statuette draped in a toga, mysteriously watchful in its shadowy immobility" (164). All of these have the quality of not being the secret agent, an image of the secret agent, or directly related to a story about the secret agent. In addition, although there are a few characters of minor importance who are not given a single line of direct or indirect speech (like Cheeseman and an amorous cat), most characters in the novel speak as if there was no clear assignment of primary and secondary roles, like Thersites in the *Iliad*. Thus, in chapter IX – concurrent in time with Winnie finding out about Stevie's death and the Greenwich explosion – there is room for the charwoman of Brett Street, Mrs Neale, to have her own act. She is given a lengthy vignette, seemingly unrelated to the primary events in the chapter:

> On all fours amongst the puddles, wet and begrimed, like a sort of amphibious and domestic animal living in ash-bins and dirty water, she uttered the usual exordium: "It's all very well for you, kept doing nothing like a gentleman." And she followed it with the everlasting plaint of the poor, pathetically mendacious, miserably authenticated by the horrible breath of cheap rum and soapsuds. She scrubbed hard, snuffling all the time, and talking volubly. And she was sincere. And on each side of her thin red nose her bleared, misty eyes swam in tears, because she felt really the want of some sort of stimulant in the morning. (140–41)

The passage is characteristic of the novel and the way irony is used for sympathy as well as for scorn. From a labor politician's perspective, she is far from an ideal representative of the virtuous poor. Her identity is not marginalized to make a point. She does not fit a social type. Her behavior is irrational but also sincere. And, as we can derive from Mrs Verloc's comments: justified. Her qualities, then, extend beyond what we get from a thematic and solution-oriented reading of *The Secret Agent*, where the title condemns Mrs Neale to the marginal – and assigns her the quality of being of secondary importance, if not wholly irrelevant, to the spy story.

The vignette of Mrs Neale, however, is a complicated structure even in isolation. Mrs Neale is not part of the Verloc family circle: her position as a worker on an hourly contract means that she can easily be discharged from the household and the reader's sympathy. (An ironic narrative perspective does not, necessarily, mean that Conrad lessens his sympathy. During the most anxiously mediated event of *Lord Jim* the title character jumps from the *Patna* on the call of "Jump, George! Jump!" 87 – although his name is Jim.) What is clear is that Mrs Neale's story cannot be reduced to context; it carries interest and independence as if it were an autonomous element of the story rather than a link along a chain.

Other characters in the novel also act out their solipsism in action and speech, without any sense of being rushed or limited in expression: "Each figure in the text takes a turn at being protagonist, fully occupying his fraction of the totality as if it were totality itself"[36] – like a character in a *Where's Wally?* drawing who does not act as if his or her main status is that of not being Wally. When *Country Life* reviewed *The Secret Agent* on September 21, 1907 they accused Conrad of "bringing in minor and inessential characters and making far too much of them"; a reason for their brazen declaration that Conrad belongs "to an earlier and less enlightened stage in our literary history."[37] As we discussed in the previous chapter, Jocelyn Baines finds that the novel consists of "a succession of only superficially related scenes" and lacks "a unifying theme."[38]

There is little validity to these observations. *The Secret Agent* could be reduced significantly in length if we are merely concerned about the most sensationalistic elements of the overarching plot. We could start by deleting every chapter apart from chapter IX. This self-contained chapter is the most direct description of the planning and execution of the Greenwich Bomb Outrage. And even here the central action is marginal; the explosion happens between two paragraphs. If we take the reductive approach further we could delete this chapter as well and the reader would be left with an empty white space that was originally to be found between two paragraphs. This paragraph break is the most direct description we have of the bomb outrage. While the explosion might be the centrifugal force of the novel, the meaning of the novel is not in this paragraph break any more than the meaning of Bruegel's painting *The Fall of Icarus* is in a zoomed-in picture of Icarus's legs.

The many side notes and vignettes in the story are not there because Conrad lost track of the main story and structure, but instead to display his skill in keeping track of the main story and structure while going off on a tangential note: like a tight-rope walker faking a fall to display total control. Similar to Bruegel's *Landscape with the Fall of Icarus* or *The Peasant Wedding* (where the viewer searches for the groom among the characters): the independence of the characters is part of the novel's intended meaning. The explosion – placed in a paragraph break – functions like other elements of Conrad's stories that are placed outside the text: like Lord Jim's jump from the *Patna.* Outside of direct description and present tense, these elements tie the story together in a tentacular manner.

A clear example of *The Secret Agent*'s tentacular quality is the way the chapters interlink. The chapters in the novel may appear as independent chronological units with occasional spatiotemporal repetitions. Still, it is worth emphasizing that chapters do more than divide ("chapter divisions") – they exclude, delete and connect. There can be temporal and thematic space between chapters. In literary studies little attention is paid to what happens in between chapters. In Conrad studies there is a notable exception: "the white space between"[39] *Victory*'s chapters four and five has been explored by Paul Kirschner in *Conrad: The Psychologist as Artist* (1968), Yves Hervouet in *The French Face of Joseph Conrad* (1990) and Robert Hampson in *Conrad's Secrets* (2012). As the latter observes: as "something which Conrad is unable – or, more accurately, is not allowed – to describe": sexual activity.[40] Conrad does not restrict the empty white space to one meaning, but fills it with multiple acts and events in his fiction, such as walking. Despite the fact that the theme of walking in *The Secret Agent* has been discussed before, no one has paid attention to its most surprising element: the persistent walking that happens between chapters.[41] In the novel, walking is repetitively used with a tentacular quality, as a structural principle to tie temporally disorganized chapters together, and to end and begin chapters. Characters walk between chapters, creating a transition for the reader by means of transportation. Out of thirteen chapters, eight chapters end with a walk or a walk that has come to end: I (Verloc), IV (Professor), VI (Chief Inspector Heat and Assistant Commissioner), VII (Assistant Commissioner), X (Assistant Commissioner), XI (Winnie), XII (Ossipon), XIII (the Professor). While readers might expect the narrative to pause between chapters, characters frequently walk between one chapter to the next: from the beginning of chapter I to the beginning of chapter II (Verloc), from the end of chapter IV to the beginning of chapter V (the Professor), from the end of chapter VI to the end of chapter VII (Assistant Commissioner), from a walk come to a standstill at the end of chapter XI to a continuation in the beginning of chapter XII (Winnie). The Assistant Commissioner, however, drives between two chapters that follow one another chronologically (VII and X): ending the former chapter with a walk to Mr Verloc's residence and continuing, we are told first in chapter X, "driven rapidly in a hansom from the neighbourhood of Soho" (162) – a journey that happened between the chapters.

Walking does not define the novel, but it defines the transitions between chapters that are frequently nonchronological. *The Secret Agent* could be classified as a novel of transportation – omnibus, train, cab, boat, foot – but it is too much of a generalization to insist that *The Secret Agent* is about walking. Yes, walking provides for uncomfortable verbal exchanges between ill-matched partners (chapters v and x) and a memorable way of illustrating Ossipon's mental state after deceiving Winnie: an aimless, circular walk around London described on less than a page. However, most events occur inside rather than outside: not on the street but in the drawing room, around the dinner table, in the bedroom, in the shop, in an Embassy, in an Italian Restaurant, in the Silenus Restaurant, in a department building, in Sir Ethelred's Office.

In *The Secret Agent*, then, walking primarily functions as a way to connect, end, and begin chapters. A chapter that ends with a walking character is not complete and self-contained; it is a dynamic ending that has a sense of continuation and openness. Walking does not divide chapters but holds them together; it is one of many ways in which the novel is structured in a tentacular fashion. As we have seen, then, the novel has tentacular bonds that interconnect disorganized characters, chapters and circumstances. For all the novel's disorder, there are multiple examples of order and organization. Like the marked contrast in style and content in *Nostromo*, "the most impressive monument to futility ever created,"[42] or between the first and second parts of *Lord Jim*, or between the assertive voice of the pilgrims in *Heart of Darkness* and Marlow's inconclusive narrative, *The Secret Agent* uses the structure and style not to mimic the subject of the text – but to convey meaning. With a tentacular grip, there is ethics in the form: in the unexpected control of the anarchist landscape.

PART III

Patterns and Preoccupations
Marginal Voices and Characters

CHAPTER 7

Voices and The Nigger of the 'Narcissus'

Although Conrad "prefers on the whole to let it appear that his writings originate in informal conversation or oral tradition,"[1] pocketbooks, notebooks, letters, labels, diaries, postscripts, pamphlets, leaflets, gazettes, records, telegrams, maps, manuscripts, newspapers and other written material – such as revolutionary literature served in soup cans in "The Informer" – play a significant part in Conrad's fiction. The main plots of *Under Western Eyes, The Arrow of Gold,* "Freya of the Seven Isles" and "The Inn of Two Witches" are according to their respective narrators based on written documents, such as a discovered manuscript or a posted notebook. And many of Conrad's books are made up of chapter-length excerpts of quoted writing, including Martin Decoud's pocketbook in *Nostromo*, H. C. Jörgenson's letter in *The Rescue*, the unnamed captain's diary in *The Shadow-Line*, and Marlow's letter to a "privileged reader" – taking up all the ten last chapters of *Lord Jim* (264).

In contrast to the noted presence of letters and other written documents in his fictional writings, Conrad has made sure that voices are heard across his writings. The banter, babble, blubber and "chitter-chatter" (*I* 173) – the swapped yarn, the after-dinner conversation, the testimonial report and the overheard rumor – are to date well-recognized elements of Conrad's fiction. Using an "extravagant and chatty prose,"[2] "Conrad was, if anything, a dialogist,"[3] "mesmerized by the spoken word,"[4] and wrote in "a style that is unmistakably a speaking voice."[5] In its (deceptively) unguarded, rambling, of-the-moment style, this ad lib speaking voice is linked to distraction and digression, two themes we discussed in Chapters 5 and 6. What drastically complicates the notion of the omnipresent voice in Conrad's prose, however, is the presentation of the voiceless, or the marginalized voice. The following chapter will listen to and amplify the voice of the "voiceless," by exploring one of Conrad's most perceptive novels: *The Nigger of the 'Narcissus'*. And, to the extent that *The Nigger of the 'Narcissus'* is an autobiographical novel, it will explore Conrad himself as a marginal subject.

Conrad once deemed *The Nigger of the 'Narcissus'* to be "the story by which, as creative artist, I stand or fall, and which, at any rate, no one else could have written. A landmark in literature, I can safely say, for nothing like it has been ever done before" (*CL* v.145), as he wrote in a slanting hand in a letter to the Irish American collector John Quinn in 1912. At first, it is difficult to understand why, in 1912, Conrad singles out this novel of 55,000 words as his most representative work as a creative artist, at a time when he had written *Heart of Darkness, Lord Jim, Nostromo, The Secret Agent* and *Under Western Eyes*. While early reviews regularly referred to *The Nigger of the 'Narcissus'* as a work of genius and a major work of fiction, the novel has also – on occasion – been considered "an apprentice work"[6] and counted "among the least popular of Conrad's works."[7] In a limited endorsement, Cedric Watts explains that with *The Nigger of the 'Narcissus'*, "Conrad's creative intelligence has not yet found the modes of co-ordination which were to result in his major achievements, *Heart of Darkness* and *Nostromo*."[8] As James E. Miller put it in a historical review of the novel's criticism: when compared with Conrad's other works and contemporary classics, the valuation of *The Nigger of the 'Narcissus'* is reliably "ambiguous."[9]

At first glance, even Conrad's enthusiastic positioning of *The Nigger of the 'Narcissus'* as a "landmark in literature" could be dismissed as a dishonest sales pitch to a collector – the letter continues by stating that Conrad wants "£80 for this MS" (*CL* v.145). Yet this explanation ignores that he expressed himself similarly enthusiastically in the Preface to the 1914 American edition of *The Nigger of the 'Narcissus'*: "It is the book by which, not as a novelist perhaps, but as an artist striving for the utmost sincerity of expression, I am willing to stand or fall" (9). In a recent essay, Marc Cyr finds more evidence for Conrad's consistent positive evaluation: given that Conrad expressed himself equally positively about the novel in multiple letters, the "1914 statement genuinely reflects his valuation of the book."[10]

One partial explanation why Conrad spoke of *The Nigger of the 'Narcissus'* so highly is that it is "the only book he ever wrote about ordinary [and able] seamen 'before the mast' (not officers, who berthed aft)."[11] Exploring this unique – for Conrad – thematic focus, I will argue that beyond being a tribute to life at sea qua life at sea, *The Nigger of the 'Narcissus'* is one of the most sympathetic portrayals of a class of people frequently considered to be marginal: a multinational group of physical laborers paid a meager wage, living in harsh and deadly conditions, doing their menial jobs heroically (with notable exceptions). This aspect of Conrad's authorship is understudied. It is not that critics have failed to notice Conrad's stated ambition: "It has been my desire to do for seamen what [the realist French painter] Millet … has done for peasants" (*CL* 1.430–31), he writes in a letter from 1897 to the influential critic Arthur Quiller-Couch. However, rather than focusing on the life of these seamen on the margins of civilized society as it is portrayed in the novel, the lion's share of criticism has de-emphasized "literal elements of the novel,"[12] stressed "the abstract and symbolic,"[13] or has "tended to focus upon such issues as the inconsistency in the narrative voice."[14]

As Brian Richardson writes in a chapter on posthumanist narration, and class and consciousness in *The Nigger of the 'Narcissus'*: "Conrad has not received sufficient credit for his positive and verisimilar portrayals of working-class characters," "such as the uncalculating generosity of men who have little, as well as a fundamental egalitarian outlook … and their uncommon capacity for endurance."[15] Although Richardson observes that the topic is understudied, his chapter focuses on the technical aspects of narration (the seemingly contradictory use of a narrative "we" and "I"). Unlike Richardson's chapter, this chapter will primarily develop the class perspective and relate it to Conrad's expressed belief that "no one else could have written" this type of novel. Of course, contemporary writers, such as Herman Melville and Richard Henry Dana Jr, also wrote sympathetically about merchant sailors before the mast. Yet Conrad's categorical and rhetorical statement about how only he could have written a novel like *The Nigger of the 'Narcissus'* is partly justified with reference to his own lived experience: not primarily because the novel is a composite of many of his own sailing voyages – including the 136-day journey on the merchant ship *Narcissus* from Bombay to Dunkirk – but because he was a foreigner in the British merchant navy in the nineteenth century, which placed him in a class of people on the margins of society. To move from the margin to the center, take up the pen and write a compelling story about this life for the middle-class literary establishment – first published in the conservative W. E. Henley's *The New Review* in 1897 – is the part of Conrad's achievement I will focus on in this chapter. I will explore how Conrad makes his readers listen to the voice of the sailors, reflect on the value of their work, and appreciate the importance of seemingly menial, physical labor – like the heroism of serving coffee, which the novel discusses.

Plot and Context

After *Almayer's Folly* and *An Outcast of the Islands*, both set in the Malay Archipelago, came *The Nigger of the 'Narcissus'*, the product of "twenty years of life, six months of scribbling" (*CL* 1.484). Unlike "A Smile of Fortune" which titles itself a "harbour story," *The Nigger of the 'Narcissus'* is primarily ship-bound – a homeward journey, taking its shipmates from a southern Bombay harbor to the Black Horse public house in London – the latter an establishment also mentioned in *Chance* – on a merchant sailing ship, during an indefinite time period, carrying a cargo that is never made known to the readers. During the journey, the ship and its "Twenty-six pairs of eyes" (27) face violence, theft, death, near mutiny and a harrowing storm of white hail, as the ship is "shaken furiously, like a toy in the hand of a lunatic" (53). The novel has a distinct place among Conrad's works; the named characters in *The Nigger of the 'Narcissus'* are found only there, except for "James," which is also the name of the protagonist in *Lord Jim*. Although *The Nigger of the 'Narcissus'* features a few place names found in other stories – it ends, for instance, where *Heart of Darkness* begins, on the River Thames in London – it primarily relates to Conrad's other writings in terms of its themes and narrative techniques. Notably, *The Nigger of the 'Narcissus'* includes those well-known characters who "populate Conrad's fiction"[16]: the voiceless.

The Simple and the Voiceless

Many instances in the novel can be read as overt attempts to counteract the presumed prejudices of the traditional, middle-class reader looking upon menial workers as "simple," "children," "unthinking," "voiceless," "inexperienced souls," and so on – words that the novel itself uses on multiple occasions. These words are, of course, self-deprecatory – Conrad spent most of his seafaring life as a sailor in the forecastle. Although the Preface explains that one aim of the novel is "to present an unrestful episode in the obscure lives of a few individuals out of all the disregarded multitude of the bewildered, the simple and the voiceless" (viii), the sailors presented in *The Nigger of the 'Narcissus'* are neither simple nor voiceless. Whilst the novel itself repeatedly stresses that the merchant sailors of Singleton's generation were "voiceless men," "strong and mute," who "lived inarticulate and indispensable" (25) – "inarticulate" and "voiceless" are more class-markers than a comment on the lack of voice or inability to communicate.[17] It certainly does not apply to the present-day crew of the

Narcissus, "who gave back yell for yell to a westerly gale" (173), as a first-person narrator summarily notes in the last sentence of the book. Despite their hailing from at least eight different native languages – Russian, Finnish, Norwegian, English, Dutch, Irish, Scottish, "West-country men" (77), there are no communication issues that prevent the merchant sailors from executing their craft.

Unlike the many taciturn characters across Conrad's fiction – such as Jim, Falk, Stevie, Stephen (in *The Sisters*), MacWhirr, Razumov, Yanko Goorall, Henry Whalley and Axel Heyst – the merchant sailors on the *Narcissus* are anything but taciturn or voiceless – except for Wamibo, who mostly communicates with the occasional grunt; his direct speech is only given on one occasion: "Hoo! Strook'im! Hoo! Hoo!" (69), as he excitedly urges Archie to use the crowbar to deliver Jimmy Wait from his prison of stout planks. And even Singleton, portrayed as the very embodiment of an older and silent generation of sailors, is given more direct-speech utterances (more than thirty) than almost any other of the able seamen in the novel. For a "taciturn" and "voiceless" character he is quite talkative (in contrast, for instance, to Kurtz in *Heart of Darkness*: although Kurtz is on multiple occasions described as a "voice" – "The man presented himself as a voice," 92; "He was very little more than a voice," 93 – readers hear his direct speech only on a few occasions: pleading, muttering and speaking in a range of abrupt utterances – "Go away," "Close the shutter," "The horror! The horror!" 117).

Throughout the voyage of the *Narcissus*, there is a constant "hubbub" (14) of yells, yelps, jeers, curses, rows, roars, groans, grunts, growls, howls, cries, squabbles, retorts, remarks, quarrels, discourses, screams, hisses, exclamations, thunders, clamors, whispers, shrieks, stammers, moans, mutters, murmurs, mumbles, shouts, blubbers, "babbling chatter" (125), "jocular abuse" (38), a "tempest of good-humoured and meaningless curses" (6), and "an impassioned screeching babble where words pattered like hail" (117). In explaining why he cannot sleep, Jimmy Wait points to an incessant "jabbering," "like a blooming lot of old women" (35). Notably, there is a vivid discussion about the characteristics of a gentleman (32), "impossible stories about Admirals" (32), arguments about whether Jimmy is shamming, superstitious talk about Jimmy ("the cause of head winds," 142), amicable disputes about the length of "homeward runs" (146), monologues such as Donkin's "impassioned orations" (101) about rights (his own, mostly), and Podmore's altercation with Charley about dried socks and his "holy row" (117) in his efforts to make Jimmy repent, so as to save his soul. During one event, Podmore, the cook who has been with the ship for more than seven years, is just like Kurtz in *Heart of Darkness*, Mr Verloc in *The Secret Agent* ("Vox et. . ." *SA* 24) or Schomberg in *Victory* and "Falk," a representative of a pure and divested voice. When he directs all of his holier-than-thou energies to save Jimmy from "everlasting fire" (116), as his Christian "heart overflowed with tenderness, with comprehension, with the desire to meddle" (115), "He was a voice – a fleshless and sublime thing" (116).

There are almost more references to "voice" and "voices" in *The Nigger of the 'Narcissus'* (about 110) than in any of Conrad's other books (*Under Western Eyes*, a significantly longer work, contains about 150 references, about the same number as *Lord Jim*). The use of direct oral speech is a significant marker of *The Nigger of the 'Narcissus'*: this novel has more than 900 direct utterances and about 400 ellipses (all of which are used to mark pauses in speech or implied and censored speech, such as swearing). Relying on statistics gathered using computer searches on the Dent collected edition (and verifying these by manual calculation), direct speech is more manifest in *The Nigger of the 'Narcissus'* than in any other Conrad narrative except *The Inheritors* and *Victory.*

In short, the voiceless create "a stormy chaos of speech" (128) in *The Nigger of the 'Narcissus'*. In a literal sense, then, Conrad's sailors are anything but voiceless. Indeed, although Marlow – a narrator in *Chance, Heart of Darkness, Lord Jim* and "Youth" – does not "represent his class" (*HD* 45), his incessant talking ("yarn spinning") is explained as a characteristic of his occupation as a sailor.[18]

The Nigger of the 'Narcissus' portrays a crew of garrulous sailors (the way most sailors are presented in Conrad's fiction) – yet its Preface maintains that the aim is to give a voice to the "voiceless." How should one make sense of these contrasting claims? In my reading, the claim that this is a novel about "voiceless" sailors is here referring to a voice that exists but that is ignored or not heard by those outside of the forecastle. Being "voiceless" is not a matter of not speaking but a matter of not being heard – of not having a listener. Along with elements of "ceremonious silence" (41), as in the response to Donkin's loss of a front tooth by the chief mate who reprimands him, or during the storm – "waiting wearily for a violent death" (61), when the entire crew is mute ("not a voice was heard," 61) – voicelessness is situational.

The subtitle of the original serial version and the first American edition of the novel spells out that *The Nigger of the 'Narcissus'* is "A Tale of the Forecastle," and the forecastle contains the sailors' living quarters, unlike the aftercastle (behind the mizzenmast) – where the captain traditionally resides. Chapter five, starting with a sentence on how "A heavy atmosphere of oppressive quietude pervaded the ship" (138), provides one example of situational voicelessness: the crew is voiceless when questioned by "the little quiet man" (135), Captain Allistoun, about their demands. When confronted by someone from a different socioeconomic group – "the ruler of that minute world" (31) – the otherwise talkative sailors fail to find their voice – or know that it is senseless to respond. When Captain Allistoun admonishes the sailors "like a Dutch Uncle" (126) in response to their protests that Jimmy should lie up in his cabin, they weakly attempt to articulate their frustration: "We don't want to go shorthanded, sir" (134) and "We did our best by her, sir" (134). These timid protests are immediately rejected by the captain's authority and sharp admonishments. While one could argue that the sailors lack a voice and "realize that they are unable to express their thoughts,"[19] it is also apparent that it is futile to speak when the authorities will not listen.

In this context, voicelessness is a metaphor for a lack of social and political power. That said, those who are typically seen as powerful – such as Kurtz in *Heart of Darkness* – have a voice in the most literal sense of the word. It is difficult to think of anyone or anything who is powerful but lacks a voice. Given that having a voice in the metaphorical sense is interconnected with having a voice in a literal sense, it is unsurprising that when we describe the sailors as voiceless, we have not explored their voice. Allan Simmons compares the voicelessness of the sailors with actual voiceless characters in Conrad's fiction, such as Yanko Goorall in "Amy Foster," who initially cannot make himself understood in English, and Stevie in *The Secret Agent*, who lacks the mental acuity to fully articulate sentences. For Simmons, "the task of the artist" in *The Nigger of the 'Narcissus'* is one of articulating and explaining the sailors' speech: "The fact that their discourse typically reduces to a 'hubbub' – there are countless synonyms for this word throughout the narrative – suggests that *this* is the task of the artist, to articulate and make sense of this 'hubbub'"; "Making something permanent out of the crew's babble of 'vanishing phrases' is the responsibility of the narrator."[20] Conrad certainly worked hard at capturing the essence of these voices. For instance, John D. Gordan has shown that although the merchant sailors express themselves hastily and unguardedly in the novel, Conrad displayed more care than usual when composing the text, and some passages exist in as many as seven versions in its holograph manuscript.[21] Whilst it is also an artistic achievement to orchestrate the individual voices into one narrative, as Simmons explains, my point is that the merchant sailors of the forecastle – unlike

Stevie or Yanko Goorall – already have a voice that is clear on its own. They are only on occasion "a group of numb men."[22] In my reading, Conrad does not merely amplify this voice, or articulate it more clearly – his rhetorical strategies remind the reader that he or she should listen. For various reasons, then, *The Nigger of the 'Narcissus'* demonstrates Conrad's success in giving voice to the voiceless; not by speaking for them, but by quoting them directly.

Cargo: "the sordid inspiration of her pilgrimage"

Giving a voice to the men in the forecastle is straightforward: as we have seen, they already have a voice, but they need listeners. The issue, of course, is also about counteracting uninformed and misleading voices. Regarding Singleton's generation, "Well-meaning people had tried to represent those men as whining over every mouthful of their food; as going about their work in fear of their lives" (*NN* 25). Yet by lauding the merchant sailors for "the iron discipline and the clockwork routines of maritime culture,"[23] Conrad can also be charged with condoning their harsh working conditions – and can falsely be labeled as a staunch conservative who does not question the merchant ethics of exacting physical labor but praises the sailors for not "whining." Indeed, Richard Ruppel summarily observes that "the underlying forces of mercantile capitalism are invisible" in this novel about shipping: "the cargo remains unidentified: it is never mentioned . . . Capital is the silent, mysterious, all-powerful and universal motivator of the narrative's action and of most of the noble impulses of the crew."[24] I take issue with the provocative idea that capital is the motivator of "most of the noble impulses of the crew" – Podmore, for instance, is a devout Christian. That said, I will offer an explanation that the sailors are praised for their exemplary labor without implying approval of the capitalist enterprise that is the source of these exacting demands.

The lack of specification of what type of cargo the *Narcissus* carries is certainly noteworthy as there are multiple references to cargo throughout Conrad's works, ranging from sugar, rice, ivory, cattle, opium, fruit, jute, petroleum, coal ("the supreme commodity of the age," *V* 3), coconuts, potatoes, timber, indiarubber, "rum, molasses, coffee, logwood" (*MS* 119), cork-wood, silver dollars, silver ingots, "rattans" ("Because of the Dollars," 140), "mail-bags" (*Y* 30), "pitch-pine deals" ("Falk," 227), "forty tons of dynamite and a hundred twenty tons of gunpowder" (*C* 17), to human passengers, such as the 800 Muslim pilgrims onboard the *Patna* in *Lord*

Jim. It is only when ships are mentioned in passing (such as the O.S.N.'s steamer *Minerva* in *Nostromo*), that there is no specification as to the cargo carried. It is therefore noteworthy that in *The Nigger of the 'Narcissus'* Conrad does not mention the primary reason for the voyage. Since the financial transaction of the narrative is staged when the story and the voyage end at the wage-table, when the shipmates are paid off for their service – why not specify the type of cargo the ship carries, the main financial reason for this specific voyage?

There are cases where the type of cargo plays a significant role in Conrad's narratives. The cargo of silver ingots that Decoud and Nostromo hide at the Isabels – "the most desperate undertaking of his life" (*N* 321) – is certainly of primary importance for the plot of *Nostromo*. The ivory tusks that Marlow's steamer in *Heart of Darkness* carries with it from Kurtz's inner station is important to the colonial dimension of the story (where ivory features prominently, but where elephants are not mentioned). The coal that spontaneously combusts in the barque *Judea* in "Youth" is at the narrative center of the story (sinking the sailing ship), although the coal itself is merely functional for the plot about sailing and mariners.

Neither sugar, rice, coconuts, potatoes nor any other cargo mentioned in Conrad's work – except for the silver ingots of *Nostromo* – can be said to be at the center of the respective stories, whether in a visible or an invisible manner. "Youth," published a year after *The Nigger of the 'Narcissus'*, contains an explanation, by a reminiscent Marlow, about the insignificance of cargo as an underlying justification and motivation for the merchant mariners: "To me she was not an old rattle-trap carting about the world a lot of coal for a freight – to me she was the endeavour, the test, the trial of life" (18). Perhaps the point about not mentioning the cargo in *The Nigger of the 'Narcissus'*, then, is to shift the focus away from the transactional value of sailing and thus demonstrate that the craft is distinct from the cargo: the value of one's work is not exclusively about how many coconuts or potatoes one transports.

Again, here we encounter a persistent Conradian theme. What is the value of merchant sailing, when its monetary rewards and even its service to society – from the utilitarian perspective of transporting cargo – at times do not appear to justify the sacrifice? Why, in the words of Donkin in *The Nigger of the 'Narcissus'*, should anyone live a "dorg's loife for two poun' ten a month? Did we think that miserable pay enough to compensate us for the risk to our lives?" (100). The same salary is reported for the sailors on *Judea* in "Youth" and here, as well, it is a cause for reflection. Although the pay is higher for chief mates and captains – for instance, Mr Bunter, a chief mate on the *Sapphire* in "The Black Mate," earns about two pounds per week – the work of merchant sailors portrayed in Conrad's stories can hardly be justified on the basis of transactional value alone. There are multiple references as to this point throughout Conrad's fiction, but it is perhaps most fully articulated in "A Smile of Fortune," where the readers are told by the unnamed captain-narrator that a man who obeys "the call for the sea" is "obviously not born for the chaffering and the bargains of the marketplace" (15–16): "Sea life unfits one for the battle of commercial wits" (15), as if the daily and constant demands that so outweigh the meager salary numb one's understanding of equitable commercial transactions. The issue or impossibility, of course, is the inherent difficulty of separating the work – and the moral worth – of the sailors from the commercial interests:

> Ah! These commercial interests – spoiling the finest life under the sun. Why must the sea be used for trade – and for war as well. Why kill and traffic on it, pursuing selfish aims of no great importance after all. It would have been so much nicer just to sail about with here and there a port and a bit of land to stretch one's legs on, buy a few books and get a change of cooking for a while. (SF 19)

A primary question these "commercial interests" pose is how to value the work of the merchant mariners when the ultimate reason for these actions (cargo transportation) appears to strip their work of heroism and honor, as in the case of a soldier fighting heroically for an unheroic cause. Conrad could have avoided the question altogether in *The Nigger of the 'Narcissus'* by explaining that the cargo was, say, a type of Indian medicine that was in great demand in London. Doing so, however, would have meant that this story about the forecastle would not have adequately reflected the reality of merchant sailing at the time, which was primarily about transporting commodities such as teak or coal. As Mark D. Larabee explains in an informative chapter on Conrad and the maritime tradition, "The historical *Narcissus* was carrying coal to India by the time of Conrad's service in her, and she would likely have been loaded with jute or another bulk cargo on the return for his single 1884 trip between Bombay and Dunkirk."[25] Jimmy, the title character in the story, hallucinates about a ship discharging grain, which is the closest suggestion to the type of cargo the fictional *Narcissus* carries.

Conrad's answer as to why merchant sailors should be lauded for their efforts is that the moral worth of the merchant crew is not measured on the basis of transactional value alone. The utilitarian calculus which maintains that a medical doctor is of higher moral standing than a cleaning person, since the doctor contributes more to the well-being of society by saving lives rather than making the living room dust-free, does not apply here. In Conrad's autobiographical reflection on sailing, *The Mirror of the Sea*, merchant sailors are provocatively compared to "Royal Academicians of a certain kind" (31). In their vocation as sailors, Conrad explains, they fought intimately with nature and this struggle "drew as much inspiration from this reality, as any man who ever put brush to canvas" (31). To evaluate merchant sailing on a strictly utilitarian basis is therefore to overlook Conrad's view of merchant sailing as "art for art's sake" (34), similar to fine arts. Moreover, in Conrad's sea stories, moral worth is attributed to how one acts *given* the circumstances in which one is placed (an idea that would have appealed to determinist philosophers such as Leibniz and Spinoza). After all, if Conrad had portrayed a society of equal opportunity where those less hard-working ended up working in menial occupations with little value to society, it would be reasonable for him to allocate little dignity to lowly work. The lack of social mobility at the time, however, means that such a valuation would be a harsh judgment on all of those who have no option but to work in so-called menial occupations: serving coffee, cooking food, cleaning the forecastle of a ship with holystones. One could therefore argue the opposite: the heroic acts are even more heroic from the perspective that the undertaking is mere transportation of cargo. *Despite* this condition on their employment the sailors behave heroically (with a few exceptions). And, as to "the sentimental voices that bewailed the hardness of their fate," these fail to recognize that "it was a fate unique and their own; the capacity to bear it appeared to them the privilege of the chosen" (*NN* 25), similar to the way many painters regard their vocation.

The Heroism of Serving Coffee

My final point concerns the heroism of serving coffee, and why it is telling that Conrad singles out this act as heroic, while downplaying other events as part of the everyday. Throughout the voyage the men endure hunger, thirst, cold, discomfort, sleep deprivation and physical fatigue. After thirty-two days at sea, the ship faces a harrowing gale. In the midst of the gale, with men swinging "on the ends of ropes, like nest robbers upon a cliff" (59), the carpenter stands ready to cut the tall masts – "inclined nearly to the horizon" (58). Yet the captain, a little "hard-faced man," shakes "his grey head" and shouts "No!" (59) – and the masts stay. Apart from

Donkin's emphatic protests, the men accept the order with stolid resignation: "They waited for the ship to turn over altogether, and shake them out into the sea; and upon the terrific noise of wind and sea not a murmur of remonstrance came out from those men, who each would have given ever so many years of life to see 'them damned sticks go overboard!'" (59). Their collective striving, physical exertions and loyalty to their occupation are also demonstrated in the saving of a crew member: James Wait, who during the gale is stuck in his cabin, "screaming and knocking . . . with the hurry of a man prematurely shut up in a coffin" (66). Digging through nails and planks with hands, hatchet and a crowbar, they save Jimmy from drowning in his collapsed cabin, on the half-submerged deck. Meanwhile, the gale provides for the display of superhuman effort and sacrifice: Singleton steers for almost two days with his white beard tucked into his oilskin coat, before he collapses on his soaked straw-bed – blaming himself for being too old. Paradoxically, these extraordinary events are part of the everyday challenges of being a merchant sailor in the nineteenth century, as Conrad seems to suggest with descriptions of other equally eventful voyages in his other stories: such as the description of an explosion in "Youth," disease in *The Shadow-Line*, and a storm in *Typhoon.*

While acknowledging these extraordinary efforts, I will focus on an aspect of seemingly menial physical labor: the serving of coffee. Another option would have been to discuss the washing of the decks, the oiling of the windlass, the heavy hauling of the main brace, the furling of the mizzen topsails, the trimming of the yards at midnight, or any other example of physical labor, where, desperate and exhausted, the crew works ceaselessly, in "the full privilege of desired unrest" (90). Serving coffee, however, is part of an everyday experience to which a cushioned middle-class reader can relate, but which in this context – of a gale at sea – is a testament to the heroism of menial labor. The heroic act takes place when the crew's energy is sapped by the stormy seas: "It was too cold for curiosity, and almost for hope. They could not spare a moment or a thought from the great mental occupation of wishing to live" (82). Yet in response to a request for fresh water by Mr Baker, the cook Podmore declares, "As long as she swims I will cook! I will get you coffee" (81). After several nighttime hours, in which the crew speculates that he must have fallen overboard, he brings hot coffee to the freezing crew, in the early morning:

> It came in a pot, and they drank in turns. It was hot, and while it blistered the greedy palates, it seemed incredible. The men sighed out parting with the mug: – "How 'as he done it?" Some cried weakly: – "Bully for you, doctor!"

> He had done it somehow. Afterwards Archie declared that the thing was "meeraculous." For many days we wondered, and it was the one ever-interesting subject of conversation to the end of the voyage . . . He remained heroic. His saying – *the* saying of his life – became proverbial in the mouth of men as are the sayings of conquerors or sages. Later, whenever one of us was puzzled by a task and advised to relinquish it, he would express his determination to persevere and to succeed by the words: – "As long as she swims I will cook!" (83)

Podmore's serving of hot coffee is "meeraculous" (83), "heroic" (84), and the cause of "fame" (100). Podmore himself – a "conceited saint unable to forget his glorious reward" (32) – remembers it as "the night when he went walking over the sea to make coffee for perishing sinners" (116). While the narrative satirizes Podmore for his self-conceit and holier-than-thou attitude ("All claim to special righteousness awakens in me that scorn and anger from which a philosophical mind should be free," *PR* 17), it is simultaneously a fond portrayal of the ship's cook reminiscent of the affectionate portrayal of Ransome, the cook with a weak heart in *The Shadow-Line*. As the voice that speaks for the crew of the *Narcissus* explains: "we did our best to conceal our admiration [of Podmore's 'heroism'] under the wit of fine irony" (83). Or as Conrad explains in a letter to the devout Calvinist Helen Watson about the description of the religious fanatic Podmore: "there was no *intention* of levity in my treatment of the cook. I did not try – and I trust I did not make him – ridiculous. Nothing was further from my thoughts than irreverence. It would have been untrue to my convictions. The worst that can be charged against me is artistic failure – failure to express the mixed sentiments the man (whom I knew) awakened in me" (*CL* 1.362). While the statement is characteristic of Conrad's diplomacy as a letter writer, his commitment to "express mixed sentiments" is an authentic expression of his writing style; like Il Conde, Conrad "had an eye for the small weaknesses of humanity. But it was a good-natured eye" ("Il Conde," 273). Or, as Conrad maintains in the "Author's Note" of *The Secret Agent* (his most sustained attempt at satire), the novel was written with the "deliberate belief" that "an ironic treatment alone would enable me to say all I felt I would have to say in scorn as well as in pity" (7).

The satirical yet fond description of Podmore and his heroic act of serving coffee, like a glorified waiter upon the sea or like Jesus offering loaves and fish, is at drastic odds with standard descriptions of sailors and heroism at sea. Lord Jim, in the eponymous book, daydreams about heroic acts at sea, in line with those portrayals he has read of in fiction: "after a course of light holiday literature his vocation for the sea had declared itself" (10–11). Yet sea life for a British merchant mariner in the nineteenth century offers a different type of heroism than that of which Lord Jim dreams, with his "head full of valorous deeds" (21) during his night watch on the ill-fated steamer *Patna*. In *The Nigger of the 'Narcissus'* the ever-ready merchant mariners are portrayed following a "roll-call to unquiet loneliness, to inglorious and obscure struggle, or to the more trying endurance of small privations and wearisome duties" (15), such as the serving of hot coffee, which accrues meaning in a storm.

It is therefore telling that Conrad does not romanticize the dangers and hardships that the crew faces. There is a death during the voyage – but even the death is slow and "unheroic," somewhat like a work-related accident rather than a swift sacrifice of life for a greater cause, the common fate of classical heroes in epic poetry. In the novel, James Wait dies after many weeks of lying in a sick-bed, unheroically and scornfully reproaching his fellow shipmates for failing to comply with his needs for compassion, silence, rest and fresh air.

A highly memorable passage is the description of his hasty burial at five o'clock in the afternoon. After the chief mate Mr Baker has read from "the prayer book" (159), Jimmy Wait, or, as he is fondly and ironically called by the crew, "Snowball," takes his "last dive" (160), with his feet weighted, in a bespoke coffin of canvas, forming a "grey package" (160). After many weeks spent lying in an improvised sick bed in his own diminutive white-painted cabin on deck, Jimmy dies in sight of land, Flores.

A number of Conrad's characters end their life at sea, but their deaths and funerals at sea are described more parenthetically and less ceremoniously, as in the case of the former captain in *The Shadow-Line*, the person Leggatt kills on the cargo ship *Sephora* in "The Secret Sharer," Laughing Anne in "Because of the Dollars," Marlow's helmsman in *Heart of Darkness*, and Captain Henry Whalley's wife in "The End of the Tether," buried "in the Gulf of Petchili" (131–32). Although Jimmy Wait dies from an unnamed disease that does not seem directly related to his life at sea (though it is exacerbated by its hard conditions), the implicit association of sea and death is not a mere coincidence, but a well-established element in Conrad's oeuvre. "Amy Foster," for instance, is the story of Yanko Goorall as the sole survivor of a large and decrepit passenger ship of emigrants, carrying families and young children. The most memorable event in "The Brute" is, arguably, the conclusion to the first mate's, Charley's, recent engagement to Maggie Colchester: she is caught up by the anchor and drowned at the end of the ship's journey. In Conrad's stories, more than fifteen named characters are buried at sea, of which six commit suicide by drowning.[26] The point is that not one of these deaths romanticizes life at sea, or associates death with an act of heroism.

When Jimmy takes his "last dive," then, this is part of what would become a Conradian convention: death and burial at sea. Even Singleton's prediction in the story that Jimmy will die in the sight of land resonates with a gruesome event in "A Smile of Fortune," where the captain's baby "died the very day we made the land" (27) for the first time in months, "only a few hours before reaching port" (22). In *The Shadow-Line* the wind picks up – as Mr Burns predicts – after they pass the late captain's burial spot at the latitude of 8 degrees 20 minutes, similar to the way the wind picks up after Jimmy's death (as Singleton predicts in *The Nigger of the 'Narcissus'*).

Although death at sea is an almost conventional occurrence in Conrad's work, those familiar with his works are hardly numbed by this motif: it is perhaps the most striking moment in *The Nigger of the 'Narcissus'*, even as one expects it. Nowhere else in Conrad's oeuvre is death and burial at sea described as extensively. Yet it is an unheroic death – part and parcel of life at sea – unlike the superhuman effort of serving coffee at sea during a storm. Rather than using the death during the voyage to romanticize life at sea, Conrad singles out the "meeraculous" (83) serving of hot coffee as heroic: "the one ever-interesting subject of conversation to the end of the voyage" (83).

Focusing on the everyday and elevating menial labor to the status of a heroic act defies clichés. Yet, rightfully worried about what "the respectable (hats off) part of the population" (*CL* 1.422) would think of a novel representative of his twenty years of experience as a merchant mariner, Conrad expressed exasperation with an early reviewer for failing to see the merchant crew in the true light: "The man complains of a lack of heroism!" (*CL* 1.418). Heroism in this novel is not the product of a singular sacrifice/event, such as death (as Lord Jim imagines from his reading of light holiday literature) but a "roll-call to unquiet loneliness, to inglorious and obscure struggle, or to the more trying endurance of small privations and wearisome duties" (*NN* 15) – in the words used to describe Mr Baker's summoning of the crew at the beginning of the novel. By avoiding ready-made descriptions of sailing and sailors, Conrad demonstrates that merchant sailing is an art of manual labor – an art that can rise to the pitch of heroism in the serving of hot coffee.

CHAPTER 8

Hats, Nostromo, *"The Secret Sharer" and* The Secret Agent

> 'Then, what clue could you have as to his identity?' / 'Only as much as we can deduce.' / 'From his hat?' / 'Precisely.' / 'But you are joking. What can you gather from this old battered felt?'
>
> Arthur Conan Doyle, "The Blue Carbuncle"

At first and second sight, a study on Conrad's hats might appear to be a mad hatter's experiment: falling within the category of esoteric trivia, exemplified by Thomas Carlyle's Professor of "Things in General" at Weissnichtwo University who has authored a book of philosophy titled *Clothes: Their Origin and Influence.* At best, it may be argued, hat study provides a superficial entry into Conrad's prose: it displaces the focus on a multifaceted person to his or her hat ("What do you think a fellow is – a scarecrow? All hat and clothes and no feeling, no inside, no brain to make fancies for himself?" *V* 398). From this perspective, a hat's proximity to the head is misleading – carrying no more connections to its thoughts and feelings than a sock.

However, as J. Hillis Miller has shown in *Poets of Reality*, by providing "glimpses of the oddity of inanimate things,"[1] what may appear to be a minor detail in Conrad's fiction often plays a significant role: such as the odd look of Almayer's house in *Almayer's Folly*, detached objects in *Typhoon*, and Mr Verloc's round hat in *The Secret Agent*, which in its normalcy is "in violent contrast to the abnormality of the situation." By displacing everyday inanimate objects and unsettling "the everyday pattern of things," Conrad changes a "web of relations."[2] Fredric Jameson similarly demonstrates, in a discussion of *Lord Jim*, that "what was secondary and inessential in one moment becomes the center and the dominant, the figure against the ground, in the next"; Conrad's prose is constructed on an "aesthetic principle" where significant details are initially made to seem "utterly insignificant."[3] This "aesthetic principle" is connected to what Beci Carver usefully labels as "Conrad's roving attentiveness to incidental detail,"[4] and what Ian Watt characterizes as Conrad's idiosyncratic focus on material things: his "steady reliance on ironic, elliptical, and paradoxical personification of an inanimate object."[5]

As a test case for Conrad's distinctive focus on details, marginal voices and characters, this chapter singles out a seemingly marginal object for further study: hats. The striking and provocative difference in theme from the previous chapter allows for focusing on a constant: Conrad's idiosyncratic writing technique and working method, and its preoccupation with marginal objects and characters. Conrad would likely have been sympathetic to a reading where his fictional hats are looked upon as bespoke pieces of the style, plot, characterization and context. For instance, after the illustrator Dudley Hardy painted Tom Lingard as wearing a fur hat in a story set in the tropics (*The Rescue*), Conrad expressed harsh disapproval: "What is it – a joke?" (*CL* VI.328). While this illustrator may have assumed that a hat was a detail of little significance, I will show that such a commonsensical assumption is at odds with Conrad's aesthetic principles and his fictional hats – their variety, number, position, meaning and function in the texts. Indeed, even though abundant secondary literature demonstrates that one can write on Conrad without writing on hats, Conrad did not seem able to write without including a full range of hats: from the bowler to the Bersagliere, there are more than twenty-five different types of hat in his fiction. They are used for fiddling, collecting nails, catching butterflies, transporting cakes, holding strips of beef, carrying secret messages, and saving a "homeless head from the dangers of the sun" (*SS* 188). Many times these hats are markers of individuality and have a visually prominent place in a story ("But the true sense of the scene he was beholding came to Ossipon through the contemplation of the hat," *SA* 213) – and may even have agency. Hats are of particular importance not only in Conrad's big city novels, *The Secret Agent* (London), *Under Western Eyes* (St Petersburg, Geneva) and *The Arrow of Gold* (Paris), but also in texts such as "The Secret Sharer," where a floppy hat saves the ship from being grounded. By looking at Conrad's hats, displayed individually and in context, on the hanger and on the head, we can approach an underexplored textual field and expand our Conradian vocabulary. We can see the hats from a nineteenth- and early twentieth-century perspective and explore both what the hats do and how to do things with hats. In particular, we can see that for Conrad the hat has both independence and agency; it functions as a telling sign of class; it unifies and marks a group of people; it serves a communicative as well as practical purpose; and, as will be shown, the hat is present even in its own absence. The hat functions partly, then, as an umbrella that covers many aspects of Conrad's style and works.

The Centrality of Literary Hats

Are there *many* hats in Conrad's fiction? Do the number of hats on their own form a uniquely large category, in relation to that of contemporary writers? There may not be anything extraordinary in Conrad's seemingly prolific writing on hats. This is apparent from looking at just a small sample case of four contemporary writers (not limited to one region, gender, nationality, style or topic). There are respectively more than twenty-five types of hat in Herman Melville's (1819–91) and Virginia Woolf's (1882–1941) writings, and more than fifteen types of hat in H. G. Wells's (1866–1946) and Vladimir Nabokov's (1899–1977) fictions.[6]

Many literary hats are clothed with meaning and are used for more than head protection. For instance, in Dickens's penultimate novel, *Great Expectations* (1861), there is a drawn-out scene of excruciating awkwardness when Joe visits Pip in London; throughout Joe struggles with his hat and where to place it. A full gamut of emotions is communicated via the hat; it is a key to a psychological state rather than a mere object of clothing. There are, however, only a few sustained studies on hats in secondary literature: Fred Miller Robinson's historical and insightful survey, *The Man in the Bowler Hat: His History and Iconography* (1993); Mark Hennelly's excellent paper on "Dickens's Immaterial Culture of Hats and the *Pickwick Papers*"; William Brevda's historicist paper on hat symbolism in *Moby-Dick*, "*Moby Dick*: A Nasty Night for Hats and Men"; Alfred Kuhn's perceptive essay on Raskol'nikov's hats; and Thomas Hanson's "Mallarmé's Hat." Hanson's essay is a blend of an academic research paper and poetical meditation,[7] but he successfully defends the notion that "Mallarmé apparently spent a fair amount of time thinking about hats."[8] Brevda demonstrates that the origin of *Moby-Dick*'s hat motif is "Melville's own psychological experience as the son of a failed father … a handsome, cosmopolitan gentleman who looked good in hats but went bankrupt trying to sell them."[9] Kuhn reads the hats as "proof of Dostoevskij's careful attention to even the smallest details in *Crime and Punishment.*" He singles out the hats for closer attention not because "they play an overwhelmingly important role in the novel," but "precisely because they are minor recurrent images."[10]

While not all minor recurrent images deserve sustained critical attention, one could argue that a topic that manages to qualify itself as uninteresting on so many accounts deserves our interest for this very reason. What do you find when you look where no one has looked? – And where no one expects you to look? (A similar type of query must have directed Sherlock Holmes in "The Blue Carbuncle," 1892, where he from the mere observation of "a very ordinary black hat" explains that the owner was "highly intellectual . . . fairly well-to-do within the last three years, although he has now fallen upon evil days," etc.[11]) Due to readers' seemingly natural inclination to treat hats as objects of minor significance and therefore pay them little attention (rather than subject them to Holmesian deduction), Conrad has a certain license to treat the hats carelessly; to use unimaginative and clichéd expressions; to employ hats that do not accord with the cultural climate; to forget whether his characters wear a hat. In short, to create a situation where hats do not yield meaning but are meaningless. Yet Conrad writes on hats with accuracy and consistency. He pays attention to details about hats that the reader is likely to ignore.[12] Conrad's hats are also more than "minor recurrent images."[13] As in "The Partner" where a ruffian's "general contempt for mankind with its activities and moralities was expressed in the rakish set of his big soft hat" (77) or in *Nostromo* where Dr Monygham's stained and old Panama hat is "an established defiance to the conventionalities of Sulaco" (45), Conrad's hats serve a wider purpose than protecting his characters' heads: they are connected, not only to attitudes such as contempt and defiance, but also to feelings, characters and plots.

"The Secret Sharer" and the Floppy Hat

In the short story "The Secret Sharer," the young and inexperienced captain risks the ship's and his crew's safety by steering the sailing ship "as close as possible" (116) to the shore of Koh-ring at nighttime. The purpose, he tells his chief mate, is to find land breezes. His real intent, however, is to allow Leggatt, the fugitive murderer and former first mate of *Sephora*, to escape to land. In this daring sailing maneuver, executed despite the fact that Leggatt is an able swimmer, the ship comes close to hitting the rocks, but is ultimately saved by the captain accidentally spotting his floppy hat floating on the water:

> Was she [the ship] moving? What I needed was something easily seen, a piece of paper which I could throw overboard and watch. I had nothing on me. To run down for it I didn't dare. There was no time. All at once my strained, yearning stare distinguished a white object floating within a yard of the ship's side. White on the black water. A phosphorescent flash passed

> under it [Leggatt swims to shore]. What was that thing? . . . I recognized my own floppy hat. It must have fallen off his head . . . And he didn't bother. (SS 118)

Thus, a list of sensory perceptions ("white," "object," "White on black water," "it," "that thing") is correctly decoded by the captain into "my own floppy hat." As a mark by which to measure the ship's movement, the white floppy hat allows the captain to safely navigate close to shore in darkness. To execute the complicated maneuver of steering straight toward the shore and then turning swiftly, the captain "needs to know whether the ship is still moving ahead, is dead in the water, or has gathered sternway." When he spots the hat slowly moving forward, he knows his "ship has gathered sternway."[14] Without the hat, there would have been a grounded ship and the ready possibility to read this event as an example of poetic justice: the punishment for helping a murderer to escape. As Porter Williams speculates about this alternative scenario: "Leggatt's murderous rage and the captain's decision to risk his ship, though not alike in terms of motivation, came surprisingly close to having the same destructive consequences in terms of human life."[15] The floppy hat prevents this situation and instead advances a plot where legal and moral rights can be seen as distinct.

Taking a less literal perspective, many have read the text as "a psychological and symbolic story of self-exploration, self-recognition, and self-mastery,"[16] where "Biblical, classical psychological, and Jungian readings have all swum to the surface like Leggatt."[17] These are worthy avenues to pursue, but they downplay the importance of the floppy hat as floppy hat: "The floppy hat variously symbolizes a Jungian archetype or a symbol of the alter ego. Or it may symbolize the instinctive violence of Leggatt, perhaps combined with the counterbalancing instinct of pity in the Captain."[18] The most extensive reference is given by Ted Billy who, in line with the tradition of reading "The Secret Sharer" from a psychoanalytic perspective, finds that the hat "comes to objectify the futile attempt to comprehend the unknowable in rational terms": the white hat "floats on the sea of consciousness, like the top of an iceberg."[19] But the hat is unlikely to represent the unknowable: the narrator's recognition of the hat saves the ship. Similarly, the sea is unlikely to represent consciousness as it is described as dark and monolithic – providing neither guidance nor mark by which to navigate. Understood literally, the floppy hat serves multiple functions in the story: as a part of the young captain's casual outfit of striped pyjamas and straw slippers; as a gift to Leggatt to make sure that he is not bareheaded when marooned in Koh-ring; as a mark by which to measure the ship's movement. In addition it becomes, in the words of the captain, "the expression of my sudden pity for his mere flesh" (118): a metonymic observation signaling that hats can say much about the thoughts and feelings of the heads they designate.

The Story of Things and Parts

Conrad frequently narrates events from an optically restricted rather than omniscient perspective: "behind that structure came out an impression of pale plumpness in a frock-coat" (*HD* 51); "a skinny forefinger beckoned me into the sanctuary" (*HD* 51). John G. Peters calls this way of seeing "primitive perception."[20] The use of primitive perception partly explains the primary importance of hats for Conrad's literature. In the *Second Meditation* (1641), Descartes uses the picture of a walking hat as an example of seeing with an innocent eye: "If I look out of the window and see men crossing the square, as I have just done, I say that I *see* the men themselves, just as I say that I see the wax; yet do I see any more than hats and coats [?]"[21] The eyes see a walking hat whereas the mind (drawing rational assumptions from previous experiences) sees a walking man.[22] Displaced from previous experience, outside of the category of cause and effect, Conrad's primitive perception tells the story of things and parts – forefingers, bells, noses, hats: "Through the middle of the street streamed, like a torrent of rubbish, a mass of straw hats" (*N* 384); "groups of sombreros set level on heads against the vertical sun were drifting away into the streets" (*N* 393). Whether these isolated parts are by necessity subordinated to a larger image is not clear: in "The Secret Sharer," "the frightful whiskers" – not the mate who wore them – "made themselves heard giving various orders" (119). In *The Secret Agent*, "Ossipon had a vision of these black-rimmed spectacles" – not the Professor – "progressing along the streets on the top of an omnibus, their self-confident glitter falling here and there on the walls of houses" (53). In *Under Western Eyes*, "the impenetrable earnestness of the blue glasses" (166), rather than that of Peter Ivanovitch, meets Razumov's stare.

Is Conrad telling the story of whiskers, black-rimmed spectacles and blue glasses? Or, of a shipmate, the Professor and Peter Ivanovitch? Is the character of the first mate introduced only to permit the use of the central image of commanding whiskers? The difficulty of answering these questions suggests that Conrad, at times, placed a focus on details over and above characters; it is in this narrative context that the hats were displayed with agency and vivid imagery as if they were in competition with static characters. As such, the hats in Conrad's fiction partly reinforce the observation that the Victorian novel "describes, catalogs, quantifies, and in general showers us with things";[23] instantiating a "kingdom of thingdom."[24]

On the one hand, a "detail" like a hat can be used to build association. For instance, in Conrad's Russian novel not only is Tekla associated with her cat and Prince K— with his grey whiskers, but also a pair of tinted spectacles and a silk top hat are the trademarks of Peter Ivanovitch, the revolutionary feminist. Inside or outside – whether he preaches, sits or walks – he is wearing his tinted glasses and his hat, on his head or beside him like extended limbs. On the other hand, Ivanovitch uses the items to create a distinct social appearance. His face is bland, featureless, shapeless, "a mere appearance of flesh and hair" (97). In contrast, his top hat has character and independence. Razumov distinctly remembers the hat in isolation: "a solitary speck reposing on the balustrade of white marble – the silk top-hat of the great feminist – asserted itself extremely, black and glossy in all that crude whiteness" (175). The hat, then, has both independence and agency – and is far from a trivial detail. While a first-time reader of *Under Western Eyes* may initially question the significance of Razumov's observation on Ivanovitch's hat and wonder why he deemed it worthy of noting in his secret journal, the silk hat tells us much about Ivanovitch. The luxurious silk hat suggests that for a revolutionary Ivanovitch lives rather well. And, along with the tinted glasses, which hint that his vision of society is limited, colored and flawed, the ostentatious hat is not part of a disguise, but revealing of his attention-seeking showmanship. The silk hat itself is a composite commercial product of international cooperation and capitalism, as well as a telling sign of class and wealth: Prince K— in *Under Western Eyes* wears a top hat, as does the financier de Barral in *Chance*, the wealthy Mr X in "The Informer," Sir Ethelred in *The Secret Agent* and, in *The Arrow of Gold*, Versoy – "a man of the world" (35). In *The Nigger of the 'Narcissus'*, the captain's brother is described as "A toff in a black coat and high hat" (165), and in *The Secret Agent* Winnie fears the legal consequences of having avenged Stevie's death: in the form of "a lot of strange gentlemen in silk hats who were calmly proceeding about the business of hanging her by the neck" (201).

For Winnie, the wearing of the silk hats unifies and marks a group of people; it is a significant fact that has implications for how she will be judged. The idea is not that, *ceteris paribus*, the members of the imaginary legal team would make better decisions if they were wearing different hats. Rather, the fact that these members wear silk hats implies that they likely have certain things in common, like being male, upper-class, and indifferent to what *The Nigger of the 'Narcissus'* classifies as "dumb fear" (*NN* 90), to characterize the irrational timidity the "obscure, forgetful, and enduring" (90) forecastle sailors have for the mores and norms of civilized society and authoritative figures. Indeed, two years after the publication of *The Secret Agent* in book form, Conrad returns to the fear of a biased jury, by referring to its members' visible traits: Leggatt laments that he cannot explain himself to "an old fellow in a wig and twelve respectable tradesmen" (*SS* 111), a jury that differs from him in dress, age, occupation – and, what is likely, beliefs and experiences (although, it is interesting that Leggatt critiques the jury for being tradesmen when he himself had a practical job, as the chief mate of the *Sephora*. That said, Leggatt is certainly not a common sailor: he has the distinction of being a former "Conway boy" (88), and would likely have regarded himself as a gentleman).

In *The Secret Agent*, the silk hat is also firmly conjoined with the upper class: "silk hats and elderly business men" (13) are both set in motion by Stevie setting off fireworks on the staircase, and "could be seen rolling independently down the stairs" (13). In *Under Western Eyes*, the revolutionist Peter Ivanovitch interestingly combines the tinted glasses with an item seemingly reserved for the upper class, a silk hat. (Ivanovitch's silk hat also hints toward the fluidity of the label "anarchist": in a letter to his outspoken socialist friend, Cunningham Graham, Conrad labels "the true anarchist ... the millionaire," *CL* III.491.) The extent to which this item is a mark of the upper class is difficult to overemphasize. Although Conrad's readers today are certainly able to identify the visual shape of a top hat, its connotations have changed drastically. This now respectable and refined hat, seen at opera houses and formal royal events, was once worn by revolutionary industrialists. Charles Blanc (1813–82), a French art critic, saw in the top hat an expression of barbarism: "Our tubular hats which artists in their everyday discourses have cast such withering scorn upon – these hats without front or back, without direction, without a culminating point, and whose frightful cylindrical shape is altogether at variance with the spherical form of the head, are assuredly the last remnant of barbarism."[25]

Blanc had every right to make the top hat an emblem of barbarism. At its first appearance in the streets of London it caused pandemonium. As a journalist noted in 1797:

> It is in evidence that John Hetherington, a haberdasher, appeared on a public highway wearing a hat which he called a silk hat, a tall structure having a shiny lustre calculated to frighten timid people. Several women

> fainted at the unusual sight, children screamed, dogs yelled, and the younger son of a cordwinder, Thomas, who was returning from a chandler's shop, was thrown down by the crowd which was collected, and his right arm was broken.[26]

While John Hetherington was fined five-hundred pounds (about £40,000 today) for inciting a riot with his choice of headwear, within fifty years the top hat became a fashion item, and "as though reflecting the locomotive stacks and industrial chimneys that proliferated, covered the pate of every Parisian gentleman."[27] Peter Ivanovitch's decision to wear a silk top hat parallels his view that "the dregs of a people" (164) are neither the "highest class" nor the "peasantry" (164), but the middle class; an opinion echoed by Mr Vladimir in *The Secret Agent*: "the middle classes are stupid" (28). Peter Ivanovitch's tinted glasses and silk hat are, then, not directly at odds with his revolutionary personality: both were contentious clothing items in the nineteenth century. Although Conrad owned a top hat (now displayed in a museum in Canterbury), he is often photographed with a bowler hat, distinctly popular with the working class in the Victorian era. Paul Langlois, a charterer in Mauritius, remembers Conrad as a sailor, even then dressed in a "black or grey bowler hat."[28]

***Nostromo*, the Bersagliere and "An immortal hero!"**

The top hat is not the only hat in Conrad's lexicon that requires historical context for understanding. The Bersagliere hat in *Nostromo* is similar to the top hat "calculated to frighten timid people." A portrait of Giuseppe Garibaldi, an Italian general and politician, is kept in the *pulperia* by Old Giorgio, who considers himself "one of Garibaldi's immortal thousand in the conquest of Sicily" (*N* 20). Old Giorgio eyes the lithograph for moral support as the rebels descend upon the *pulperia*: "He grounded his old gun, and, turning his head, glanced at the coloured lithograph of Garibaldi in a black frame on the white wall; a thread of strong sunshine cut it perpendicularly" (21). Old Giorgio, of course, is already familiar with the portrait. Yet its visual details – "the red of the shirt, the outlines of the square shoulders, the black patch of the Bersagliere hat with cock's feathers curling over the crown" (21) – are a comforting reminder: "An immortal hero!" (20). There may be an element of intended irony here: Garibaldi was never a member of the Bersagliere; in fact, "they stopped his march to Rome." Garibaldi "was accidentally shot by Luigi Ferrari, a 36-year-old Bersaglieri lieutenant . . . To avoid a fractural war, Garibaldi ordered his volunteers not to return fire and was captured."[29]

The picture of Garibaldi with a Bersagliere hat is historically accurate, if inventive, from the perspective that both Garibaldi and the elite unit are renowned for their extraordinary military feats in the unification of Italy. Founded in 1836 in the Kingdom of Sardinia, the Bersagliere have always been a high-mobility light infantry unit, operating in loose formations without direct command, and frequently serving as assault troops. Yet the Bersagliere hat that Garibaldi wears in the lithograph serves as more than a comment on military history; the wide-brimmed hat itself is an intriguing visual object: it is typically decorated with hundreds of black capercaillie feathers, which serve as camouflage and sunshade. Conrad's Anglophone readers are not expected to know what an Italian Bersagliere hat looks like; the present-day editions by Penguin and Oxford contain explanations beyond Conrad's own ("cock's feathers curling over the crown").

In *Nostromo*, the visual form of the Bersagliere hat contributes to the powerful nature of the portrait of Garibaldi. It is a hat that makes a statement. The Bersagliere, a flamboyant war hat, is the absolute opposite of an everyday, practical hat: the hat has limited practical function; it is primarily decorative and symbolic. The wearer of the Bersagliere becomes the peacock. The Bersagliere hat, although powerful on its own, is not only part of military uniform but could also be a mark of individuality – like the cufflinks of the accountant in *Heart of Darkness* that set him apart from his pyjama-wearing co-workers.

To the Anglophone reader, without knowledge of the appearance of such hats, the descriptor "Bersagliere" functions merely to communicate foreignness, in language and meaning. Readers with fuller knowledge can see the hat in all its flamboyance and splendor: they can see what Old Giorgio sees, without accepting Giorgio's unthinking idolatry, which overlooks that his military hero is wearing the mark of defeat on his head.

The Displaced, Repurposed and Absent Hat

In "Thing Theory," Bill Brown writes on the possibility of locating a thing's identity outside its function as an object. If you reduce a thing (like a hat) to its function, you see an object or tool rather than a thing. An object's thingness is emphasized when it stops executing its expected function. There is a clear thingness to many objects in Conrad's prose. For instance, apart from odd hats, there are hats used in odd ways. Stein in *Lord Jim* uses his hat to catch butterflies ("One step. Steady. Another step. Flop!" 160); Sotillo in *Nostromo* uses his hat to steal a gold watch; the crew in *The Nigger of the 'Narcissus'* collects nails with hats in the process of saving Jimmy; Attilio in *Suspense* has hidden a bundle of papers in Cosmo's hat ("dangerous documents," 165); Montero's army in *Nostromo* transports "strips of raw beef twined round the crowns of their hats" (385); Peter Ivanovitch uses his hat to carry cakes to Mme de S— : he "returned instantly with a parcel wrapped up in white glazed paper, which he must have extracted from the interior of his hat" (*UWE* 169). Then, in *Under Western Eyes*, there is the oddity of not wearing a hat when walking in a snowy Geneva – an oddity congruous with Razumov's dejected state and newly acquired deafness. As if the hat is such a potent symbol in Conrad that it is present even in its own absence, both Tekla and a driver distinctly remember the fact that Razumov was bareheaded: "a bedraggled, soaked man without a hat" (280). Bareheadedness codes for vulnerability, as in "The Secret Sharer," where the unnamed captain gives his floppy hat to Leggatt to save his head from the scorching sun.

Although being bareheaded outdoors can be a sign of vulnerability, wearing a hat indoors is not a sign of strength. As a domesticated double agent, Adolf Verloc in *The Secret Agent* does not seem to be the most revolutionary of anarchists – living the life of a well-fed married shop-owner with a cleaning lady. However, he regularly breaks the social code by wearing a hat indoors. "Mr Verloc loved to take his ease in hat and overcoat" (119) on a horse-hair sofa in his living room. Although he takes off his hat when visiting State Councillor Wurmt and Mr Vladimir, at home he eats dinner with his hat on and on two occasions wears his hat at breakfast. This seemingly trivial fact about Mr Verloc's use of his hat is a partial response to a set of questions posed in a thematic precursor to *The Secret Agent*, "The Informer": what does it mean to be an anarchist in an everyday situation, during "the routine acts of daily life" (75)? Does someone "still remain an anarchist when alone, quite alone and going to bed, for instance?" (75). Whereas "The Informer" explicitly spells out the absurdity of navigating an organized life with the mindset of an anarchist ("I would never be able to compose myself sufficiently to sleep or eat," 75), in *The Secret Agent* the reader is left to connect the dots through the lens of the absurd details that make up Mr Verloc's everyday existence: such as his wearing a hat when having supper with his family in the privacy of their home.

The displaced hat here reinforces the Conradian theme that minor, everyday details are important to safeguard sanity: "the trivialities of daily existence were an armour for the soul" (48), Razumov explains in *Under Western Eyes*; "These little things make all the great difference" (94), Marlow tells his listeners in *Heart of Darkness*. In *Typhoon*, the narrator asserts that it is the "little habits that chain us to the weary round life" (85). It is therefore interesting that Conrad pays so much attention to Mr Verloc's hat in *The Secret Agent*, especially as a contrast to the fanciful notion of Mr Verloc's strict dinner etiquette; on the assumption that Mr Verloc would have been "inexpressibly pained and shocked by any deficiency of cleanliness at meal times" (34), Winnie always makes sure that Stevie washes his hands and face before dinner. The expectations for Mr Verloc's behavior are different. Whereas Mr Verloc gets angry when his wife wears a "confounded hat" (192) indoors, Winnie tolerates that her husband wears his hat at home to dinner or breakfast. Although Winnie has prepared the food and it is served in the comfort of his home, he "ate as if in a public place, his hat pushed off his forehead, the skirts of his heavy overcoat hanging in a triangle on each side of the chair. And across the length of the table covered with brown oil-cloth Winnie, his wife, talked evenly at him the wifely talk" (139). Like a "homeless couch" (67) found outside in an alley in the novel, Mr Verloc's use of the hat indoors communicates displacement: Verloc lives in a hazy dream state of "intense meditation" (120), separated from the everyday concerns of hat etiquette. With a constant "air of having wallowed, fully dressed, all day on an unmade bed" (120), he seems to lack the mental focus to make the effort to remove the hat when indoors. I will suggest that readers also lack the capacity to remove Mr Verloc's hat: it is difficult to imagine Verloc hatless.

On the way to Mr Verloc's residence, the Assistant Commissioner visits "a peculiarly British institution" (115): the Italian restaurant. He observes that the guests and the restaurant seem made for one another, so that one cannot imagine either one of them independently. The same is the case for Mr Verloc and his hat – they go not hand in hand, but head in hat. The hat is a distinct trademark of Verloc's appearance. So, whereas both Sir Ethelred and his silk hat look "expanded" (106); Michaelis wears a round hat for his "round head" (44); the evening visitors to Verloc's store are identified as "the men with collars turned up and soft hats rammed down" (10); the definition of Mr Verloc includes his "hat and stick," in three references (18, 21, 23). This aligns with John Lyon's observation that in *The Secret Agent*, "inanimate objects," like Mr Verloc's hat, "appear aggressively animated."[30] ("There is a rebellious soul in things," 201, to borrow a phrase from *Lord Jim*.) Indeed, whilst there is an element of somnolence and inaction to Mr Verloc, his hat is actively employed in several scenes.

The hat plays a part in Mr Verloc's decision to use Stevie to detonate the X2 green powder in the planned anarchist attack on the Greenwich observatory (a false-flag operation orchestrated to promote vigilance and protect property). After Stevie has swiftly and "reverently" (140) borne off Mr Verloc's hat to the kitchen, Winnie answers her husband's surprise: "*You* could do anything with that boy, Adolf" (140). Verloc's hat also frames his final moments, from when he returns from Greenwich – "with his hat rammed down upon his forehead" (144) – to his final rest on the sofa in his living room. During this time, the hat is seemingly positioned everywhere except on a rack: the hat travels from his head, to under the sofa, to his hands, to under the table, to the middle of the floor. Conrad keeps track of the hat – seemingly a marginal detail – through deeply unsettling events. Rather than lying forgotten under the table, where it was placed several pages earlier, it moves when Winnie rushes against the table on her way out. (As a marginal detail, it is reminiscent of how in *The Nigger of the 'Narcissus'* the cat Tom reappears in the narrative after being absent for several chapters.) Staying on the theme, chapter XI ends with a vision of the hat: "Then all became still. Mrs Verloc on reaching the door had stopped. A round hat disclosed in the middle of the floor by the moving of the table rocked slightly on its crown in the wind of her flight" (199). Ending the chapter with a vision of a round hat is reminiscent of theatrical staging – as is the ending of chapter IV, where a mechanical piano plays out Ossipon to "the tune of 'Blue Bells of Scotland'" (65). The hat is not a cliffhanger; neither is it a resolution, nor a summary judgment. But the final word is not given to a voiceless hat: the hat is a carrier of meaning – a meaning intrinsically connected to Mr Verloc's existence. As Ossipon will notice, the displaced hat marks and contextualizes Mr Verloc's death.

After speaking with the Professor and finding out who was responsible for the explosion in Greenwich, Ossipon goes to 32 Brett Street to see Winnie ("Fasten yourself upon the woman for all she's worth," 64). He finds her outside. When returning to Winnie's house, Ossipon is shocked at finding Mr Verloc at rest on a sofa when he was supposed to have blown himself up in the park (according to Ossipon's mistaken view of the situation). But

> the true sense of the scene he was beholding came to Ossipon through the contemplation of the hat. It seemed an extraordinary thing, an ominous object, a sign. Black, and rim upward, it lay on the floor before the couch as if prepared to receive the contributions of pence from people who would come presently to behold Mr Verloc in the fullness of his domestic ease reposing on the sofa. (213)

Although the hat calls attention to Mr Verloc, it is Conrad who has marked the scene with a hat: the upturned hat associates the dramatic death of Mr Verloc with the banality of a street performance or freak-show, undertaken for gratuities. It is a comic scene in a domestic drama: the constantly tired Mr Verloc, devoted to "fanatical inertness" (16), has found final rest on the sofa. As we would imagine the guests in the Italian restaurant to cease to exist if they left it, Mr Verloc's death separates him from his hat.

Setting the Scene: Upturned Hat, Carving Knife, Pool of Blood

The Secret Agent was first printed (1905–06) as eleven installments in *Ridgway's: A Militant Weekly for God and Country.* Without Conrad's assistance, the story was heavily edited – Mrs Neale and the butchery boy were pruned out;[31] the *Ridgway's* publication has the appearance of a draft in relation to the book, published by Methuen in 1907, which is one third longer. In the book, the hat plays a more significant part; especially in the last chapters, where it is given agency and a cohesive narrative. The following section cannot be found in *Ridgway's*: "Mr Verloc flung himself heavily upon the sofa, disregarding as usual the fate of his hat, which, as if accustomed to take care of itself, made for a safe shelter under the table" (*SA* 194–95). In *Ridgway's*, Mr Verloc's hat plays a diminutive role: it does not conclude a chapter, and it is not used to mark Mr Verloc's death. Rather than seeing an upturned hat, Ossipon sees "the handle of the carving knife in Mr. Verloc's side" (46) and exclaims (without an exclamation point): "You've murdered him" (46). Ossipon's exclamation, which Conrad later deleted, repeats what is already clear from the scene. In contrast, by the time Ossipon sees the knife handle in the book version, he is already aware that Winnie is responsible for Mr Verloc's death.

Conrad had successfully worked on limiting over-explanation in previous texts: the manuscript version of *Heart of Darkness*, where Kurtz calls for "More blood, more of heads on stakes, more adoration rapine and murder," was limited in published form to the more enigmatic: "The horror! The horror!" (*HD* 117). Here, the less obvious is the more interesting. Another reason for why Conrad communicated Mr Verloc's death to Ossipon through an upturned hat (rather than a carving knife) may stem from the way the illustrator Henry Patrick Raleigh told the story in *Ridgway's*.

Apart from working with painting, etching and lithography, Raleigh illustrated for *Vanity Fair* and *Saturday Evening Post*, and for Agatha Christie, F. Scott Fitzgerald and H. G. Wells. Raleigh was one of the most famed and affluent illustrators of the time – an artist in his own right. In a 1923 interview, Raleigh says that "the most beautiful picture is one

Figure 8.1 A Henry Raleigh illustration for the American serialization of *The Secret Agent* in *Ridgway's*. Part 11 of 11 (December 15, 1906), page 43. Butler Library, Columbia University, New York.

which the observer is left free to complete for himself. The illustrator should be able to select the essential elements in any subject which will convey to the layman the entire scene in the simplest and most direct way, avoiding mere details which tend to cause either monotony or confusion."[32] Raleigh's drawing of Mr Verloc's death includes an upturned hat next to the sofa (Figure 8.1). Applying Raleigh's own artistic credo, the hat in this drawing is not a mere detail but serves to convey the scene, as Conrad perhaps realized when he later included the hat in the same position in the novel.

S. W. Reid compares Raleigh's drawings for *The Secret Agent* to those accompanying a standard "comic-book."[33] Laurence Davies finds that the drawing reproduced above is "crude but atmospheric."[34] Cedric Watts classifies Raleigh's interpretations as "line-drawings in a style verging on caricature."[35] Yet Raleigh's twenty-five drawings cannot be reduced to one style (linear) and message (caricature). The drawing reproduced above is painterly rather than committed to line and contour: the style is impressionistic, not caricatural (the aforementioned comments are more fitting for the actual comic-book adaptation by John K. Snyder of the story in 2013). The drawing correctly identifies the shadow Mr Verloc sees on the wall as deriving from Winnie's placement in front of the fireplace and the grate, objects mentioned in the story. To classify the drawings as illustration is to assume that they are subservient to the text and lack independence. If, as suggested above, Conrad was influenced by Raleigh's drawing of an upturned hat, they were co-writers of a scene: the later version of *The Secret Agent* illustrates Raleigh's hat scene with words. Although there is plenty of evidence that Conrad was both directly and indirectly influenced by other writers, the idea that an illustrator influenced his story is new. However, similar creative relationships between writers and illustrators have been proposed previously: George Cruikshank, one of Dickens's most prolific illustrators, claimed "to have originated some of the characters and situations of *Oliver Twist*."[36]

For Stephen Donovan, the upturned hat next to Mr Verloc's body exemplifies "the tableau designer's practice of foregrounding small objects through which spectators could imaginatively enter into the display."[37] The idea is that everyday, familiar objects (such as hats) can be used as stepping stones for the mind by which to reach an understanding of the unusual; the everyday object can be a channel for communicating dramatic events. Following this logic, although it is difficult to picture Stevie's "mangled remains" (*SA* 70), Conrad uses the reader's awareness of a familiar image – "an inexpensive Sunday dinner" (*SA* 71) – to explain the unfamiliar notion of "violent disintegration" (*SA* 178). Conrad also associates an everyday material object with death in *Heart of Darkness*, where Marlow's bloodied shoes – subsequently thrown overboard – mark the death of his speared helmsman.[38] Although an everyday object can certainly limit the dramatic sense of a scene (like the sombrero which hides a dead man's face in *Nostromo*), it can also open the reader's imagination – as in the case of Marlow's bloodied shoes and Mr Verloc's upturned hat.

Whereas one might expect the theatrical and imagistic style of *The Secret Agent* would make it easily translatable into a stage play, *The Secret Agent* flopped on its first performance in November 1922. The *Daily Mirror* deemed it too focused on written dialogue: it was "not like a stage play, but like portions of a book read out by characters in costume."[39] The criticism occurred although Conrad himself adapted the novel to a play, and had prior experience adapting three stories into plays: "To-morrow," "Because of the Dollars" and "Gaspar Ruiz." Looking at the script for *The Secret Agent*, it differs significantly from the book and the serial version. For instance, three different objects produce Ossipon's realization that Mr Verloc is dead: carving knife (serial version), upturned hat (book) and pool of blood (play). The variety here testifies to the effort Conrad invested in thinking through this scene, which, perhaps, needed to be communicated in different ways across different media. Although Conrad uses Mr Verloc's hat extensively in the play ("Takes hat off and throws it in the corner of the room," 167), the subtlety of seeing the "true sense of the scene" (*SA* 213) by looking at an upturned hat is left for the book version. While faithful to many visual details in the book, a modern cinematic interpretation of *The Secret Agent* (directed by Christopher Hampton and released in 1996) also displays Verloc's death without a focus on the hat – and therefore misses one of the most powerful images in the novel. One explanation is that not every part of a novel can be translated into a cinematic scene, as with a play. Another explanation is that there is here an over-reliance on spoken dialogue whereas images and inanimate objects that speak have been silenced.

The peculiar picture in *The Secret Agent*, where a hat reveals the "true sense of the scene" (213), is one of many examples of the importance of hats for Conrad's fiction. The béret, calotte, shako, sombrero, Bersagliere, toque, mitre, fez, coif, boina, nightcap, turban, felt hat, solah topi, smoking hat, tarpaulin hat, beaver hat, cocked hat, bowler hat, opera-hat, top hat, Tyrolese hat, Panama hat, Astrakhan cap, canvas cap, skull cap, tam-o'-shanter, feather hat, "that old three-cornered hat" (*S* 114), "tall stove-pipe hat" (*LJ* 247), "gaff-topsail hat" (*NN* 107) and "shore-going round hats" (*NN* 107), are also revealing of Conrad's authorship – in variety and function. The hats are not trivial details but distinctive elements of his writing style, and of importance for plot, characterization and context. Comparing Conrad's prose with its own references to writers reinforces this perspective. Whereas public writers in Conrad's fiction are concerned with promoting big categories, Conrad's own writing seems to persistently deconstruct categories through dominant details. The image of Mr Verloc eating a family dinner, indoors, while wearing his round hat takes us to the heart of the family dynamics of *The Secret Agent* and defies traditional depictions of anarchism. A material object, then, undermines anarchism – not by its identity as a decontextualized commodity but when presented in its full social context: as an object connected to a subject. Mr Verloc's round hat, Ivanovitch's shiny silk hat and Garibaldi's Bersagliere leave us with the idea that while we may think that we wear hats, hats are clothed in meaning and may even wear us; there is no clear boundary between object and person; an everyday material object can be a key to understanding a complex individual and vice versa. In this reading, the hats are not just a crowning achievement of the literary enterprise; they are symptomatic of Conrad's distinctive and persistent focus on details.

"Evviva! Evviva! / Hat in the air. / (Intermezzo ends.)" (CL III.4)

CHAPTER 9

Animals, Heart of Darkness *and "The Planter of Malata"*

> The contemplation of the infirm and lonely steed overcame him.
>
> *The Secret Agent*

> Razumov went on studying the stripes of the grey fur of the cat.
>
> *Under Western Eyes*

> I respected the intense, almost passionate, absorption with which he looked at a butterfly.
>
> *Lord Jim*

As a result of drastic changes to the climate and biosphere, how to read and how to understand nonhuman animals have been defined as two of the most "pressing political questions of our times."[1] Animal studies, a quickly expanding field in literary studies, has succeeded in answering complex epistemological questions about the status and nature of nonhuman animals. However, there is room for complementing the often theoretical discussions in animal studies with a closer look at the literary fauna. There are many detailed studies of one or a few animals, but there is next to no comprehensive information about the number and types of animals in an author's work. For instance, critics have claimed that the author of *Moby-Dick* (1851) showed no great interest in animals other than whales.[2] I found that in Melville's extant prose fiction, totaling about 1,400,000 words, there are more than 350 distinct animal species. At a minimum, this aggregate number of animal species is an argument for the specificity and variety of Melville's writing, a testament to his tendency to meticulously label and categorize phenomena, and evidence of Melville's expansive interest in nonhuman animals.

Using manual data collection in an effort to provide a comparative numerical context, I found more than 400 distinct animal species in Vladimir Nabokov's fiction; 300 animal species in Virginia Woolf's fiction; and 150 species of animals in Joseph Conrad's fiction.[3] The reason this chapter is focused on Conrad's animals is because they are surprisingly odd, unreal and implausible, as well as relatively unexplored. As if the animals did not deserve more sustained attention than a collection of hats, Conrad criticism only mentions a few animals, and then only briefly.[4] Because of this critical uninterest, many questions remain unanswered: what types of animals are in Conrad's fiction? Do these animals have any characteristics in common? What roles do they serve in Conrad's narratives?[5] The urgency of these questions emerges when we consider the sheer size and variety of Conrad's animal collection:

REPTILES: alligator, crocodile, lizard, snake (adder, cobra, viper), tortoise, turtle.

INSECTS AND ARACHNIDS: ant, bee (bumble-bee), beetle (buprestidae, coleoptera, longicorn), bug, butterfly, centipede, cicada, cockroach, flea, fly (bluebottle, gadfly), glowworm, gnat, hornet, locust, mite, mosquito, moth, spider, wasp.

BIRDS: albatross, blackbird, canary, cockatoo, crow, dove, duck, eagle, fowl (seafowl), fruit pigeon, goose, gull, hawk, heron, lark, lovebird, magpie, mynah, nightingale, orpington, ostrich, owl, parrot, partridge, penguin, petrel, pheasant, pigeon, popinjay, rice bird, seabird, skylark, snipe, sparrow, starling, swallow, swan, thrush, turkey, vulture, waterfowl, *ya-acabo, zamuro.*

LAND MAMMALS: alpaca, antelope, baboon, badger, bat, bear, boar, buffalo, bull, camel, cat (Angora), cattle, deer, dog (Alsatian, bulldog, greyhound, labrador, mastiff, mongrel, pig, pug, retriever, spaniel), donkey, elephant, fox, gazelle, goat, gorilla, guanaco, hare, hedgehog, hippo, horse, hyena, ichthyosaurus, jaguar, leopard, lion, macaque, mastodon, mole, monkey (capuchin), mouse, mungo, ox, panther, pig, porcupine, rabbit, rat, sable, sheep, skunk, springbok, squirrel, tiger, wildcat, wolf.

MARINE MAMMALS: porpoise, seal, shark, walrus, whale.

FISH: carp, dog-fish, eel, goldfish, manta, minnow, raven, salmon, sardine, shellfish, sprat, stickleback.

AMPHIBIANS, MOLLUSKS, CRUSTACEANS AND MARINE INVERTEBRATES: argonaut, cockle, conch, coral, frog (salamander), lobster, oyster, scorpion, slug, sponge, toad, trepang, urchin.

The list includes both the category and subcategory of the same animal (thus the buprestidae and longicorn are counted along with the beetle). However, the list excludes Conrad's mythological animals and fantasy creatures (basilisk, bogy, centaur, cerberus, demon, dragon, fairy, genie, ghost, ghoul, giant, griffin, hobgoblin, hydra, imp, incubus, maenad, merman, minotaur, monster, ogre, phantom, sibyl, unicorn and vampire) and denotations that are not taxonomical within a zoological system: "scarecrow," "hawbuck," "milch-cow" and "poll-parrot." Relying on the common understanding of animals as nonhuman, "human" and "homunculus" are excluded from the list. The albatross, eel and heifer are included in the list, although they are not mentioned in Conrad's fiction, but in his letters.

Even this impressive list of about four marine mammals, eight reptiles, twelve fish, twenty-four insects, forty-five bird species, sixty land mammals, and a range of amphibians, arachnids, mollusks, crustaceans and marine invertebrate does not do justice to the number of animals populating Conrad's oeuvre. There are more than fifty references to bird(s), more than one hundred references to horse(s), more than two hundred references to dog(s), and – in a character's imagination – "Millions of pink toads" (*LJ* 45). Beyond the sheer weight of numbers, there is thematic importance to these animals: imagine reading *Heart of Darkness* or "An Outpost of Progress" without ivory, *Nostromo* without its symbolic birds, *Lord Jim* without the chief engineer's hallucinations about pink toads, *The Secret Agent* without its "dramas of fallen horses" (13), *Chance* without the dog that prevents Flora's suicide attempt, or *A Personal Record* without Mr Nicholas B eating Ruthenian roasted dog.

Yet, Conrad's works include no attempt to understand an individual animal with the sustained focus of Melville's *Moby-Dick* (1851), Stevenson's *Travels with a Donkey in the Cévennes* (1879), Kafka's *Die Verwandlung* (1915), Thomas Mann's *Herr und Hund* (1918) or Virginia Woolf's *Flush: A Biography* (1933). Moreover, Conrad's oeuvre is no exception to the commonplace hypothesis that "the metaphorical far outnumber the literal animals in literature."[6] At times, literal animals are conspicuously absent from Conrad's writings. Jeffrey Myers, writing on evolution, ecology and imperialism in *Heart of Darkness*, observes that "the myriad species of African wildlife do not appear in this narrative of Africa" and neither do "plants or other features of the landscape except the Congo River itself." There are no individual species, "just a solid undifferentiated mass."[7] While there are a few exceptions to these observations,[8] it is important to recognize that the lack of naming is a structural component of the novella that extends beyond its engagement with environment: *Heart of Darkness* is a novella of nameless characters, chapters, rivers, rites, experiences and landscapes (Marlow and Kurtz are the only living persons introduced with a proper name) – not just nameless animals. This, in turn, is not necessarily because Conrad writes an anthropocentric, Eurocentric story with – as Chinua Achebe puts it – Africa as a setting and background: as a metaphysical battlefield.[9] Instead, Conrad frequently places *significant* events in the margins of his texts or even outside the texts themselves. For instance, Leopold, Belgium and the Congo are not mentioned by name in *Heart of Darkness* but are nevertheless essential to the novella. A clear example of a present-absent is given by Myers himself; he was the first to argue that the conspicuous absence of elephants in *Heart of Darkness* can be a strong argument for their near extinction in a novella that is ivory-centric.[10] Moreover, while there are only a few direct references to real-life animals in *Heart of Darkness*, the metaphors alone refer to thirteen animals.[11]

I argue that critics may have overlooked Conrad's animals because they most frequently appear in metaphors and similes: at first sight, they lack physical presence and independent meaning (to this extent, these fantastical animals partly escape Cheryll Glotfelty's widely accepted definition of ecocriticism as "the study of the relationship between literature and the physical environment," xviii[12]). Also, texts in which animals predominantly appear in metaphors may appear to contradict an ideal of animal studies, whereby texts should be evaluated according to "the degree to which an animal is presented [as] true to himself or herself," "with some measure of autonomy, agency, voice, character, and as a member of a species with a nature that has certain typical capabilities and limitations."[13] According to Randy Malamud's *Poetic Animals and Animal Souls* (2003), however, whether a text can make its readers think more consciously about animals is not necessarily contingent on how accurately it describes animals. If a text is "difficult and challenging" it can open a "portal into the world of animals," by virtue of making the reader think more critically about animals.[14] Conrad's odd, unreal and surreal metaphorical animals frequently inspire the reader to ask and answer questions about animals in new contexts. Indeed, the paradox is that Conrad's animal metaphors and similes capitalize on their marginality. The "short-sighted, but indulgent and very meagre lion that peers at the unicorn across a plum-cake" (*I* 65) is more interesting than the person who supposedly resembles this lion: Mr Churchill, the stereotypical old man besotted by a young girl (the unicorn). The lean lion cast as a dreamer opposes clichés, indulging its fantasy rather than its appetite. The same is true of the "sentimental bat" (35) in "The Planter of Malata" and the "bloodthirsty pigeon" (112) in *Romance*: they support the idea that Conrad's animal metaphors are seldom mere explanatory tools; their primary purpose is not to explain, but to raise questions – sometimes to cause confusion – and to provoke the reader's imagination, as if these writings on animals were constructed to counteract the tendency of the reader who skims or skips passages that are not directly related to character, plot, theme and the human.[15]

Conrad's bewildering, provocative animal metaphors can be placed in a modernist context. As Judith Paltin observes, "modernist nature" is an environment with specific characteristics: it "operates as an agile breaching force, exploding perceptual illusion and readerly comfort in a series of confrontational anti-mimetic pulses."[16] Her article is subtitled "Modernist Nature as the Ground of Anti-Realism," a characterization echoed in Conrad's metaphors that consistently challenge everyday expectations about animals, by introducing seemingly impossible and patently unrealistic animals and animal behaviors. As I will show, Conrad's metaphorical animals are strange even in comparison to his imaginative non-animal metaphors and serve to invoke what I will designate as an "unreality effect" (in contrast to Barthes's reality effect). The metaphors, in this reading, illustrate recent theories about the function and meaning of metaphors, where the "effect" itself is the primary source of meaning. In short, Conrad's unconventional animal metaphors deserve attention and should, to borrow Marlow's words regarding Kurtz's memory, not "rest in the dust-bin of progress, amongst all the sweepings and, figuratively speaking, all the dead cats of civilization" (*HD* 96).

The Dreamwork of Language

> Can one imagine a loathsome insect in love?
>
> *Lord Jim*

> if one could imagine such a thing as a passionate fish . . .
>
> "A Smile of Fortune"

In the late 1970s analytic philosophers argued that metaphors are primarily effect-making machines. In a deceptively simplistic and counterintuitive position, Donald Davidson maintains that the metaphor is not a vehicle for indirectly conveying the author's intended meaning: to suppose a metaphor "can be effective only by conveying a coded message is like thinking a joke or a dream makes some statement which a clever interpreter can restate in plain prose."[17] Instead, the function of the metaphor is to provoke the reader's imagination and thought process – turning the reader into an explicit co-creator: "Metaphor is the dreamwork of language, and, like all dreamwork, its interpretation reflects as much on the interpreter as on the originator."[18] Richard Moran labels this function the "'framing-effect' and 'perspective' to speak of the dimension of metaphor that is distinct from what is asserted either literally or metaphorically."[19] Conrad's animal metaphors can be explained from this theoretical standpoint of a frame, perspective and effect; their primary function is not to convey a specific message but to engage the reader's imagination and thinking.

This effect-oriented reading explains Conrad's metaphors because many of them are provocatively and distinctly nonsensical; they are thus suitable examples for explaining metaphor's nonassertive qualities. Conrad's animal metaphors frequently set up highly implausible comparisons. On these occasions, Conrad is not revealing himself as a non-native to English and its idiomatic expressions: with exceptional command of the language, he demonstrates his ability to willfully write unidiomatic English. Consider, for example, the manner in which Brown in *Lord Jim* explains that the "water was smooth, and the bay dark, 'like the inside of a cow'" (267) (instead of descriptions like "pitch dark" or "dark as night"). Conrad may even seem to share the peculiarity of expression of the butterfly collector and German native, Stein, who "did make use of funny expressions" (179) when speaking English; and that of the half-caste shipmaster in *Lord Jim* who explains in non-native English that the Rajah was a "laughable hyaena" and "somebody else was many times falser than the 'weapons of a crocodile'" (181). Hyenas are known for laughing, not for being laughable; the weapons of a crocodile are its teeth and jaws – it is crocodile tears that are false. Marlow notes the odd phraseology and remarks that the shipmaster's "flowing English seemed to be derived from a dictionary compiled by a lunatic" (181). Many of the animal similes we encounter in Conrad's fiction also fall far outside the range of a standard dictionary. Whereas Conrad's creations – Brown, Stein and the half-caste shipmaster in *Lord Jim* – are unaware of the infelicity of their wording, Conrad deviates from established, ready-made clichés in a systematic manner, on purpose.

In one of the most memorable examples of this idiosyncratic writing, Conrad uses the adjective "sentimental" in a manner that is diametrically opposed to any clichés. Although sentimentality is usually considered a human trait, "The Planter of Malata" challenges us to consider the possibility of a sentimental bat: "he was more of a figure in a nightmare, hovering about the circle of chairs in his dress-clothes like a gigantic, repulsive and sentimental bat" (35). The indirect voice in the passage belongs to the pioneering planter of vegetable silk in Malata, Geoffrey Renouard. The sentimental bat in question is William Dunster. He is part of the search party for Felicia Moorsom's runaway fiancé Arthur: "Willie's soft heart's enlisted in the cause" (23). Renouard knows that Arthur is dead but withholds the information from the search party. He is in love with Felicia and unsentimentally maintains that Arthur has left the island ("The dead don't mind," 56), and is consequently frustrated by the "sentimental Willie's" (72) search for Arthur. Although William "affected a great horror of insects of all kinds" (35), he is arguably bat-like in his ability to come out late at night (for dinner with Renouard and the Moorsoms), and in his ability to inspire repulsiveness in the human animal; Renouard finds him and his "spatulous nose," "absurd eyebrows" and "spongy skin" "repulsive" (35).

Yet, what is here more interesting? The idea of a sentimental bat or that William appeared like one? Does the simile help us understand the person in discussion and/or does it pose a question about what a sentimental bat would be like? Is a sentimental bat a contradiction in terms, like a square circle? A fanciful, imaginary being who exists purely in the realm of fiction? Or is it simply an excessively emotional bat inclined to ready tears and the hoarding of old letters? Does the simile assume that the reader knows the difference between a sentimental and non-sentimental bat? And, in what way is the person in discussion like a sentimental bat – in its behavior, appearance or mental state? Is it in its dark fur, vascular wings, echolocating navigation and ability to sleep upside down, hanging from its feet? Or is the bat "sentimental" according to Decoud's definition of the term in *Nostromo*, seeing one's life as "a moral romance derived from the tradition of a pretty fairy tale" (158)?

"Sentimental bat" is not necessarily an example of nonsense language. Renouard's conception of William as a sentimental, nocturnal and repulsive creature, as well as the questions above, suggest that a "sentimental bat" could be an expression of multiple meanings. The solution to the metaphorical puzzle, however, is not to provide an exhaustive catalogue of possible meanings. There is no single, correct reading: "endlessness is a familiar fact about poetic metaphor."[20] Moreover, according to the effect-theory, metaphor functions somewhat like a chemical compound that produces a different effect depending on who is doing the stirring. Rather than communicating a specific message from sender to receiver, then, what is invariant and intriguing about living metaphors is that they produce a response in the reader, and are characterized by "the *effects*" they "have on us."[21]

Metaphors that function as effect-making machines can be said to have cognitive autonomy – they are not a mere vessel for a statement. When

Conrad's sentimental bat is seen as an individual, the need for it to be representative or symbolic of something or someone else disappears. A sentimental bat is just a sentimental bat and cannot be reduced to the sum of its parts. In this reading, a sentimental bat is sui generis – unrepresentative of both sentimentality and batness. To get to the meaning of Conrad's text we must accept the sentimental bat, in all its irreconcilable ambiguity, rather than explain its existence by what is already familiar. Of course, it is useful to reflect on the sentimental bat and how it connects to Renouard's understanding of William, but the sentimental bat is not shorthand for something else; it is its own essence. Indeed, Thomas Nagel makes a similar argument in his influential paper, "What Is It Like to Be a Bat?" (1974), where he argues at length for the seemingly commonsensical position that it is a specific, unique and untranslatable experience to live life as a bat; bat sonar, for instance, "is not similar in operation to any sense that we possess, and there is no reason to suppose that it is subjectively like anything we can experience or imagine."[22] Bat consciousness, in this argument, is ultimately impenetrable by the thought of another organism – it is its own irreducible entity. Another example of irreducible subjectivity can be found in the mantis-shrimp, which sees primary colors we cannot even imagine; while most animals have three color receptors (red, blue and yellow), the mantis-shrimp has twelve.

The idea of a *sentimental* bat at once challenges and reinforces this notion of irreducible subjectivity. The metaphor appears stretched in two directions – a literal and a metaphorical. Following Davidson's focus on metaphorical effects, the late twentieth-century theorist Paul Ricœur suggests that metaphors bewilder and make the reader discover new modes of coherence and "*models* for reading reality."[23] Unlike Davidson, however, Ricœur is more explicit on how the metaphorical effect works. According to Ricœur, the able reader unifies these two contrasting layers of the metaphor in imagination – so that the reader comprehends the literal and the metaphorical layers simultaneously and in symbiosis; to read a metaphor requires "the ability to entertain two different points of view at the same time."[24] This creates a sense of defamiliarization, where "imagination provides *models* for reading reality in a new way."[25] Out of context, this might appear commonsensical. But the focus here is on the creation of a new system of understanding, similar to the understanding of a new dialect. It is not, to return to Conrad's simile, sufficient to recognize that someone resembles a sentimental bat – and, perhaps, picture the person sentimentally hovering about the circle of dining chairs at night. One needs to tap into a mood and way of understanding, where it is sensible and coherent to speak of a sentimental bat as a dinner companion.

It is not just sentimental bats that provoke this type of challenge and effect. While the sentimental bat embodies singularity (one-of-a-kind-ness), it is typical – in its singularity – of many of Conrad's animal metaphors. Indeed, this pattern of complexity repeats itself; a situation where we as readers tend to focus more on the metaphor than its referent: on the vehicle rather than the tenor, to use I. A. Richards's contested terminology.[26] In *Almayer's Folly*, for instance, Babalatchi is presented walking on a dusty path, "his body swaying, his chin with its few grey hairs pushed forward, resembling an inquisitive goat bent on some unlawful expedition" (45). In addition to clarifying Babalatchi's method of walking and emphasizing his "reckless confidence" (45), as he freely shares information given to him in strict confidence, the metaphor introduces the question of what an inquisitive goat is and what is legal and nonlegal in goat-context. When *The Rescue* explains that "he stared at her like an offended owl" (54), we think not only about Shaw's appearance but also about that owl. Although owls are well known for their large round eyes, the possibility that they have the capacity for feeling offended, and that this could be reflected in their appearance, is unfamiliar. That said, an offended owl is somewhat like a winged horse; it can be grasped by the imagination (unlike a square circle) even if it does not exist in nature. Indeed, the idea of an offended owl is no more implausible than the idea of a wise owl, with glasses and a mortarboard. The difference is that wise owls are prevalent in the fictional landscape, while offended owls are not. If you were to compare an acquaintance to a Selenite or mooncalf, the person unfamiliar with H. G. Wells's *The First Men in the Moon* (1901) might be more interested in the Selenite or mooncalf than in the acquaintance. Conrad's comparisons to other imaginary creatures, like the offended owl, detract from the tenor in the same way.

A similar mechanism is at work in *Heart of Darkness* when Marlow uses a visual image to describe sound: "A deadened burst of mighty splashes and snorts reached us from afar, as though an ichthyosaurus had been taking a bath of glitter in the great river" (63). Given that Marlow feels as though he wanders "on a prehistoric earth" (79) and was "travelling back to the earliest beginnings of the world" (77), it is perhaps fitting that he conjures up an extinct marine reptile in his imagination rather than, say, a paddle-boat. Yet consider the remarkable specificity of Marlow's fantastical sound-image. Marlow can neither see nor identify what produces the sound. He can only speculate. He muses that the *sound* is consistent with an ichthyosaurus taking a bath of glitter. The idea that an ichthyosaurus taking a bath of glitter produces a distinct sound is highly complicated, as is the visual picture of this bathing dinosaur: its glittering bath conjures up images of luxurious bath bombs (inventions at odds with the prehistoric age) and pampered dinosaurs. As a simile, the vehicle is more complicated than the unseen tenor: no reader has seen or heard an ichthyosaurus taking a bath of glitter. Similarly, when Marlow explains that he is justified in laying Kurtz's memory among "the dead cats of civilization" (96), he introduces questions about an unheard-of category: is Kurtz among these dead cats of civilization? Who else is a member? What aspects of Kurtz's memory place him alongside these dead cats or in this category? Marlow raises these implicit questions without answering them.

Despite the unmistaken singularity of the aforementioned Conradian animals, unconventional animal similes and metaphors are common in his work. For example, in *Romance*, the narrator says that Tomas Castro swelled his breast and "stepped on his toes before me like a bloodthirsty pigeon" (112). Pigeons are generally hungry for seeds, not thirsty for blood. The dove, a bird in the same clade as the pigeon, symbolizes peace. Tomas Castro is not a bloodthirsty tiger but an animal outside of its natural state, swelling its breast to adapt to its newfound predatory role.

How do we make sense of these metaphors stylistically and treat them as conscious literary products? What do these metaphors do? They create an *effect* of unreality, of a world in which a bat can be sentimental or a pigeon bloodthirsty. For instance, we expect a bat to be repulsive and bloodthirsty, like Bram Stroker's fictional bats, or "horrid," like Conrad's own bat in *The Arrow of Gold*, or "weak-eyed" (Hardy, *Jude the Obscure*, 72), with "better eyes for the darkness than for the light" (Dickens, *Pickwick Papers*, 717), but not sentimental. Whereas the idea of a sentimental animal is unoriginal – Herman Melville's *Moby-Dick* describes a type of whale as having "sentimental Indian eyes of a hazel hue"[27] – a sentimental bat is a rare fictional creature. To my knowledge, Conrad's is the only direct reference to a sentimental bat in the history of literature.[28]

This sentimental bat draws, in part, on the expectation that the reader will understand that bats are not by nature sentimental creatures. If one of the main qualities we associated with bats were a sentimental nature, the metaphor would be less striking – along the lines of busy bees and brave lions. Sentimentality is conventionally seen as a human quality, so the metaphor about the person who looks like a sentimental bat insists on the separation of human and animal even as it collapses it. Put differently, the sentimental bat appears here in order to challenge the reader; even an expert on bats, reading the text, would find it impossible to distinguish between a bat that is sentimental and one that is not. Conrad has therefore shifted the reader's interest from the object of comparison to the metaphor itself. Rather than just explaining a situation or object, this metaphor brings a new life-form into existence – a being itself in need of further explanation: a new type of winged horse. Conrad's sentimental bat falls neither in the category of fantasy nor myth, but exemplifies a type of nature writing that challenges the commonsensical assumption, spelled out by Kate Rigby, "that the natural world to which it refers is presumed to pre-exist the written text," in the way nature serves as a given, uncomplicated backdrop.[29]

The unreality effect is an apt term for this phenomenon: it highlights that nature is not a mere background or "setting": "the common omnibus term used for designating the sphere of the nonhuman environment in literary works."[30] It therefore differs from Barthes's notion of a reality effect. According to Barthes, there are details in a text that are independent of narrative, structure, meaning and symbol, "which no function (not even the most indirect) can justify."[31] The "significance of this insignificance"[32] is to produce an effect: to instantiate and authenticate a sense of concrete reality. By themselves and in isolation, these descriptive details serve no other purpose. "Flaubert's barometer, Michelet's little door finally say nothing but this: *we are the real*; it is the category of 'the real' (and not its contingent contents) which is then signified ... the *reality effect* is produced, the basis of that unavowed verisimilitude which forms the aesthetic of all the standard works of modernity."[33] Modernist nature functions differently; it does not instantiate reality but challenges our conception of reality – "exploding perceptual illusion and readerly comfort in a series of confrontational anti-mimetic pulses," to borrow Paltin's useful observation.[34]

The unreality effect, by challenging the reader, certainly fits in with the confrontational aspect of modernist nature. However, it is beyond the scope of this chapter to claim that the unreality effect can automatically be applied to the writings of Conrad's contemporaries. Authors who influenced Conrad – such as Crane, Dickens, Dostoevsky, Flaubert, Hardy, James, Stevenson, Zola – use animal metaphors to varying degrees of complexity. Yes, there are admittedly certain similarities in structure; Hardy's emphasis that "To fling elaborate sarcasms at Tess, however, was much like flinging them at a dog or cat"[35] functions similarly to "But Fyne was as impervious to sarcasm as a turtle" (*C* 55). These writers also occasionally employ unusual and striking metaphors, as when

Dickens in *Hard Times* (1854) writes: "It was a town of machinery and tall chimneys, out of which interminable serpents of smoke trailed themselves for ever and ever"; "the piston of the steam-engine worked monotonously up and down, like the head of an elephant in a state of melancholy madness."[36] Here Dickens is using an extraordinarily imaginative simile to describe the sooty Coketown, an industrialized city devoid of fancy and wonder. Dickens is generally not this fanciful with his animal similes, but the simile about the melancholy-mad elephant serves a unique purpose: it seems consciously constructed to go against the workaday speech of Mr Gradgrind and Mr Bounderby ("I call a spade a spade"[37]).

That said, the opening paragraph of *Bleak House* (1852–53) is remarkably fanciful in its animal imagery: "As much mud in the streets, as if the waters had but newly retired from the face of the earth, and it would not be wonderful to meet a Megalosaurus, forty feet long or so, waddling like an elephantine lizard up Holborn Hill."[38] A muddy London conjures up the idea of a Megalosaurus, just as in *Heart of Darkness* the deadly river reminds Marlow of an ichthyosaurus. While *Heart of Darkness* raises multiple questions about what this ichthyosaurus looks like and what sound it produces, a similar unreality effect cannot be said to function in *Bleak House*'s prehistoric simile, which contains details about the size and the look of a Megalosaurus. So, although even the briefest of comparisons shows that there are parallels in how these two writers use animals, Dickens's metaphors do not seem to be systematically odd, surreal and implausible – for the sake of being odd, surreal and implausible. For instance, Dickens also found use for less fanciful figures of speech – clichés: "busy as a bee" (*The Life and Adventures of Martin Chuzzlewit*), "the busy Bee" (*Bleak House*), "as the crow flies" (*Oliver Twist*), "brave as a lion" (*David Copperfield*), "quiet as a mouse" (*Bleak House*), "strong as an ox" (*Barnaby Rudge*). Most of these conventional sayings figure in the speech of characters, as part of appropriately realistic dialogue. Among contemporary writers, Conrad's use of animals in figures of speech appears singular in *persistently* inspiring the reader to pause and wonder, "does that make sense?" For instance, despite the numerous references to animals in Hardy's pastoral prose – populated by "Rabbits, hares, snakes, rats, mice" and ornamented by "the flanks of infinite cows"[39] – his metaphors do not spill over into the realm of the unreal.

Conrad could be said to anticipate a postmodern treatment of animals: his fanciful animals are reminiscent of Beckett's constipated cockatoo in *Mercier and Camier* (written in 1946) and Salman Rushdie's "insomniac cow" (49) and "constipated goose" (22) in *Midnight's Children* (1981), a work which also contains the expression, "silly as an owl" (15).

"Yes! Cat, dog": Animal Metaphors and Similes in Context

Assuming that Conrad used metaphors and similes in the way suggested above, why did he so frequently use animals for this purpose? He sometimes constructed similar unconventional figures of speech with inanimate objects; to express a character's lack of expected emotion or inexpressive response, Conrad could write:

- "This white man was like a senseless stone" (*AF* 122)
- "looking himself as incapable of an emotional display as a sack of meal" (*LJ* 110)
- "as incapable of an attitude as a bed-post" (*C* 87)
- "You might as well try to make a bedpost understand" (*T* 71)
- "She was no more self-conscious than a flower" (*N* 209)

Compare these to the case of Fyne in *Chance*:

- "But Fyne was as impervious to sarcasm as a turtle" (55).

On one level, this last reference to a turtle is arguably less absurd than the others, because a turtle, like a person, has a capacity for feeling (if not for emotion), whereas a stone, flower or sack of meal does not.

Conrad uses similar rhetorical devices in creating metaphors of all kinds. He frequently employs a transferred epithet (hypallage), using an adjective that often modifies an animate object to modify an inanimate object. The resulting observation is a poetic expression at odds with literal meaning. Examples from *Victory* of a transferred epithet include "The drowsy afternoon was slipping by" (37), "sleepy leaves" (96), "the slumbering silence" (46), "the offended door" (184). The sentimental bat and bloodthirsty pigeon resemble these nouns modified by a transferred epithet. Indeed, what is interesting about Conrad's descriptions of animals is that they are constructed with similar detail, precision and variety as other parts of the prose. The animals range in size from ants to whales; are colored pink, yellow, red, white, black, piebald, chestnut, sorrel, slate or dapple-grey; stretch over thirty years of literary production; are made of glass, flesh, wood, stone, paper, paint; are found in Eastern-bound ships, the Malayan jungle, the vertical sunshine of South America, snowbound Russia, gas-lit London, a narrator's dream in *Romance*, and, the fantasy about prehistory in *Heart of Darkness* (or the fantasy that is *Heart of*

Darkness; there are no alligators in its presumed setting, the Congo). This attention to animals and marginal details may be frustrating to certain readers; *Nostromo* asks us, Guerard judges, "to record too many visual impressions, down to the white eye of Gould's 'slate-coloured beast'."[40] (The argument can be extended to the green eyes of the cat Tom in *The Nigger of 'Narcissus'*.) Yet it is also this attention to particularities that makes Conrad Conrad: it is criticism that sets off his animals in parentheses and dashes. By turning a zoological gaze on Conrad, we gain a large element of the textual corpus. With the smell of dead hippo in our nostrils, traveling along a snake-shaped river on a beetle-like steamer in *Heart of Darkness*, or from the vantage point of a mule overlooking "the Paradise of snakes" in *Nostromo*, we – Conrad's readers – do well to examine the Conradian fauna. This not only because the textual animals are many and various, but also because ignoring them is as limiting as ignoring a painter's frequent use of a specific color.

Curiously, this focus on textual form and empirical data (like the critic who counted forty-five species of flowers in William Cullen Bryant's poems and remarked that "it is rather odd that none, save the violet, reappears more than once or twice"[41]) is not typical for ecocriticism: "Ecocriticism is basically an *expanded* mode of contextual criticism"[42] – a view echoed by critics like Sven Birkerts, David Taylor, Susie O'Brien and Lawrence Buell.[43] In contrast, this chapter on Conrad's animals focuses on the metaphors and similes, and makes a case for reading them for their effect rather than their veiled meaning (more precisely, it deems the effect itself to be the primary source of meaning). This focus on literary form over context is unusual for ecocriticism but hopefully responds to the appeal, recently articulated by Sarah Ensor, that "ecocriticism, a field whose focus has largely been on the thematic or mimetic representation of environment in literature, also stands to benefit from an increased attention to literary form and style."[44] Indeed, Laura Brown's *Homeless Dogs and Melancholy Apes* (2010) proves the fruitfulness of this approach by focusing "on the realm of representation."[45] By this she means that there is also room to study animals in literature from a strictly formal perspective: to treat them as grammatical components rather than as flesh-and-blood creatures. Specifically, this chapter supports a recent development, where analyses of modern and contemporary poetics have started to identify the productive role of metaphor "as a literary portal into the world of animals."[46] If a text makes us think critically and deeply about the animals in an author's work, regardless of whether those animals are described in a realistic manner, "we may also learn from example how to understand and appreciate animals in the world around us."[47] Thus, whether an author writes realistically about animals is not the single criterion by which a text can be relevant for animal studies. Animal references that are provocative and challenging can make us more diligent and perceptive readers of real-life animals: "We might apply, in our thoughts about animals at large, many of the same skills we invoke when we grapple with a difficult and challenging poem: diligent, deliberate attention to detail and nuance; careful concentration; willingness to transcend pedestrian, conventional processes of cognition and representation."[48] The skill-set gained from reading and understanding fictional animals can be applied to real-life animals.

This possibility allows for animal studies to explore how authors can write sympathetically, provocatively and attentively on animals, while simultaneously placing them in metaphors and similes. In short, a writer's relevance for animal studies can be made in relation to whether he or she writes on animals in a manner that promotes reflection, rather than on the basis of whether the animals are portrayed as realistic and independent beings, or conspicuously present, as protagonists or as essential elements of the plot.

Thus, like Stevie in *The Secret Agent*, who gave in to "the attractions of stray cats and dogs, which he followed down narrow alleys into unsavory courts" (13), I maintain that the many animals in Conrad's fiction are worthy of further investigation (both formal and contextual) – a somewhat surprising stance given the limited attention paid to animals in the history of Conrad studies. Still, the appearance of these animal metaphors and similes as a relatively constant factor of Conrad's authorship, from *Almayer's Folly* to *Suspense*, implies that they constitute a significant element of his style. The persistent disruption of one's conventional understanding about animals – his examples of "an outraged cockatoo" (*LJ* 145), a "lion that peers at the unicorn across a plum-cake" (*I* 65), "an ichthyosaurus taking a bath of glitter" (*HD* 63), "loathsome insect in love" (*LJ* 215), "passionate fish" (*SF* 55), "intelligent mule" (*The Rover*, 17), "industrious gorilla" (*T* 79), "obese raven" (*AG* 260), "shameless mynah" (*OI* 155), "ponderous insect" (*N* 367), gullible owl (*SA* 27), respectable hen (*I* 55), lonely crow, offended owl, bloodthirsty pigeon, inquisitive goat, sentimental bat, and the dead cats of civilization – hint at the complex ways Conrad presents and uses animals.

This complexity occurs throughout his writing and impacts his prose in multiple ways. The similes and metaphors hint at the extent to which a writer can place animals in the margin – yet still, and perhaps for that very reason, allow them to play a central part in the text. The marginal placement becomes abrupt and declares a conspicuous absence, leaving the reader searching for an explanation. This search, as we have discussed, is itself meaningful, and inversely connected to the Barthesian reality effect. While the Barthesian reality effect advances the idea of superfluous detail in a text – a type of filler that only serves to say "*we are the real*"[49] – the unreality effect, which I have argued unites Conrad's unconventional animal metaphors, has the opposite purpose: it confronts the reader to question the reality of the fictional construct. The unconventional sayings that produce this unreality effect all say: we have the appearance of a marginal, incidental detail but we are one of the most complicated structures in the text. This unreality effect is distinctly confrontational – like Socrates's gadfly – and leaves the readers wondering, even when we come to the last sentence, what a sentimental bat is.[50]

Conclusion

P.P.P.S.

CL II.69

End! Finis!

Lord Jim

finished!!!!!!

CL VI.505

I concloode

The Nigger of the 'Narcissus'

[Marlow:] I like to think my summing-up would not have been a word of careless contempt. Better his cry – much better.

Heart of Darkness

[Mr Verloc, indirect voice:] For to exaggerate with judgment one must begin by measuring with nicety.

The Secret Agent

As is hopefully clear by this point, my critical approach is closer to analytic philosophy than continental philosophy and the dominant strands of literary theory. This means that the methods in my work are different from many contemporary approaches to reading fiction and Conrad, and that a chapter on hats or doodles is not the product of levity, but of an underlying belief in a different method, valuation and philosophy.

What is arbitrary, insignificant and even unseen from a macroscopic perspective can gain meaning, structure and coherency close-up. For instance, as I show in Chapter 8, even though abundant secondary literature demonstrates that one can write on Conrad without writing on hats, Conrad did not seem able to write without including a full range of hats. Far from being arbitrary details, top hats, sentimental bats and secret cats are telling fingerprints of Conrad's authorship. These details can also provide a more precise understanding of certain categories and larger themes. For instance, the absurd details that make up Mr Verloc's everyday existence, such as his wearing a hat when having supper with his family in the privacy of their home, take us to the heart of the meaning of anarchism in *The Secret Agent*.

While much focus has been given to historical movements and theoretical concepts, such as colonialism, anarchism and modernism, a complementary focus on the marginal details that uniquely identify Conrad's texts is needed. In the most extreme search for theoretical abstractions, we have acted like someone who confuses the cookie jar with the cookies – the container with the content – and is terribly offended when caught in the act of chewing on the lid. The details of Conrad's fiction are, after all, not subservient to larger structures any more than the ontological reason for why cookies exist is so that we can have cookie jars, or any more than the sole reason plants exist is to explain Linnaeus's taxonomic system (rather than the other way around).

Like an individual plant in Linnaeus's system, a detail is part of a larger structure. A detail is its own category. It might therefore seem peculiar to prioritize details over categories, if they are one and the same. Even the definitions of "detail" and "category" are unspecific. For instance, if a category is a category because it fits the definition of a category, a third definition is required to explain why a category and the definition of a category are both categories. This is Plato's so-called third man argument. The aim of this monograph has not been to correct Plato (on this point). As my embroidered throw pillow says: a certain degree of metaphysical uncertainty is necessary for living and for engaging with Plato's ideas.

Discussing details and margins is not necessarily more valuable than discussing larger issues – it is merely a different perspective, and it allows for the inclusion of overlooked material. The French *en détail* is opposed to *en gros* – to buy in bulk, wholesale. The word "detail" originally comes from tailoring and the act of cutting into pieces for a bespoke look. Applying this original meaning to Conrad's prose, my ambition has been to engage with the tailor-made aspects. The focus has been on those elements that, like *The Nigger of the 'Narcissus'*, form a story that "no one else could have written" (*CL* v.145).

Going against assumptions of Conrad as a methodical and philosophical writer, the monograph argues – with doodles, details and delayed decodings – that Conrad's own texts are inherently eclectic, like the harlequin's patched-together clothing in *Heart of Darkness* or Donkin's assorted and assembled outfit in *The Nigger of the 'Narcissus'*. This overarching argument about eclecticism, joined with the idea about Conrad as an artist with a modern mindset, is likely unsurprising to many who are familiar with Conrad's writings. However, engaging with this eclecticism as a unifying element is simultaneously in opposition to "the right way of going to work" (*HD* 81), to appropriate Marlow's words about the seamanship manual in *Heart of Darkness*. The academic approach has long been to prioritize the generalization above the detail ("Thinking usually consists in passing from concepts to things, and not from things to concepts"[1]). That said, the chapter on decoding and miscoding in this monograph shows that Conrad's fiction is structured the other way around – prioritizing "the specific detail to the generalization, images to ideas, obscure facts to clear symbols, and the discovered wild fruit to the synthetic jam,"[2] to borrow the words used by Nabokov (an author dismissive of Conrad) to explain his own artistic preferences. Similarly, Chapter 6 on *The Secret Agent* shows that the order and unity of the novel can be found through its scattered and eclectic details.

Recording these defining features is anything but a passive, innocent and mimetic endeavor. Seeking merely to zoom in on Conrad's texts and record their eclectic interests in doodles, sticks, arrows, maps, bats, hats and cats, this monograph has resulted in new critical concepts – delayed miscoding, unreality effect, unprofessional narrator, distracted reading, *in medias distractionis*, nonlinguistic texts – and the introduction of new names to Conrad studies from art history. The focus on Conrad's detail-rich prose has also required linking the analytic philosophy of Bertrand Russell with Conrad's delayed decoding, and, in the chapter on animals, using the thoughts of analytic philosophers to understand Conrad's metaphors as effect-making machines.

This monograph has, furthermore, brought Conrad criticism closer to Conrad's authorship by introducing and reproducing many of his hitherto unpublished nonlinguistic texts: maps, doodles and drawings. Similar to approaches and methodologies common in digital humanities, the monograph uses newly digitized images and "text-mining" to build a layered and comprehensive understanding of Conrad's authorship, to understand his commitment to the marginal, and to make a major argument about the importance of the minor details of Conrad's prose. This layered approach, with sharp changes in topic between and within chapters, may make the monograph appear disjointed in comparison to standard works of criticism. However, my argument is that Conrad's margins and details are so significant that they affect Conrad's writings in multiple ways, and can be observed across different media and in a diverse selection of his writings. A multilayered approach also allows for using lists, numbers and drawings to make Conrad's texts visible in nontraditional formats (and maybe for nontraditional readers). As I hope this monograph demonstrates, Conrad was fiercely and philosophically opposed to overreliance on generalizations and theoretical abstractions, and this outlook affected his writing. He consistently favors the particular above the abstract: in his leaning toward analytic philosophy, in his identity as a marginal subject with an ability to give voice to the "voiceless," and in his preprint and published documents, which demonstrate a clear interest in margins and details.

From a beginning with chapters on drawings and doodles, to chapters on decoding and miscoding, to chapters on specific details, the monograph addresses a few gaps between secondary and primary literature. The monograph gradually uncovers more of Conrad's artistic creations, from newly digitized sources, to large segments of texts that are underexplored. As a step-by-step argument, the monograph demonstrates Conrad's commitment to a modern worldview – where the transient, changing and temporary count as true, and where the detail is prioritized above the generalization. This is apparent not only in Conrad's writings but also in his drawings. By using the negative space and a painterly technique, his drawings demonstrate an ability to solve an intellectual puzzle of representation with a modern mindset. By consulting underexplored sources, it becomes apparent that Conrad's artistry hinges on an anti-Platonic truth hierarchy, where the marginal is often central – and the trivial is significant. From distracted writing to delayed decoding, Conrad's corpus gives the detail autonomous value. While this detail may illuminate other aspects of the text, the value of the detail is not exclusively or primarily contingent on this function.

The research presented is written in support of and in tribute to extant Conrad scholarship. Yet, it is apparent that these stumbling steps are just the beginning – there is much more room for varied observations and so-called distracted reading; for allowing Conrad's distracted prose to guide the critic. There is the possibility of looking further at doodles and other aspects of the nonlinguistic text, and thereby exploring and expanding the very concept of writing – both the noun and the verb. There is also room to approach verbal texts in nontraditional ways. Other scholars will likely identify even larger sections of texts that resist top-down categorization, or they might find an explanation for why no critical commentary is itself a commentary. There is also the opportunity to further investigate the many ways in which macroscopic and microscopic readings on Conrad inform and support one another, in mutually beneficial ways. The last word, then, is hopefully not mine.

Notes

Introduction

1 Morelli, *Italian Painters*, 21, 37.
2 *Ibid.*, 43, 48.
3 *Ibid.*, 37.
4 *Ibid.*, 7.
5 Schmitt, "Tidal Conrad," 10.
6 Higdon, "His Helpless Prey," 113; Galef, *Supporting Cast*, 1.
7 Guerard, *Conrad the Novelist*, 102.
8 Forster, "Joseph Conrad," 137.
9 Follett, *Joseph Conrad*, 73.
10 Watt, *Conrad in the Nineteenth Century*, 357.
11 Higdon, "His Helpless Prey," 114.
12 J. Hillis Miller, "Should We Read," 124.
13 A chapter of this monograph will connect Conrad's writing to an ideal language in philosophy that treats texts as autonomous beings, namely Bertrand Russell's logical atomism. It is important, then, to state that I think Conrad's intentions are important for how to read his texts. On the subject of analytic philosophy, it is interesting that when the theory of "intentional fallacy" was published in the 1950s, a counter-argument already existed in the form of P. F. Strawson's fine essay, "On Referring" (1950) – itself an argument against Russell's autonomous language.
14 Skinner, "Obscurity," 95.
15 For an argument that "it is the very conception of presence that undergoes a radical transformation in Conrad's writing" so that the "clear categorical distinction between absence and presence is thus subverted," see Levin, *Tracing the Aesthetic Principle*, 3.
16 Said, *Beginnings*, 11–12.
17 Knapp Hay, "Joseph Conrad and Impressionism"; Johnson, "Conrad's Impressionism"; Peters, *Conrad and Impressionism*; Watt, *Conrad in the Nineteenth Century*.
18 In opposition to Ulmer's wish that the criticism of modernism needs to become modern, Percy Lubbock wished that the criticism of modernism

had lagged behind its object of study even further: he "wished that the modern novel had been invented a hundred years sooner, so that it might have fallen into the hands of the critical schoolmen of the seventeenth century … it missed the dry light of academic judgment" (*Craft of Fiction*, 22).

19 I am indebted to Peters's helpful division of the major trends of Conrad criticism, outlined in *Joseph Conrad's Critical Reception* (2013) that surveys more than 360 mostly book-length studies. For a critical survey that includes more journal articles, consider Knowles, *Annotated Critical Bibliography.*

20 J. Hillis Miller, "Foreword," 2.

21 Danto, *Beyond the Brillo Box*, 28.

22 Nietzsche, "On Truth and Lies," 117. "Denken wir besonders noch an die Bildung der Begriffe: jedes Wort wird sofort dadurch Begriff, dass es eben nicht für das einmalige ganz und gar individualisirte Urerlebniss, dem es sein Entstehen verdankt, etwa als Erinnerung dienen soll, sondern zugleich für zahllose, mehr oder weniger ähnliche, d.h. streng genommen niemals gleiche, also auf lauter ungleiche Fälle passen muss. Jeder Begriff entsteht durch Gleichsetzen des Nicht-Gleichen. So gewiss nie ein Blatt einem anderen ganz gleich ist, so gewiss ist der Begriff Blatt durch beliebiges Fallenlassen dieser individuellen Verschiedenheiten, durch ein Vergessen des Unterscheidenden gebildet" (Nietzsche, "Über Wahrheit und Lüge," 879–80).

23 Rooney, "Form and Contentment," 37.

24 Nabokov, *Lectures on Literature*, 381.

25 Loughery, "Telling Detail," 464.

26 Best and Marcus, "Surface Reading," 17.

27 Peters, *Conrad and Impressionism*, 14.

28 Focillon, *Life of Forms*, 33–34.

29 The concept of "detail" may appear to be an innocent, self-explanatory term. However, its history is much more interesting, and fitting to Conrad's prose, than what one may at first assume. The word "detail" derives etymologically from French, from tailoring and the practice of cutting out a piece of fabric. The clothier makes ready-made products for sale, *en gros*, the tailor makes bespoke products – *en détail.* Taken to its extreme, the tailor's job becomes a piece-by-piece production – a collection of details (cuttings). Conrad, the self-proclaimed craftsman of fiction, tailors his prose with individually cut pieces. An example of Conrad's style of writing and simultaneously a metaphorical illustration of his tailored writing can be found in the so-called Harlequin's clothes in *Heart of Darkness*: "it was covered with patches, all over with bright patches, blue red and yellow – patches on the back, patches on front, patches on elbows, on knees, coloured binding round his jacket, scarlet edging at the bottom of his trousers, and the sunshine made him look extremely gay and wonderfully neat withal, because you could see how beautifully all this patching had been done" (98).

30 The contrast between modern and premodern philosophy is succinctly summed up by Henri Bergson (1859–1941) in his *Introduction to Metaphysics* (1903): "The whole of the philosophy which begins with Plato

and culminates in Plotinus is the development of a principle which may be formulated thus: 'There is more in the immutable than in the moving, and we pass from the stable to the unstable by a mere diminution.' Now it is the contrary which is true" (75).

31 Watt, *Rise of the Novel*, 11.

32 Barthes, *Rustle of Language*, 148.

Chapter 1

1 Battles, *In Praise of Doodling*, 108.

2 Jessie Conrad, *Joseph Conrad*, 19.

3 *Ibid.*, 146.

4 Battles, *In Praise of Doodling*, 108.

5 *Ibid.*, 105.

6 Andrade, "What Does Doodling Do?"

7 Smith, "Hidden Narrative," 33.

8 Karl, *Joseph Conrad*, 598.

9 Eggert, "Conrad's Working Methods," 5.

10 Watt, *Essays on Conrad*, 23; Knowles, "Preprint Documents," 25.

11 John Conrad, *Joseph Conrad*, 161.

12 Batchelor, "Conrad's Truancy," 126.

13 T. S. Eliot, "Tradition and the Individual Talent," 45.

14 Batchelor, "Conrad's Truancy," 121.

15 *Ibid.*

16 Eggert, "Conrad's Working Methods," 5.

Chapter 2

1 Hampson, "Passion for Maps," 44.

2 Clemens, "Conrad as Geographer," 460.

3 Najder, "Century of *Nostromo*," 232. Ian Watt has traced the developments of the mappings of Costaguana's Occidental Republic: "The first published map was that of E. M. Tillyard, in 1958, and since then at least three others have appeared; and they are supplemented by at least a score of writings on the novel's geography" (*Nostromo*, 16). The research has taken on unexpected, scientific proportions. According to Gene M. Moore, Hans van Marle tried to "remember enough trigonometry to test the accuracy of the proposed maps of Sulaco with reference to the angle at which the light from the sunrise above Higuerota enters the windows of Casa Gould" ("Introduction," 9).

4 Early key texts in the field of critical cartography include Harley, "Deconstructing the Map" and Harley "Cartography, Ethics and Social Theory"; Monmonier, *How to Lie with Maps* (1991); Moretti, *Atlas of the European Novel* (1999). The multivolume work *History of Cartography* (1987–), founded by J. B. Harley and David Woodward, is a significant

contribution to the field. For an overview of the field and its developments, consider Crampton and Krygie, "Introduction to Critical Cartography."

5 For exceptions, consider my two recent full-scale publications of two of Conrad's maps: Warodell, "Conrad's Unpublished Map of his Congo Journey" and "Query: Joseph Conrad's Unpublished 'Map of Russias'."

6 Berthoud et al., "Notes," 493.

7 In passing, Simmons (*Joseph Conrad*, 305) refers to a doodled "map of the courtyard" in *An Outcast of the Islands*, and in an accompanying footnote lists the maps in the "Author's Note" to *Almayer's Folly*, in the holograph of *Nostromo* and in the holograph of *Victory*.

8 These documents were first published in 1925 in *Blue Peter* by Richard Curle as "Joseph Conrad's diary (hitherto unpublished) of his journey up the valley of the Congo in 1890." On its publication they contained a map made by Curle, titled "ROUGH MAP of the ROUTE followed by JOSEPH CONRAD on his overland JOURNEY in the BELGIAN CONGO from MATADI to NSELEMBA in 1890." Regarding Conrad's own doodles and sketches, the Cambridge edition of *Last Essays* reproduces four of the sketches of the terrain (out of twelve) in "The Congo Diary," and one sketch from the "Up-river Book" out of twelve. Józef Miłobędzki's journal article "Dziennik Kongijski Josepha Conrad/Joseph Conrad's Congo Diary" reproduces all seven of the navigational maps of the Lulanga river passage.

9 A small selection of the sketches in the manuscripts of the "Up-river Book" and "The Congo Diary" are published in the Cambridge Edition of *Last Essays* (1926) and four maps – or "conjectured plans" – are published in the Cambridge Edition of *'Twixt Land and Sea* (1912). To date, the other editions of Conrad's books (by Cambridge, Oxford, Penguin and other book publishers) have not reproduced the maps in Conrad's handwritten manuscripts. The exclusion of most of the maps in the authoritative Cambridge Editions follows the established procedure of editors to ignore doodles – no matter their visual complexity, frequency and meaning. To take one example, the Cambridge Edition of *Victory*, seeking to present a raw and unedited Conrad constructed directly from primary sources, follows its predecessors by overlooking the most visually striking way in which the handwritten manuscript differs from the printed edition: the doodles on almost every page.

10 At Beinecke Research Library I have accessed part or complete holograph manuscripts of *Suspense, The Rover, Heart of Darkness, Under Western Eyes, Chance, The Shadow-Line*, "The Warrior's Soul," "The Smile of Fortune: A Harbour Story," "An Outpost of Progress," "Amy Foster," "The End of the Tether," "Falk: A Reminiscence" and "The Nature of a Crime." At Rosenbach Research Library: *Almayer's Folly, Lord Jim, Nostromo, The Secret Agent, The Nigger of the 'Narcissus'*, "Initiation," "The Informer," "The Inland Sea," "The Polish Question," "Because of the Dollars," "The Inn of the Two Witches," "The Partner." At Houghton Library: "The Congo Diary" and the "Up-river Book." At the Harry Ransom Center: *Chance* and *Victory*. The locations of some of Conrad's holograph manuscripts are unknown and not all leaves of

every manuscript have been preserved. A substantial portion of "The End of the Tether" was lost due to lamp fire; "Karain" is now located at 41° 43' N, 49° 56' W, at a depth of 12,500 feet, along with the *Titanic*; and some texts are held in private collections, such as a manuscript for Conrad's unfinished novel *The Sisters*. "A Descriptive Location Register of Joseph Conrad's Literary Manuscripts," compiled by Gene M. Moore, provides a comprehensive list of Conrad's manuscripts and their locations.

11 Donald Rude discusses the preprint documents of the Saxtons' map and demonstrates how the published map, despite input from Conrad, "did not accurately reflect Conrad's intentions" ("Letters to Saxton," 56). Although the Saxtons' map along with Conrad's written comments accurately document the sailing routes, the artist responsible for drawing the map for publication carried out the "wishes of the author in a confusing way" (*ibid.*, 56). On its first publication, the map gives an inaccurate route for *Judea* and an inaccurate description of where it caught fire.

12 Hampson, "Spatial Stories," 56–57.

13 *Ibid.*, 57.

14 *Ibid.*

15 Great Britain Hydrographic Office, *Chart Relating to the Gulf of Siam: Original Navigation Chart Used By Joseph Conrad*. A high resolution photo negative is available at the Beinecke Rare Book and Manuscript Library.

16 The topographical map of Higuerota is on a manuscript page of *Nostromo*, numbered 345, located at the Rosenbach Museum and Library, Philadelphia. The map was first reproduced in Knapp Hay, *Political Novels of Joseph Conrad* (1961), with the caption "a relief map of the coast of Costaguana – his imaginary republic on the west coast of South America" (173). In a letter to Conrad, the novelist Arnold Bennett calls Higuerota "the principal personage in the story" (quoted in Watt, *Nostromo*, 16).

17 Najder, *Chronicle*, 457.

18 Woodward, "Introduction," 7.

19 Harley, "Deconstructing the Map," 1.

20 Moretti, *Atlas*, 3.

21 Harley, "Deconstructing the Map," 7.

22 Harley, "Text and Contexts," 36.

23 Jeremy Black, *Maps and History*, i.

24 Bushell, "Mapping Victorian Adventure Fiction," 630.

25 Bushell, "Paratext," 187.

26 Borges, "Travels of Praiseworthy Men," 131.

27 Kimpel and Eaves, "Geography," 48, 53.

28 Derrick, "Mapping Axel Heyst's Island," 44.

Chapter 3

1 Ford, *Tiger, Tiger*, 495.

2 Jessie Conrad, *Joseph Conrad*, 282, 146.

3 Stape, *Several Lives*, 154; Meyers, *Joseph Conrad*, 234.

4 Warodell, "Conrad's Painterly Drawings."
5 Najder, "The Sisters," 77.
6 In *The Political Unconscious: Narrative as a Socially Symbolic Act* (1981), Fredric Jameson connects Conrad's work ethic to that of the Protestant. This is slightly misleading given the strong associations between the Protestant work ethic and industrialization. The context in which Conrad praises work is frequently with reference to the craftsmanship of a preindustrial era. In *The Mirror of the Sea*, for instance, he speaks about the craft of sailing. Like John Ruskin and William Morris, he also sees himself as a craftsman in his work as a writer. He resists, in other words, the modern convention of distinguishing art from manual craftsmanship. This resistance is not part of Conrad's characteristic strategy of self-deprecation (he speaks complimentarily about other writers as craftsmen too). The word-choice is more likely a reaction to the lessened status of the craftsman that the Industrial Revolution implied. The advent of the steam engine resulted, after all, not just in cheapened machine-made imitations – but also in steamships that, due to their efficiency, implied the loss of a class of skilled workers.
7 Yelton, *Mimesis and Metaphor*, 14.
8 Meyer, *Joseph Conrad*, 49.
9 Karl, *Joseph Conrad*, 363.
10 Watt, *Conrad in the Nineteenth Century*, 13; Jones, *Conrad and Women*, 91.
11 Najder, "The Sisters," 25–34.
12 *Ibid.*, 77, 72.
13 "They were water colors and in them the fierce tropical nature and the physiognomies of cannibals appeared as if seen through a softening mist" (Purdy, "Manuscript of *Victory*," 106).
14 Stape, "Gaining Conviction."
15 Najder, "The Sisters," 72.
16 Curle, *Joseph Conrad*, 122; Rothenstein, *Men and Memories*, 41.
17 He saw an exhibition by Augustus John in London and maintains that he has seen a painting by John Lavery, which at that time was displayed at the Goupil Gallery, London.
18 Jessie Conrad, *Joseph Conrad*, 5.
19 Warodell, "Conrad's Painterly Drawings."
20 Jones, "Conrad's Debt," 19.
21 Johnston, *Nineteenth-Century Fashion*, 80.
22 Fashion Institute, http://sites.fitnyc.edu/depts/museum/RetroSpective/Gigot-Sleeve-1.html.
23 Gernsheim, *Victorian and Edwardian Fashion*, 84.
24 "The Idiots" relies on this equation ("the elongated, gracefully flowing lines of the clear Parisian toilette," 59), as does *Under Western Eyes* ("The Egeria of the 'Russian Mazzini . . . A witch in Parisian clothes'," 214–15), *The Arrow of Gold* ("The latter was eminently elegant . . . Very Parisian indeed," 12) and *Nostromo*, wherein Don Martin Decoud sports an "elegant Parisian overcoat, with a pearl-grey silk lining" (229).

25 Rothenstein, *Men and Memories*, 43.

26 One of the foundational art historians, Giorgio Vasari (1511–74), is known for having written informatively about the Mona Lisa (La Gioconda), without admitting that he had never seen the painting. Vasari, in turn, deemed the Florentine architect Leon Battista Alberti (1404–72) much better at writing on architecture than practicing it: in writing "he even surpassed those artisans who actually surpassed him in the practice of their craft" (*Lives of the Artists*, 179). Similarly, according to Clement Greenberg, Kant had limited knowledge of visual art – "Yet his capacity for abstraction enabled him, despite many *gaffes*, to establish in his *Critique of Aesthetic Judgment* what is the most satisfactory basis for aesthetics we yet have" (*Collected Essays*, 249).

27 This list can be extended to include those who dream of a different political future, like Michaelis, Ossipon, Karl Yundt and the Professor in *The Secret Agent*.

28 Woolf, *Jacob's Room*, 167.

29 Danto, *After the End of Art*, 46.

30 Najder, "The Sisters," 78–79.

31 Danto, *What Art Is*, 1.

32 Greenberg, *Late Writings*, 36.

33 Belting, *End of the History of Art*, 14.

34 For a fuller investigation of the concept of family resemblance (*Familienähnlichkeit*), see Wittgenstein's *Philosophische Untersuchungen* (1953) and his *Preliminary Studies for the 'Philosophical Investigations'* (1958).

35 Danto, *What Art Is*, 1. Consider Danto, *After the End of Art* (1997); Greenberg, *Late Writings* (2003); Gombrich, *Art and Illusion* (1962); Wölfflin, *Kunstgeschichtliche Grundbegriffe* (1917). To say that art history, unlike other arts, has a history is not necessarily a way to dismiss the art form. For instance, art history cannot be dismissed as unscientific due to its lack of development (in the way ordinary language philosophers explained the non-teleological history of philosophy as a problem of miscommunication).

36 Gombrich, "Reflections."

37 Belting, *End of the History of Art*, 6, 23.

38 Wölfflin quoted in Gombrich, *Art and Illusion*, 4.

39 Danto, *After the End of Art*, 46.

40 Danto, *What Art Is*, 108, 110. Photography is today, of course, concerned with more than mimetic representation: "Not even photography, the self-proclaimed medium of objective documentation, kept its promise: instead it became, in the hands and with the eyes of the photographer, a highly individual vehicle for the interpretation of reality" (Belting, *End of the History of Art*, 24).

41 Danto, "End of Art," 128.

42 Ambrosini, *Conrad's Fiction*, 2.

43 An irony of this reading is that a unidirectional art history has also been conceived of as an illustrated Bildungsroman stretching over millennia. In this fanciful reading, Stephen is part of the Zeitgeist that carves out a new

direction for visual art – as sui generis and ahistorical – although his own personal history is evolutionary.

44 Baines, *Joseph Conrad*, 167–68.

45 To further complicate the discussion: Conrad's tendency to revise manuscripts heavily before publication means that one should be cautious about treating *The Sisters* as a finished product; it may compare unfavorably to other texts simply by virtue of being at an earlier stage in the production process.

Chapter 4

1 Margaret Moran, "Bertrand Russell and Joseph Conrad"; Knowles, "Joseph Conrad and Bertrand Russell."

2 Peters, *Conrad and Impressionism*, 168.

3 *Ibid.*, 16.

4 Russell, *Portraits from Memory*, 89.

5 *Ibid.*, 87.

6 Russell, *Philosophy of Logical Atomism*, 22.

7 Conrad's comment on the unreliability of language is taken from a lengthy correspondence with Cunningham Graham, the first ever socialist member of the Parliament of the United Kingdom. In the letter to Graham, Conrad discusses the possibility of reform when "we don't even know our own thoughts," and when "Faith is a myth and beliefs shift like mists on the shore; thoughts vanish; words, once pronounced, die; and the memory of yesterday is as shadowy as the hope of to-morrow" (*CL* II.18).

8 Russell, *Philosophy of Logical Atomism*, 135.

9 In the same letter to the writer Henry Newbolt, Conrad writes that "the notions of truth, justice and beauty are clear enough as long as we abstain from definitions whose intellectual effort only blurrs [*sic*] and diminishes the mental image" (*CL* III.328)

10 For an introduction to Russell's philosophy, consider the chapter "The Philosophy of Logical Analysis," in Russell's *History of Western Philosophy* (1945), and the chapter "Knowledge by Acquaintance and Knowledge by Description" in Russell's *The Problems of Philosophy* (1912). For a more sophisticated and nuanced view on Russell by Russell, consider "On Denoting" (1905), *The Philosophy of Logical Atomism* (1918) and "Logical Atomism" (1924).

11 Russell, *Philosophy of Logical Atomism*, 16.

12 *Ibid.*, 2, 21.

13 *Ibid.*, 25.

14 *Ibid.*, 11, 110.

15 "Knowledge by Acquaintance," 12.

16 These words, or a version of them, are used with such frequency in *Notes on Life and Letters* that no specific page numbers have been provided here.

17 Russell, *Contemplation and Action*, 499.

18 "A Glance at Two Books" exemplifies how an uncritical and amorous treatment of one's fictional characters undermines their realism: Thackeray "was in love with the sentiments they [his heroines] represented. He was, in fact, in love with what does not exist – and that is why Amelia Osborne does not exist, either in colour, in shape, in grace, in goodness" (133). Michaelis in *The Secret Agent* says: "All idealisation makes life poorer. To beautify it is to take away its character of complexity – it is to destroy it. Leave that to the moralists, my boy" (33).

19 Russell, *Portraits from Memory*, 87.

20 James, *Principles of Psychology*, vol. II, 224.

21 Russell, *Philosophy of Logical Atomism*, 17.

22 Conrad's "method of work" is, if we trust his voice in correspondence, based "on fidelity – in the words of a writer now dead – 'remorseless fidelity to the truth of my own sensations'" (*CL* III.12). This dictum recurs throughout Conrad's texts.

23 Cecil Roberts, "Joseph Conrad," 127.

24 Nabokov, *Strong Opinions*, 4.

25 Russell, *Philosophy of Logical Atomism*, 25.

26 *Ibid.*, 26.

27 Conrad does not deem the reader's contribution to be negligible: "one writes only half the book; the other half is with the reader" (*CL* I.370). Indeed, one of Conrad's letters to Hugh Clifford strongly emphasizes the importance of leaving room for the reader's imagination: "if you read the sentence in its place on the page You will see that the word frightened (or indeed any word of the sort) is inadequate to express the true state of that man's mind. No word is adequate. The imagination of the reader should be left free to arouse his feeling" (*CL* II.201).

28 Russell, *Philosophy of Logical Atomism*, 26.

29 *Ibid.*, 59.

30 Thus, in "Language and Metaphysics" Russell notes that Plato infers "properties of the world from properties of language" (*Basic Writings*, 221). In *The Philosophy of Logical Atomism*, Russell explains that "unless you are fairly self-conscious about symbols, unless you are fairly aware of the symbol to what it symbolizes, you will find yourself attributing to the thing properties which only belong to the symbol" (10).

31 Watt, *Conrad in the Nineteenth Century*, 175.

32 *Ibid.*, 174.

33 These reasons possibly account for a recent surge in criticism that considers the ambiguity of *Heart of Darkness* to be external to the text's formalistic aspects, so that our presumptions about its inherent ambiguity are what makes it difficult to approach. Artese, who in *Testimony on Trial* (2012) re-evaluates early modernism in these terms, maintains that the text itself is not inherently ambiguous but is understood this way since scholars have classified it "modernist."

34 Watt, *Conrad in the Nineteenth Century*, 175, 176–79.

35 Johnson, "Conrad's Impressionism," 57, 55, 70. In earlier sections of the essay Johnson engages with the idea of absolute relativism, where the existence of a truth hierarchy is senseless: "a good part of Conrad's 'delayed decoding'" is consistent with the recognition "that here is no such thing as an isolated and meaningful fact or event or object" (60); "preconceived 'nets' of meaning instantly trap an event" (61). He further speculates in the direction against a truth hierarchy when he associates Conrad's delayed decoding with Husserl's phenomenology: "The true spirit of *epoché* refused to establish quickly and prejudicially hierarchies of what might be very real, less real, or not so real about the experience" (68).
36 Towheed, "Geneva v. Saint Petersburg," 11.
37 These descriptions derive from the following: Chantler, *Character Studies*, 50; Faris, "Dehumanization," 318; Hampson, *Conrad's Secrets*, 21; Finkelstein, "Hope and Betrayal," 20; Jones, *Conrad and Women*, 178; McLeod, "Disturbing the Silence," 117; Galef, On the Margin," 137; Watts, *Conrad's Heart of Darkness*, 162; and Levin, "Conrad, Freud, and Derrida," 100.
38 The critics cited are White, "Conrad and Modernism," 173; Knowles and Moore, *Oxford Reader's Companion*, 175; Cantor and Hufnagel, "Empire of the future," 36; and Gorra, "Joseph Conrad," 561.
39 Johnson, "Conrad's Impressionism," 57.
40 For a representative discussion of Conrad's anti-logocentric aesthetic, see Said, "Conrad and Nietzsche."
41 Watt, *Conrad in the Nineteenth Century*, 178.
42 Peters, *Conrad and Impressionism*, 7.
43 Carabine, *The Life and the Art*, xxv.
44 Harkness, "Introduction," xxxii.
45 Andrew Michael Roberts, "Conrad, Theory and Value," 197.
46 Fowler, *Linguistic Criticism*, 216.
47 Hawthorn, *Language*, 31.
48 Watt, *Conrad in the Nineteenth Century*, 176–77.
49 Johnson, "Conrad's Impressionism," 55.
50 Reginald Davey Cooper, *Hunting and Hunted*, 195–96.
51 *Ibid.*, 122.
52 De Quatrefages, *Pygmies*, 84.
53 Stanley, *Autobiography*, 365.
54 Watt, "Pink Toads," 28, 29.

Chapter 5

1 In *Mimesis: The Representation of Reality in Western Literature* (1946), Erich Auerbach explains (among many other things) the way digressive details function and why they are a hallmark of the oral style. In Virginia Woolf, for instance, "realistic depth is achieved in every individual occurrence" (552): in the attempt "to put the emphasis on the random occurrence, to exploit it not in the service of a planned continuity of action but in itself. And in the

process something new and elemental appeared: nothing less than the wealth of reality and depth of life in every moment to which we surrender ourselves without prejudice" (552). It is in this category of realism I place Conrad's references to distractions that admittedly appear, at first blush, to be insignificant elements of the narrative.

2 For a fuller account of this element of Conrad's personality, see John Batchelor's chapter "Conrad's Truancy" in *The Art of Literary Biography* (1995). The chapter explores how, for Conrad, procrastination and productivity worked in delayed symbiosis.

3 Conrad was far from the first to pay attention to those who do not pay attention. The most conspicuous artist in this genre might be a visual artist. According to art historian Michael Fried, Jean-Baptiste-Siméon Chardin's (1699–1779) defining contribution to art history was to translate the rapturousness of religious painting into the absorption of the ordinary: "he located the experience of absorption in the home, or at any rate in absolutely ordinary surroundings" (46). Chardin's iconic images of young people playing and amusing themselves, such as of a boy blowing a soup bubble, "are not of time wasted but of time *filled*... they embody a new, unmoralized vision of distraction as a vehicle of absorption ... an unofficial morality according to which absorption emerges as good in and of itself" (*Absorption and Theatricality*, 51). Distraction, then, can be viewed as a normative concept, where absorption would be a more neutral descriptive term.

4 Donald Davidson's fine paper "Joseph Conrad's Directed Indirections" (1925) is an exploration of the nonchronological nature of Conrad's work; it is not a discussion about distraction.

5 North, *Problem of Distraction*, 5.

6 Allen, "Dazed and Confused," 48.

7 Crary, *Suspensions of Perception*, 23.

8 Batchelor, "Conrad's Truancy," 126. Other stories also grew far beyond their expected length; *The Nigger of the 'Narcissus'* was intended to be a part of a collection of short stories: "I am letting myself go with the *Nigger*. He grows and grows" (*CL* 1.312). "First Command" became *The Shadow-Line*. *An Outcast of the Islands* was originally conceived as a short story.

9 There are a few notable exceptions. Apart from *Heart of Darkness*, *The Secret Agent* has proven particularly open to detailed readings. Recent studies, like Kim Salmons's "Anarchic Appetites: Vegetarianism in *The Secret Agent*" (2012), Judith Paltin's "Conrad's Agile Crowds" (2013) and James Purdon's "Secret Agents, Official Secrets: Joseph Conrad and the Security of Mail" (2015), have demonstrated the possibility of constructing a cohesive narrative from minor "details." Another excellent paper in this style is David Leon Higdon's "Conrad's Clocks" (1991).

10 Greaney, *Conrad, Language, and Narrative*, 82.

11 From one perspective, secondary literature cannot be keen on these sideshows; once you have devoted sustained attention to an idea/image, then you have rescued it from marginality.

12 Guerard, *Conrad the Novelist*, 130.

13 Watt, *Rise of the Novel*, 291.
14 All too often, Edward Said notes, "Conrad's text is searched for supervening sub-texts or privileged meanings of the sort that seem more important than the book itself" ("Narrative," 118).
15 Watt, *Conrad in the Nineteenth Century*, 56.
16 *Ibid.*, 206.
17 Woolf, "Joseph Conrad," 226.
18 *Ibid.*, 47.
19 Hagan, "Design," 149.
20 Baines, *Joseph Conrad*, 408.
21 Guerard, *Conrad the Novelist*, 224.
22 To list a few notable examples: "(I had straw slippers on my feet)" (*SS* 107); "(she had splendid teeth)" (*C* 41); "the cousin (who took snuff during the interview)" (*HD* 120) – and to specify the look of Almayer's pyjamas: "(enormous flowers with yellow petals on a disagreeable blue ground)" (*PR* 74).
23 Erich Auerbach famously makes the case in *Mimesis* that "the Homeric style knows only a foreground, only a uniformly illuminated, uniformly objective present" (7). It is ultimately senseless to divide the *Odyssey* into foreground/background, center/aside, digression/focus: it is arbitrary to speak of one element of the story as more interesting and important than another.
24 Guerard, *Conrad the Novelist*, 229.
25 *Ibid.*, 231.
26 Stallman, "Time," 101.
27 Erdinast-Vulcan *Modern Temper*, 5.
28 J. Hillis Miller, *Poets of Reality*, 45.
29 Hagan, "Design," 154.
30 Jessie Conrad, *Joseph Conrad*, 19.
31 Quoted in Najder, *Joseph Conrad: A Life*, 128.
32 Leavis, *Great Tradition*, 128.
33 Guerard, *Conrad the Novelist*, 218.
34 Carlyle, "Nigger Question," 84.
35 Watts, *Conrad's Heart of Darkness*, 67.
36 *Heart of Darkness*, writes Michael Greaney, "might well be seen as a text that plays all too easily in the hands of deconstruction, a text only too happy to lead the reader into an epistemological cul-de-sac" (*Conrad, Language, and Narrative*, 76).
37 Captain Brierly's suicide is surprising and out of character, like the final act of the cowardly Hirsch in *Nostromo*: he boldly spits his torturer in the face.
38 Ambrosini, *Conrad's Fiction*, 199.
39 North, *Problem of Distraction*, 4. North's excellent monograph is highly informative and takes its root in philosophical history. To avoid tautology, and define the one in terms of the other, North probes the possibility of understanding distraction as a concept independent of attention (which is different from how Conrad understood distraction).
40 Eagleton, *How to Read Literature*, 9.

41 Watt, *Conrad in the Nineteenth Century*, 56.
42 T. S. Eliot, *Four Quartets*, 73.
43 Ford, *Remembrance*, 171.
44 A belief shared to some extent with Conrad himself: "the man believes in the [Copernican] system without, often, knowing as much about it as its name" (62), he writes in *Notes on Life and Letters*. Marlow, in *Lord Jim*, defines astronomy as "a sort of scientific scandal mongering" (166).
45 Berthoud, *Major Phase*, 133.
46 To picture a sine wave, imagine that you put a pen on wheel and move it along an axis next to a wall – the drawing on the wall is the sine wave. If you extend and flatten a spiral along a wall, you also get a sine wave.

Chapter 6

1 Reiss, "True Classic."
2 Erdinast-Vulcan, "Sudden Holes."
3 Stallman, "Time," 114.
4 Simmons, *Joseph Conrad*, 135.
5 Stape, "Conrad the Impressionist," 482.
6 Schnauder, *Free Will*, 208.
7 Davidson, "Directed Indirections," 167.
8 Watts, *Conrad's Heart of Darkness*, 64.
9 Consider Ian Watt's collection of essays in *Conrad: The Secret Agent. A Casebook* (1973). With essays on "Order and Anarchy" by Irving Howe, "A Version of Anarchy" by Albert Guerard, "Irony as Theme" by Robert Spector and "The Symbolic World of *The Secret Agent*" by Avrom Fleishman, the collection is representative of the tendency to read the novel from an overarching argument or theme (order, anarchy, irony, symbolism).
10 Howe, "Order and Anarchy," 141.
11 Erdinast-Vulcan, "Sudden Holes," 207.
12 Greaney, *Conrad, Language, and Narrative*, 136.
13 J. Hillis Miller, *Poets of Reality*, 39.
14 Eloise Knapp Hay finds certain accusations of callousness unwarranted; contemporary newspapers reported the Greenwich bombing, on which the novel is partly based, with the same tone and "effect of humor-seasoned-by-distance" (*Political Novels*, 223). Journalism, of course, can be seen as a weak criterion by which to judge morality and ethics.
15 Stallman, "Time," 107.
16 Eagleton, "Form," 27.
17 Dostoevsky, *The Devils*, 106.
18 His respect for private property can be seen as irreconcilable with anarchism, or as its natural manifestation in the individuals who uphold it as a belief system. Mr Verloc's identity as a pretend anarchist is reminiscent of a passage in Dostoevsky's *The Devils*: "why is it that all these desperate socialists and communists are . . . such believers in private property, and indeed, the bigger

the socialist, the more extreme he is, the stronger is his instinct for private property – why is it?" (90–91).

19 Oliver, "Conrad's Grotesque Public," 210.

20 Harrington, *Conrad's Sensational Heriones*, 11.

21 Stevie's attack on Greenwich meantime might have been more successful than the book originally calculated. With the use of GPS (Global Positioning System), recent research demonstrates that the actual meridian is placed at a distance of about 100 meters from the original line. If Stevie accidentally reached this position, he would have been ahead of his time.

22 Apart from in *The Secret Agent*, a clock is used to mark the time of death in *Under Western Eyes* and *Lord Jim*.

23 To make sense of time and space constraints, Sutherland suggests Mrs Dalloway must have taken an invisible taxi from Upper Bond Street to her home in Westminister, a distance the character covers in less than ten minutes in the novel ("Clarissa's Invisible Taxi," in *Jane Eyre*). For a distinction between the notions of inconsistency and ambiguity in Conrad, consider Hawthorn, "Incoherences."

24 "Athenaeum," 48.

25 Watts, *Joseph Conrad: Secret Agent*, 28.

26 Auerbach, *Mimesis*, 4–5.

27 *Ibid.*, 7.

28 Schwarz, *Conrad*, 28.

29 Walkowitz, *Cosmopolitan Style*, 44.

30 Watts, *Joseph Conrad: Secret Agent*, 28.

31 Stallman, "Time," 113.

32 "The Dial."

33 Greaney, *Conrad, Language, and Narrative*, 139.

34 Danto, *Transfiguration*, 120.

35 *Ibid.*, 118.

36 Harpham, *One of Us*, 43.

37 "Country Life," 31.

38 Baines, *Joseph Conrad*, 408.

39 Hampson, *Conrad's Secrets*, 129.

40 *Ibid.*, 128.

41 "I had to fight hard to keep at arm's length the memories of solitary and nocturnal walks all over London in early days" (7), writes Conrad in the "Author's Note" to *The Secret Agent*. This theme is more often remarked upon than examined; consider Ray, "Landscape," and Hampson, "Topographical Mysteries." The most sustained discussion of walking in the novel is Kao, "Flâneur."

42 Baines, *Joseph Conrad*, 373.

Chapter 7

1 Greaney, *Conrad, Language, and Narrative*, 3.

2 Said, *Fiction of Autobiography*, 4.

3 Fogel, *Coercion to Speak*, 22.

4 Greaney, *Conrad, Language, and Narrative*, 2.
5 Guerard, *Conrad the Novelist*, 2.
6 Messenger, "Jimmy Wait," 65.
7 Livingstone, "Seeing through Reading," 133.
8 Watts, "Introduction," xxvii.
9 James E. Miller, "Re-examination," 911.
10 Cyr, "Dramatized and Embodied Artist," 145.
11 Jasanoff, *Dawn Watch*, 110.
12 Yates, "Social Comment," 185.
13 Guerard, *Conrad the Novelist*, 102.
14 Simmons, "Story-Telling," 43. For a range of representative readings of the novel, consider John Palmer's collection of critical essays in *Twentieth-Century Interpretations of The Nigger of the 'Narcissus'* (1969).
15 Richardson, "Posthumanist Narration," 213.
16 Simmons, "Story-Telling," 46.
17 I here associate inarticulateness with socioeconomic class in relation to those inarticulate characters in, say, Dickens who only seem able to speak in a format that is as marginal and secondary as their own position in society: "Mrs Piper has a good deal to say, chiefly in parenthesis and without punctuation, but not much to tell" (*Bleak House*, 176).
18 Thus, in response to the length of *Lord Jim* and the unreasonableness that its narrator could talk for so long in one sitting, as Marlow is supposed to have done as its oral narrator, Conrad answers in its "Author's Note" that he is personally aware of times when sailors have spoken for multiple hours: "Men have been known, both in the tropics and in the temperate zone, to sit up half the night 'swapping yarns'" (5). Conrad is therefore using yarn-spinning – sailor's talk – as the plausible starting point for Marlow as an oral narrator.
19 Ambrosini, *Conrad's Fiction*, 67.
20 Simmons, "Story-Telling," 47–48.
21 Gordan, *Making of a Novelist*, 141–44.
22 Ambrosini, *Conrad's Fiction*, 70.
23 Greaney *Conrad, Language, and Narrative*, 63.
24 Ruppel, *Political Genealogy*, 18.
25 Larabee, "Maritime Tradition," 56.
26 Captain Brierly in *Lord Jim* commits suicide with the help of four iron belaying-pins from the mainmast, which he puts in his pockets "to help him down" (52). Decoud in *Nostromo* puts four silver ingots in his pockets, shoots himself with a revolver in the chest and then rolls overboard. In *The Mirror of the Sea* a person named Cesar drowns strapped with a gold-belt. Henry Whalley, the nearly blind captain of the steamer *Sofala* in "The End of the Tether," commits suicide with the help of "pieces of iron" (247) to send himself to the depths. The captain on the ill-fated steamer *Burgmester Dahl* in "Falk" reportedly commits suicide by jumping into the sea. Renouard in "The Planter of Malata" commits suicide by calmly swimming with his eyes fixed on a star, until he sinks from exhaustion. In *Suspense*, Father Carpi remembers

Clelia's mother "who was found drowned years ago in a remarkably shallow pond ... It might have been an accident. He had consented to bury her in consecrated ground" (118). Even in *The Secret Agent*, a story set in London, Winnie Verloc commits suicide by jumping from a ship; prior to the act she contemplates throwing herself into the river from a bridge. In *Victory*, Lena confesses to Axel Heyst that she has contemplated drowning herself – "make a hole in the water" (78) – to escape from Zangiacamo's orchestra. Flora in *Chance* looks out over a cliff on the ocean contemplating suicide.

Chapter 8

1 J. Hillis Miller, *Poets of Reality*, 22.
2 *Ibid.*
3 Jameson, *Political Unconscious*, 212.
4 Carver, *Granular Modernism*, 32.
5 Watt, *Conrad in the Nineteenth Century*, 98.
6 I have consulted five books from each writer, manually counted the number of hats and afterwards done a computer search to verify the results. By 'hat' I mean any shaped covering for the head. Virginia Woolf's *Jacob's Room, Orlando, Mrs Dalloway, To the Lighthouse* and *The Waves* contain the following references to distinct types of hats: billycock, bonnet, bowler, cap, coronet, cocked hat, crown, felt hat, furred hat, deer-stalker's hat, Homburg hat, mantilla, Panama hat, silk hat, "slouched hat" (*Orlando*, 40), straw hat, shooting cap, top hat, turban, tarpaulin hat, tweed cap, whimple, "Welshwomen's hats" (*Jacob*, 103), "the conical white hat of a pierrot" (*Jacob*, 99), "an organ grinder's monkey's hat" (*Dalloway*, 126), "hats-emerald and white, lightly wreathed or drooping beneath deep-dyed feathers" (*Jacob*, 167). Herman Melville's *Typee, Redburn, Billy Budd, Moby-Dick, White-Jacket* contain the following references to distinct types of hat: bonnet, crown, cocked hat, lace hat, Maltese cap, Payta hat, sou'-wester, tarpaulin hat, turban, "a shako of badger skin" (*Redburn*, 145), "a tasseled Chinese cap" (*Redburn*, 179), "tasseled smoking-cap" (*Redburn*, 336), "tasselled caps of red worsted" (*MD* 443), "the laced chapeau of Mowanna" (*Typee*, 18), "one of those red-billed savage sea-hawks" (*MD* 585), "his slouched and gaily-ribboned hat" (*MD* 273), "a huge chapeau bras, waving with ostrich plumes" (*Typee*, 7), "fanciful turban of purple velvet, figured with silver sprigs, and surmounted by a tuft of variegated feathers" (*Typee*, 8), "I put round the apology for a hat which I had been forced to construct for myself out of palmetto leaves" (*Typee*, 162). H. G. Wells's *The Invisible Man, The Time Machine, The Shape of Things to Come, The War of the Worlds, The Island of Doctor Moreau* contain the following references to distinct types of hat: bowler, "fashionable hats with heavy plumes" (*Invisible*, 31), "furry silk hat" (*Invisible*, 39), helmet, "a high hat" (*Invisible*, 62), silk hat, slouch hat, "soft felt hat" (*Invisible*, 5), straw hat, "small round caps" (*Worlds*, 37), "three-cornered hat" (*Shape*, 91), turban, top hat and "wide-brimmed straw hat"

(*Moreau*, 82). Vladimir Nabokov's *Luzhin, Despair, Pnin, Lolita, Pale Fire* contain the following hat references: boater, bowler, cap with earflaps, coxcomb cap, fedora, opera hat, plumed hat, sieve-pitted cap, silk nightcap, steel cap, straw hat, top hat, trilby, turban and a Russki factory worker cap.

7 Mallarmé's hat is not only "the womb of the parthenogenesis which poetry demands," but also "caused the death of the larynx. I interpret this strangulation as an epilepsy-like orgasmic eroticization of the entire body, an upward displacement of ejaculation (the physical analogue of the verticality described by Richard above) which, for reasons you now know, failed to transcend the *ici-bas*, in a suffocating act of love-death, those opposing realms which are bounded, encircled and linked by a hat" (Hanson, "Mallarmé's Hat," 226–27).

8 Hanson, "Mallarmé's Hat," 216.

9 Brevda, "Nasty Night," 424.

10 Kuhn, "Raskol'nikov's Hats," 425.

11 Doyle, *Adventures of Sherlock Holmes*, 151–52.

12 Conrad's attention to "trivial" details can be viewed as a telling aspect of his authorship. For a general debate about the importance of factual consistency in fiction, consider L. C Knights, "How Many Children Had Lady Macbeth? An Essay in the Theory and Practice of Shakespeare Criticism" (1964), or Julian Barnes's *Flaubert's Parrot* (1984), where he discusses Christopher Ricks's and Enid Starkie's lectures on mistakes in literature. John Sutherland wrote three canonical books that all explore, directly and indirectly, the question of factual consistency: *Is Heathcliff a Murderer?* (1996), *Can Jane Eyre be Happy? More Puzzles in Classic Fiction* (1999), *Who Betrays Elizabeth Bennet? Further Puzzles in Classic Fiction* (2000).

13 Kuhn, "Raskol'nikov's Hats," 425.

14 Foye et al., "Sailing Maneuver," 122.

15 Williams, "Matter of Conscience," 627.

16 Guerard, "Introduction," 10.

17 Johnson and Garber, "Secret Sharing," 629.

18 Foye et al., "Sailing Maneuver," 121.

19 Billy, *Wilderness of Words*, 24.

20 Peters, *Conrad and Impressionism*, 37.

21 Descartes, *Discourse on Method*, 57.

22 The extent to which it makes sense to speak about the eyes' vision as different from that of the mind has not been established either in philosophy or medicine. The aim of the paragraph is to elaborate on Descartes's reasoning – not evaluate it.

23 Freedgood, *Ideas in Things*, 1.

24 Hennelly, "Dickens's Immaterial Culture," 79.

25 Blanc, *Art and Ornament*, 96.

26 Quoted in Hanson, "Mallarmé's Hat," 215.

27 Quoted *ibid.*

28 Quoted in Watt, *Conrad in the Nineteenth Century*, 19.

29 Curreli, "Garibaldian Names," 87.
30 Lyon, "Introduction," xxi.
31 For an account of how *Ridgway's* edited the text, consider Emily Dalgarno, "Conrad's Attitude to his Text" (1977); S. W. Reid, "American Markets, Serials, and Conrad's Career" (2003); Joseph Conrad, *The Secret Agent*, ed. Bruce Harkness and S. W. Reid (1990).
32 Raleigh, "Henry Patrick Raleigh."
33 Reid, "American Markets," 60.
34 Davies, "Dark Side."
35 Watts, *Joseph Conrad: Secret Agent*, 105.
36 Stein, "Dickens and Illustration," 168.
37 Donovan, *Popular Culture*, 40.
38 Given that Marlow throws one pair of shoes overboard and gives a second pair away to the Russian harlequin, he must have brought a minimum of three pairs of shoes and one pair of slippers with him to Kurtz's station (although I am unsure Conrad knew that Marlow packed so many shoes).
39 "Our Dramatic Critic," "Conrad's Play."

Chapter 9

1 Vint, *Animal Alterity*, 17.
2 Where *Moby-Dick* is framed as "a sustained exploration of the symbolism of the non-human," "everything relates back to the master symbol of the white whale" (Simons, *Animal Rights*, 113); the whale is a "metonym" for the "non-human universe" (Hecht, "Scarcity," 111). Hobart Smith and Rozella Smith even conclude that in *Moby-Dick* "astonishingly little knowledge is revealed of marine life other than whales – no more than of terrestrial life, which was itself meager" ("Herpetology," 9). It is "obvious that Melville was not a naturalist ... His mastery of whale lore was arduous for him, and was single-tracked, not a product of cosmopolitan interest in biology" (Smith and Smith 9).
3 For a computer search to be accurate and comprehensive, it would need to scan for all named animal species (1.5 million) multiplied by the number of languages used in an author's text. The available computer programs for calculation, classification and listing generate false positives and fail to identify most regionalisms, neologisms, misspellings and idiosyncratic spellings. I have therefore relied on manual calculation. The numbers of animal species listed in the chapter derive from reading all of Conrad's, Melville's, Nabokov's and Woolf's prose fiction (Warodell, "Melville's Fiction," "Nabokov's Fiction," "Woolf's Fiction").
4 The most sustained exploration of Conrad's animals is Michael John Di Santo's "Dramas of Fallen Horses" (2010). There, Di Santo partly explores the trope of the suffering horse in an effort to construct Stevie as a Conradian response to Dostoevsky's and Nietzsche's thinking. Palmer's *Joseph Conrad's*

Fiction (1968) discusses the symbolism of the many serpents in Conrad's work. Watt's *Conrad in the Nineteenth Century* discusses the pink toads in *Lord Jim* in a section on symbolism; Newell's " Yellow-Dog Incident" (1971), perfunctorily mentions the dog in *Lord Jim*, as does Attridge in "Yellow-Dog Thing" (2010). Multiple studies mention the butterflies in *Lord Jim*, such as Tagge's "Butterfly Hunters" (1996). And, as noted in the introduction of this chapter, many have discussed the absence of living elephants in the ivory-trade-centric *Heart of Darkness*.

5 Animals and animal studies are not represented in Knowles and Moore's comprehensive *Oxford Reader's Companion to Conrad* (2000), Peters's *Joseph Conrad's Critical Reception* (2013) or discussions about Conrad's marginal characters, such as Galef's "On the Margin" (1990). Schneider-Rebozo et al. (eds.), *Conrad and Nature* (2019), addresses elements of this gap in secondary literature.

6 Mary Allen, *Animals*, 6.

7 Myers, "Anxiety of Confluence," 103.

8 The word Congo is never used in the novella, so "the Congo River itself" cannot be said to appear among an otherwise nameless environment. The observation that "except for one desultory reference to hippos and alligators sunning themselves on a bank, the myriad species of African wildlife do not appear in this novel, not even mosquitoes" (Myers, "Anxiety of Confluence," 103), can be countered with the four scattered references to flies in the novella. Apart from a reference to a fish that leaped, there are references to donkeys and hens; both of these two species are native to Africa. The ancestor to the modern donkey is a subspecies of the African wild ass. It is further difficult to insist that plants and the landscape are exclusively described as one monolithic mass (as "wilderness"): the novella describes the grass, a twig, capers, reeds, treetops, thickets, mangroves, "trunks, branches, leaves, boughs, festoons" (63) and other aspects of the environment.

9 Achebe, "Image of Africa," 782.

10 Myers, "Anxiety of Confluence"; McCarthy, "Choice of Nightmares"; Huggan and Tiffin 2010; Murphy, "Exterminating the Elephant"; Atkinson, "Elephant in the Text."

11 A mouse, a cat, a horse, a hyena, a monkey, a beetle, a snake, a dog, a bird, a pug-nose, bees, flies and magpies.

12 In the "Introduction" to *The ISLE Reader: Ecocriticism, 1993–2003*, Branch and Slovic declare that Glotfelty's early statement is "the closest thing we have to a general definition of the field" (xvii). However, it is not directly apparent how this general definition incorporates the animals of fantasy and science fiction, although these two fields have benefited from "the emergence of ecocriticism" (Baratta, "Introduction," 2).

13 Shapiro and Copeland, "Animal Issues," 344.

14 Malamud, *Poetic Animals*, 59.

15 Sven Birkerts hypothesizes that most readers are prone to ignore place-based passages ("Only God").

16 Paltin, "Infected Carrier," 779.
17 Davidson, "What Metaphors Mean," 46.
18 *Ibid.*, 31.
19 Richard Moran, "Seeing and Believing," 108.
20 *Ibid.*, 94.
21 Davidson, "What Metaphors Mean," 46.
22 Nagel, "What Is It Like to Be a Bat," 438.
23 Ricœur, "Metaphorical Process," 157.
24 *Ibid.*, 154.
25 *Ibid.*, 157.
26 "Richards has suggested using the words 'tenor' and 'vehicle' for the two '*thoughts*' which, in his view, are 'active together' . . . But this picture of two *ideas* working upon each other is an inconvenient fiction. And it is significant that Richards himself soon lapses into speaking of 'tenor' and 'vehicle' as 'things'" (Max Black, *Models and Metaphor*, 47). Although the precise terminology is unclear, many have found it useful to speak of a metaphor's double structure, and Black criticizes Richards's tenor/vehicle distinction to offer his own (frame/focus).
27 Melville, *Moby-Dick*, 156.
28 An indirect reference can be found in Charles Derennes's *La chauve-souris* (1922) – *The Life of the Bat*; it was published in a collection titled *Bestiaire sentimental* (*The Sentimental Bestiary*).
29 Rigby, *Writing After Nature*, 357.
30 Buell, "Representing the Environment," 177.
31 Barthes, *Rustle of Language*, 141.
32 *Ibid.*, 143.
33 *Ibid.*, 148.
34 Paltin, "Infected Carrier," 779.
35 Hardy, *Tess of the d'Urbervilles*, 327.
36 Dickens, *Hard Times*, 27.
37 *Ibid.*, 37.
38 Dickens, *Bleak House*, 13.
39 Hardy, *Tess of the d'Urbervilles*, 124, 152.
40 Guerard, *Conrad the Novelist*, 180.
41 Bassett, "Nature in Bryant's Poetry," 12.
42 Slovic, "Roundtable Discussion," 463.
43 Birkerts, "Only God"; Taylor, "What Is Ecocriticism?"; O'Brien, "Back to the World"; Buell, "Ecocritical Insurgency."
44 Ensor, "Spinster Ecology," 431.
45 Laura Brown, *Homeless Dogs*, x.
46 Malamud, *Poetic Animals*, 59.
47 *Ibid*, 94.
48 *Ibid.*
49 Barthes, *Rustle of Language*, 148.

50 In *Apology*, Plato famously compares Socrates to a gadfly: an uncomfortable goad, provocatively stirring the Athenian political scene, which Plato likens to a dimwitted horse.

Conclusion

1 Bergson, *Introduction to Metaphysics*, 40.
2 Nabokov, *Strong Opinions*, 4.

Bibliography

Achebe, Chinua. "An Image of Africa." *Massachusetts Review* 18/4 (1977): 782–94.

Allen, Mary. *Animals in American Literature*. Urbana: University of Illinois Press, 1983.

Allen, Stan. "Dazed and Confused." *Assemblage* 27/48 (1995): 47–54.

Ambrosini, Richard. *Conrad's Fiction as Critical Discourse*. Cambridge University Press, 1991.

Andrade, Jackie. "What Does Doodling Do?" *Applied Cognitive Psychology* 24/1 (2009): 100–06.

Artese, Brian. *Testimony on Trial*. University of Toronto Press, 2012.

"Athenaeum 28 September 1907." Watt (ed.), *Conrad: The Secret Agent*, 47–49.

Atkinson, William. "The Elephant in the Text: Toward a Post-Humanist Reading of Heart of Darkness." *Critical Approaches to Joseph Conrad*. Ed. Agata Szczeszak-Brewer. Columbia: University of South Carolina Press, 2015. 59–70.

Attridge, John. "'The Yellow-Dog Thing': Joseph Conrad, Verisimilitude, and Professionalism." *ELH* 77/2 (2010): 267–96.

Auerbach, Erich. *Mimesis: The Representation of Reality in Western Literature*. Trans. Willard R. Trask. Princeton University Press, 2013.

Baines, Jocelyn. *Joseph Conrad: A Critical Biography*. London: Weidenfeld & Nicolson, 1959.

Baratta, Chris. "Introduction." *Environmentalism in the Realm of Science Fiction and Fantasy Literature*. Ed. Chris Baratta. Newcastle: Cambridge Scholars, 2012.

Barnes, Julian. *Flaubert's Parrot*. London: Jonathan Cape, 1984.

Barthes, Roland. *The Rustle of Language*. Trans. Richard Howe. Berkeley: University of California Press, 1989.

Bassett, John Spencer. "Nature in Bryant's Poetry." *South Altantic Quarterly* 4/17 (1918): 10–17.

Batchelor, John. "Conrad's Truancy." *The Art of Literary Biography*. Ed. John Batchelor. Oxford University Press, 1995. 115–28.

Battles, Matthew. "In Praise of Doodling." *American Scholar* 73/4 (2004): 105–08.

Belting, Hans. *The End of the History of Art?* Trans. Christopher Wood. University of Chicago Press, 1987.

Bergson, Henri. *An Introduction to Metaphysics.* Trans. T. E. Hulme. New York: G. P. Putnam's Sons, 1912.

Berthoud, Jacques. *Joseph Conrad: The Major Phase.* Cambridge University Press, 1978.

et al. "Notes." *'Twixt Land and Sea.* Ed. Jacques Berthoud et al. Cambridge University Press, 2008.

Best, Stephen and Sharon Marcus. "Surface Reading: An Introduction." *Representations* 108/1 (2009): 1–21.

Billy, Ted. *A Wilderness of Words: Closure and Disclosure in Conrad's Short Fiction.* Lubbock: Texas Tech University Press, 1997.

Birkerts, Sven. "Only God Can Make a Tree: The Joys and Sorrows of Ecocriticism." *Boston Book Review* 3/1 (1996): 5–7.

Black, Jeremy. *Maps and History: Constructing Images of the Past.* New Haven, CT: Yale University Press, 1997.

Black, Max. *Models and Metaphor.* Ithaca, NY: Cornell University Press, 1962.

Blanc, Charles. *Art and Ornament in Dress.* New York: Scribner, Welford & Armstrong, 1877.

Borges, Jorge Luis. "Travels of Praiseworthy Men." *A Universal History of Infamy.* Ed. Norman Thomas Di Giovanni. Harmondsworth: Penguin, 1975.

Branch, Michael P. and Scott Slovic. "Introduction." *The ISLE Reader: Ecocriticism, 1993– 2003.* Ed. Michael P. Branch and Scott Slovic. Athens: University of Georgia Press, 2003.

Brevda, William. "Moby Dick: A Nasty Night for Hats and Men." *Texas Studies in Literature and Language* 59/4 (2017): 421–56.

Brown, Bill. "Thing Theory." *Critical Inquiry* 28/1 (2001): 1–22.

Brown, Laura. *Homeless Dogs and Melancholy Apes: Humans and Other Animals in the Modern Literary Imagination.* Ithaca, NY: Cornell University Press, 2010.

Buell, Lawrence. "The Ecocritical Insurgency." *New Literary History* 30/3 (1999): 699–712.

"Representing the Environment." *The Green Studies Reader: From Romanticism to Ecocriticism.* Ed. Laurence Coupe. London and New York: Routledge, 2000. 177–81.

Bushell, Sally. "Mapping Victorian Adventure Fiction: Silences, Doublings, and the Ur-map in Treasure Island and King Solomon's Mines." *Victorian Studies* 57/4 (2015): 611–37.

"Paratext or Imagetext? Interpreting the Fictional Map." *Word and Image* 32/2 (2016): 181–94.

Cantor, Paul A. and Peter Hufnagel. "The Empire of the Future: Imperialism and Modernism in H. G. Wells." *Studies in the Novel* 38/1 (2006): 36–56.

Carabine, Keith. *The Life and the Art: A Study of Conrad's "Under Western Eyes."* Amsterdam: Rodopi, 1996.

Carlyle, Thomas. "The Nigger Question." *Miscellaneous Essays*, vol. VII. London: Chapman & Hall, 1888. 79–110.

Carver, Beci. *Granular Modernism*. Oxford University Press, 2014.
Chambers, Ross. *Loiterature*. Lincoln: University of Nebraska Press, 1999.
Chantler, Ashley. *Heart of Darkness: Character Studies*. London: Continuum, 2008.
Christie's Auctions & Private Sales. "Printed Books and Manuscripts: British Authors." Sale 7964, Lot 146. New York, October 7, 1994.
Clemens, Florence. "Joseph Conrad as a Geographer." *Scientific Monthly* 51/5 (1940): 460–65.
Conrad, Jessie. *Joseph Conrad as I Knew Him*. London: Heinemann, 1926.
Conrad, John. *Joseph Conrad: Times Remembered*. Cambridge University Press, 1981.
Cooper, Reginald Davey. *Hunting and Hunted in the Belgian Congo*. Ed. R. Keith Johnston. London: Smith, Elder, 1914.
"Country Life." Watt (ed.), *Conrad: The Secret Agent*, 27–32.
Crampton, Jeremy W. and John Krygie. "An Introduction to Critical Cartography." *ACME* 4/1 (2005): 11–33.
Crane, Stephen. *The Red Badge of Courage*. Ed. Anthony Mellors and Fiona Robertson. Oxford University Press, 2008.
Crankshaw, Edward. *Joseph Conrad: Some Aspects of the Art of the Novel*. London: Macmillan, 1976.
Crary, Jonathan. *Suspensions of Perception: Attention, Spectacle, and Modern Culture*. Boston: Massachusetts Institute of Technology, 2001.
Curle, Richard. *Joseph Conrad: A Study*. Garden City, NY: Doubleday, 1914.
"Joseph Conrad's Diary (Hitherto Unpublished) of His Journey up the Valley of the Congo in 1890." *Blue Peter* 43/5 (1925): 317–64.
Curreli, Mario. "Garibaldian Names in 'Nostromo'." *The Conradian* 33/2 (2008): 80–97.
Cyr, Marc. "The Dramatized and Embodied Artist in *The Nigger of the 'Narcissus'*." *Conradiana* 45/2 (2013): 145–62.
Dalgarno, Emily. "Conrad's Attitude to his Text." *Conradiana* 9/1 (1977): 3–16.
Danto, Arthur C. *After the End of Art: Contemporary Art and the Pale of History*. Princeton University Press, 1997.
Beyond the Brillo Box: The Visual Arts in Post-Historical Perspective. Berkeley: University of California Press, 1998.
"The End of Art: A Philosophical Defense." *History and Theory* 37/4 (1998): 127–43.
The Transfiguration of the Commonplace: A Philosophy of Art. Cambridge, MA: Harvard University Press, 1981.
What Art Is. New Haven, CT: Yale University Press, 2014.
Davidson, Donald. "Joseph Conrad's Directed Indirections." *Sewanee Review* 33/2 (1925): 163–77.
"What Metaphors Mean." *Critical Inquiry* 5/1 (1978): 31–47.
Davies, Laurence. "The Dark Side and the Bright: Conrad in *Ridgway's* and *The Metropolitan Magazine*." *Conrad First*. Ed. Stephen Donovan. 10 March 2015. www.conradfirst.net/conrad/scholarship/authors/davies.html

De Quatrefages, Armand de Breau. *The Pygmies*. Trans. Frederick Starr. London: Macmillan, 1895.

Derrick, John. "Mapping Axel Heyst's Island: The Limits of Allegory in Conrad's *Victory*." *Ilha do Desterro* 4/10 (2008): 33–53.

Descartes, René. *Discourse on Method and Meditations on First Philosophy*. Trans. Donald Cress. Indianapolis: Hackett, 1998.

"The Dial." Watt (ed.), *Conrad: The Secret Agent*, 51.

Dickens, Charles. *Bleak House*. Ed. Nicola Bradbury. London: Penguin, 2011.

Hard Times. Ed. Kate Flint. London: Penguin, 2003.

Pickwick Papers. Ed. James Kinsley. Oxford University Press, 2008.

Di Santo, Michael John. "Dramas of Fallen Horses: Conrad, Dostoevsky, and Nietzsche." *Conradiana* 42/2 (2010): 45–68.

Donovan, Stephen. *Joseph Conrad and Popular Culture*. Basingstoke: Palgrave Macmillan, 2005.

Dostoevsky, Fyodor. *The Devils*. Trans. David Magarshack. Harmondsworth: Penguin, 1969.

Doyle, Arthur Conan. *The Adventures of Sherlock Holmes*. Oxford University Press, 2008.

Dryden, Linda. *Joseph Conrad and the Imperial Romance*. Basingstoke: Macmillan, 2000.

Eagleton, Terry. "Form, Ideology and *The Secret Agent*." *Against the Grain: Essays 1975–1985*. London: Verso, 1986. 23–32.

How to Read Literature. New Haven, CT: Yale University Press, 2013.

Eggert, Paul. "Conrad's Working Methods in *Under Western Eyes*: The Editorial Challenge." *Under Western Eyes: Centennial Essays*. Ed. Allan Simmons, J. H. Stape and Jeremy Hawthorn. Amsterdam: Brill, 2011.

Eliot, George. *The George Eliot Letters, in Seven Volumes*, vol. IV: *1862–1868*. Ed. Gordon S. Height. New Haven, CT: Yale University Press, 1955.

Eliot, T. S. *Four Quartets*. New York: Harcourt, Brace, 1943.

"Tradition and the Individual Talent." *The Sacred Wood: Essays on Poetry and Criticism*. London: Faber & Faber, 1997. 39–49.

Ensor, Sarah. "Spinster Ecology: Rachel Carson, Sarah Orne Jewett, and Nonreproductive Futurity." *American Literature* 84/2 (2012): 409–35.

Erdinast-Vulcan, Daphna. *Joseph Conrad and the Modern Temper*. Oxford: Clarendon Press, 1991.

"'Sudden Holes in Space and Time': Conrad's Anarchist Aesthetics in *The Secret Agent*." Moore (ed.), *Conrad's Cities*, 207–22.

Faris, Wendy B. "The 'Dehumanization' of the Arts: J. M. W. Turner, Joseph Conrad, and the Advent of Modernism." *Comparative Literature* 41/4 (1989): 305–26.

Fashion Institute of Technology. http://sites.fitnyc.edu/depts/museum/RetroSpective/Gigot-Sleeve-1.html. November 22, 2013.

Finkelstein, Sue. "Hope and Betrayal: A Psychoanalytic Reading of 'Amy Foster'." *Conradiana* 32/1 (2000): 20–31.

Fleishman, Avrom. "The Symbolic World of the Secret Agent." *ELH* 32/2 (1965): 196–219.

Focillon, Henri. *The Life of Forms in Art*. Trans. Charles B. Hogan and George Kubler. 1989. New York: Zone, 1996

Fogel, Aaron. *Coercion to Speak: Conrad's Poetics of Dialogue*. Cambridge, MA: Harvard University Press, 1985.

Follett, Wilson. *Joseph Conrad: A Short Study of His Intellectual and Emotional Attitude Toward His Work and of the Chief Characteristics of His Novels*. New York: Doubleday, 1915.

Ford, Ford Madox. *Joseph Conrad: A Personal Remembrance*. Boston: Little, Brown, 1924.

"*Tiger, Tiger*." New York: Bookman, 1928.

Forster, E. M. "Joseph Conrad: A Note." *Abinger Harvest*. Boston, MA: Mariner Books, 1950. 136–41.

Fowler, Roger. *Linguistic Criticism*. Oxford University Press, 1996.

Foye, Paul et al. "The Sailing Maneuver in 'The Secret Sharer'." *Journal of Modern Literature* 2/1 (1971): 119–23.

Freedgood, Elaine. *The Ideas in Things: Fugitive Meaning in the Victorian Novel*. University of Chicago Press, 2006.

Fried, Michael. *Absorption and Theatricality: Painting and Beholder in the Age of Diderot*. University of Chicago Press, 1988.

Galef, David. "On the Margin: The Peripheral Characters in Conrad's *Heart of Darkness*." *Journal of Modern Literature* 17/1 (1990): 117–38.

The Supporting Cast: A Study of Flat and Minor Characters. University Park: Pennsylvania State University Press, 1993.

Garnett, Edward. "Introduction." *Letters from Joseph Conrad 1895–1924*. Ed. Edward Garnett. Indianapolis: Bobbs-Merrill, 1928.

Gernsheim, Alison. *Victorian and Edwardian Fashion: A Photographic Survey*. New York: Dover, 1981.

Gillon, Adam. *Joseph Conrad: Comparative Essays*. Ed. Raymond Brebach. Lubbock: Texas Tech University Press, 1994.

Glotfelty, Cheryll Burgess. "Introduction." *The Ecocriticism Reader*. Ed. Cheryll Burgess Glotfelty and Harold Fromm. Athens: University of Georgia Press, 1996. xv–xxxvii.

Gombrich, Ernst Hans. *Art and Illusion: A Study in the Psychology of Pictorial Representation*. London: Phaidon, 1962.

"Reflections on Teaching Art History in Art Schools." *The Gombrich Archive*. https://gombricharchive.files.wordpress.com/2011/04/showdoc34.pdf.

Gordan, John D. *Joseph Conrad: The Making of a Novelist*. Cambridge, MA: Harvard University Press, 1963.

Gorra, Michael. "Joseph Conrad." *Hudson Review* 59/4 (2007): 541–71.

Greaney, Michael. *Conrad, Language, and Narrative*. Cambridge University Press, 2002.

Greenberg, Clement. *The Collected Essays and Criticism*, vol. III. Ed. John O'Brian. University of Chicago Press, 1986.

Late Writings. Ed. Robert Morgan. Minneapolis: University of Minnesota Press, 2003.

Guerard, Albert. *Conrad the Novelist*. Cambridge, MA: Harvard University Press, 1958.

"Introduction." *Heart of Darkness and The Secret Sharer*. By Joseph Conrad. New York: Signet, 1950.

Hagan, John. "The Design of Conrad's *The Secret Agent*." *ELH* 22/2 (1955): 148–64.

Hampson, Robert. *Conrad's Secrets*. Basingstroke: Palgrave Macmillan, 2012.

"'A Passion for Maps': Conrad, Africa, Australia, and South-East Asia." *The Conradian* 28/1 (2003): 34–56.

"Spatial Stories: Joseph Conrad and James Joyce." *Geographies of Modernism*. Ed. Peter Brooker and Andrew Thacker. Abingdon-on-Thames: Routledge, 2005. 54–64.

"'Topographical Mysteries': Conrad and London." Moore (ed.), *Conrad's Cities*, 207–22.

Hanson, Thomas. "Mallarmé's Hat." *Yale French Studies* 54 (1977): 215–27.

Hardy, Thomas. *Jude the Obscure*. Ed. Patricia Ingham. Oxford University Press, 2008.

Tess of the d'Urbervilles. Ed. Simon Gatrell and Juliet Grindle. Oxford University Press, 1983.

Harkness, Bruce. "Introduction." *The Secret Agent: A Simple Tale*. Ed. Bruce Harkness and S. W. Reid. Cambridge University Press, 1990. xxiii–xli.

Harley, J. B. "Cartography, Ethics and Social Theory." *Cartographica* 27/2 (1990): 1–23.

"Deconstructing the Map." *Cartographica* 26/2 (1989): 1–20.

"Text and Contexts in the Interpretation of Early Maps." *The New Nature of Maps: Essays in the History of Cartography*. Ed. Paul Laxton. Baltimore, MD: Johns Hopkins University Press, 2001. 33–50.

Harley, J. B. and David Woodward (eds.). *The History of Cartography*. 6 vols. University of Chicago Press, 1987–.

Harpham, Geoffrey Galt.. *One of Us: The Mastery of Joseph Conrad*. University of Chicago Press, 1996.

Harrington, Ellen Burton. *Conrad's Sensational Heroines: Gender and Representation in the Late Fiction of Joseph Conrad*. Cham: Palgrave Macmillan, 2017.

Hawthorn, Jeremy. "The Incoherences of *The Nigger of the 'Narcissus'*." *The Conradian* 11/2 (1986): 98–115.

Hecht, Jamey. "Scarcity and Compensation in *Moby-Dick*." *Massachusetts Review*, 40 (1999): 111–30.

Language and Fictional Self-Consciousness. Lincoln: University of Nebraska Press, 1979.

Hennelly, Mark. "Dickens's Immaterial Culture of Hats and *The Pickwick Papers*." *Dickens Studies Annual* 42 (2011): 77–122.

Hervouet, Yves. *The French Face of Joseph Conrad*. Cambridge University Press, 1990.
Higdon, David Leon. "Conrad's Clocks." *The Conradian* 16/1 (1991): 1–18.
"'His Helpless Prey': Conrad and the Aggressive Text." *The Conradian* 12/2 (1987): 108–21.
Howe, Irving. "Conrad: Order and Anarchy." Watt (ed.), *Conrad: The Secret Agent*, 140–49.
Huggan, Graham and Helen Tiffin. *Postcolonial Ecocriticism: Literature, Animals, Environment*. Abingdon: Routledge, 2010.
James, William. *The Principles of Psychology*, vol. I. New York: Cosimo Classics, 2007.
The Principles of Psychology, vol. II. New York: Holt, 1890.
Jameson, Fredric. *The Political Unconscious: Narrative as a Socially Symbolic Act*. Ithaca, NY: Cornell University Press, 1981.
Jasanoff, Maya. *The Dawn Watch: Joseph Conrad in a Global World*. London: William Collins, 2017.
Johnson, Barbara and Marjorie Garber. "Secret Sharing: Reading Conrad Psychoanalytically." *College English* 49/6 (1987): 628–40.
Johnson, Bruce. "Conrad's Impressionism and Watt's 'Delayed Decoding'." *Conrad Revisited: Essays for the Eighties*. Ed. Ross C. Murfin. Tuscaloosa: University of Alabama Press, 1985. 51–70.
Johnston, Lucy. *Nineteenth-Century Fashion in Detail*. London: Victoria and Albert Museum, 2009.
Jones, Susan. *Conrad and Women*. Oxford: Clarendon Press, 1999.
"Conrad's Debt to Marguerite Poradowska." *Conrad: Intertexts and Appropriations: Essays in Memory of Yves Hervout*. Ed. Gene Moore and Owen Knowles. Amsterdam: Rodopi, 1997. 7–28.
Kao, Pei-Wen Clio. "The Flâneur/Flâneuse and the Benjaminian Law of 'Dialectic at a Standstill' in Joseph Conrad's *The Secret Agent*." *Conradiana* 45/2 (2013): 125–44.
Karl, Frederick R. *Joseph Conrad: The Three Lives*. New York: Farrar, Straus and Giroux, 1979.
Kimpel, Ben and Duncan Eaves. "Geography and History in 'Nostromo'." *Modern Philology* 5/56 (1958): 45–54.
Kirschner, Paul. *Conrad: The Psychologist as Artist*. Edinburgh: Oliver & Boyd, 1968.
Knapp Hay, Eloise. "Joseph Conrad and Impressionism." *Journal of Aesthetics and Art Criticism* 34/2 (1975): 137–44.
The Political Novels of Joseph Conrad: A Critical Study. University of Chicago Press, 1963.
Knights, L. C. "How Many Children Had Lady Macbeth? An Essay in the Theory and Practice of Shakespeare Criticism." *Explorations*. New York: George W. Stewart, 1964. 15–54.
Knowles, Owen. *An Annotated Critical Bibliography of Joseph Conrad*. New York: St Martin's Press, 1992.

"Joseph Conrad and Bertrand Russell: New Light on their Relationship." *Journal of Modern Literature* 17/1 (1990): 139–52.

"Preprint Documents." *The Shadow-Line*. Ed. John Stape and Allan Simmons. Cambridge University Press, 2013. 121–25.

Knowles, Owen and Gene M. Moore (eds.). *Oxford Reader's Companion to Conrad*. Oxford University Press, 2000.

Krishnan, Sanjay. "Animality and the Global Subject in Conrad's *Lord Jim*." *Reading the Global: Troubling Perspectives on Britain's Empire in Asia*. New York: Columbia University Press, 2007. 133–64.

Kuhn, Alfred. "A Note on Raskol'nikov's Hats." *Slavic and East European Journal* 15/4 (1971): 425–32.

Larabee, Mark. "Joseph Conrad and the Maritime Tradition." *A Historical Guide to Joseph Conrad*. Ed. John Peters. Oxford University Press, 2010. 47–76.

Leavis, F. R. *The Great Tradition: George Eliot, Henry James, Joseph Conrad*. New York: George W. Stewart, 1950.

Lees, David E. "Conrad's Unpublished Pen and Ink Sketches for *The Secret Agent: A Drama*." *Conradiana* 8/3 (1976): 253–56.

Levin, Yael. "Conrad, Freud, and Derrida on Pompeii." *Partial Answers: Journal of Literature and the History of Ideas* 3/1 (2005): 81–100.

Tracing the Aesthetic Principle in Conrad's Fiction. New York: Palgrave Macmillan, 2008.

Livingstone, Robert Eric. "Seeing through Reading: Class, Race and Literary Authority in Joseph Conrad's *The Nigger of the 'Narcissus'*." *NOVEL: A Forum on Fiction* 26/2 (1993): 133–50.

Loughery, John. "The Telling Detail." *Hudson Review* 50/3 (1997): 463–69.

Lubbock, Percy. *The Craft of Fiction*. London: Jonathan Cape, 1921.

Lyon, John. "Introduction." *The Secret Agent*. By Joseph Conrad. Ed. John Lyon. Oxford University Press, 2004.

Malamud, Randy. *Poetic Animals and Animal Souls*. New York: Palgrave Macmillan, 2003.

Marcus, Miriam. "Writing, Race, and Illness in *The Nigger of the 'Narcissus'*." *The Conradian* 23/1 (1998): 37–50.

McCarthy, Jeffrey Mathes. "'A Choice of Nightmares': The Ecology of *Heart of Darkness*." *Modern Fiction Studies* 55/3 (2009): 620–48.

McLeod, Deborah. "Disturbing the Silence: Sound Imagery in Conrad's *The Secret Agent*." *Journal of Modern Literature* 33.1 (2009): 117–31.

Mégroz, R. L. *Joseph Conrad's Mind and Method: A Study of Personality in Art*. London: Faber & Faber, 1931.

Melville, Herman. *Moby-Dick*. Ed. Harrison Hayford, Hershel Parker and Thomas Tanselle. London: Penguin, 2013.

Moby-Dick; or, The Whale. Ed. Coralie Bickford-Smith. London: Penguin, 2013.

Redburn. Ed. Harold Beaver. London: Penguin, 1977.

Typee: A Peep at Polynesian Life. Ed. John Bryant. London: Penguin, 1996.

Messenger, Nigel. "'We did not want to lose him': Jimmy Wait as the Figure of Abjection in Conrad's *The Nigger of the 'Narcissus'*." *Critical Survey* 13/1 (2001): 62–79.

Meyer, Bernard. *Joseph Conrad: A Psychoanalytic Biography*. Princeton University Press, 1970.

Meyers, Jeffrey. *Joseph Conrad: A Biography*. New York: Cooper Square Press, 2001.

Miller, James E. "*The Nigger of the 'Narcissus'*: A Re-Examination." *PMLA* 66/1 (1951): 911–18.

Miller, J. Hillis. "Foreword." *Conrad in the Twenty-First Century: Contemporary Approaches and Perspectives*. Ed. Carola M. Kaplan, Peter Lancelot Mallios, and Andrea White. Abingdon: Routledge, 2005. 1–16.

Poets of Reality: Six Twentieth-Century Writers. Cambridge, MA: Belknap Press, 1965.

"Should We Read *Heart of Darkness*?" *Joseph Conrad's Heart of Darkness*. Ed. Harold Bloom. New York: Chelsea House, 2008. 115–30.

Miłobędzki, Józef. "Dziennik Kongijski Josepha Conrad/Joseph Conrad's Congo Diary." *Nautologica* 1 (1972): 3–55.

Monmonier, Mark. *How to Lie with Maps*. University of Chicago Press, 1991.

Moore, Gene M. "A Descriptive Location Register of Joseph Conrad's Literary Manuscripts." *The Conradian* 27/2 (2002): 1–93.

"Introduction." Moore (ed.), *Conrad's Cities*, 9–12.

(ed.). *Conrad's Cities: Essays for Hans van Marle*. Amsterdam: Rodopi, 1992.

Moran, Margaret. "Bertrand Russell and Joseph Conrad." *Russell: The Journal of Bertrand Russell Studies* 2/1 (1982): 29–46.

Moran, Richard. "Seeing and Believing: Metaphor, Image, and Force." *Critical Inquiry* 16/1 (1989): 87–112.

Morelli, Giovanni. *Italian Painters: Critical Studies of Their Works*. Trans. Constance Jocelyn Ffoulkes. London: John Murray, 1900.

Moretti, Franco. *Atlas of the European Novel*. Guildford: Verso, 1999.

Moser, Thomas. *Joseph Conrad: Achievement and Decline*. Cambridge, MA: Harvard University Press, 1957.

Murphy, Ryan Francis. "Exterminating the Elephant in *Heart of Darkness*." *The Conradian* 38/2 (2013): 1–17.

Myers, Jeffrey. "The Anxiety of Confluence: Evolution, Ecology, and Imperialism in Conrad's *Heart of Darkness*." *Interdisciplinary Studies in Literature and Environment* 8/2 (2001): 97–108.

Nabokov, Vladimir. *Lectures on Literature*. Boston, MA: Houghton Mifflin Harcourt, 1982.

Strong Opinions. London: Penguin, 2011.

Nagel, Thomas. "What Is It Like to Be a Bat?" *Philosophical Review* 83 (1974): 435–50.

Najder, Zdzisław. "A Century of *Nostromo*." *Conradiana* 40/3 (2009): 233–46.

Joseph Conrad: A Chronicle. New Brunswick, NJ: Rutgers University Press, 1983.

Joseph Conrad: A Life. Trans. Halina Najder. New York: Camden House, 2007.
"The Sisters: A Grandiose Failure." *Conrad in Perspective: Essays on Art and Fidelity*. Cambridge University Press, 1997. 68–80.

Newell, Kenneth. "The Yellow-Dog Incident in Conrad's *Lord Jim*." *Studies in the Novel* 3/1 (1971): 26–33.

Nietzsche, Friedrich. "On Truth and Lies in a Nonmoral Sense." *The Nietzsche Reader*. Ed. Keith Ansell Pearson and Duncan Large. Malden, MA and Oxford: Blackwell, 2006. 114–23.
"Über Wahrheit und Lüge im aussermoralischen Sinne." *Die Geburt der Tragödie: Unzeitgemäße Betrachtungen I-IV: Kritische Studienausgabe*. Ed. Giorgio Colli und Mazzino Montinari. Germany: de Gruyter, 1999. 873–90.

North, Paul. *The Problem of Distraction*. Stanford University Press, 2012.

O'Brien, Susie. "'Back to the World': Reading Ecocriticism in a Postcolonial Context." *Five Emus to the King of Siam: Environment and Empire*. Ed. Helen Tiffin. Amsterdam: Rodopi, 2007.

Oliver, Matthew. "Conrad's Grotesque Public: Pornography and the Politics of Reading in *The Secret Agent*." *Twentieth-Century Literature* 55.2 (2009): 209–31.

"Our Dramatic Critic." "Conrad's Play: Anarchist Types and Theories in The Secret Agent – Unrehearsed Incident." *Daily Mirror*, November 3, 1922, 2.

Palmer, John A. *Joseph Conrad's Fiction: A Study in Literary Growth*. Ithaca, NY: Cornell University Press, 1968.
(ed.) *Twentieth-Century Interpretations of The Nigger of the 'Narcissus'*. Englewood Cliffs, NJ: Prentice-Hall, 1969.

Paltin, Judith. "Conrad's Agile Crowds". *The Conradian* 38/1 (2013): 1–21.
"'An Infected Carrier of the Past': Modernist Nature as the Ground of Anti-Realism." *ISLE: Interdisciplinary Studies in Literature and Environment* 20/4 (2013): 778–94.

Peters, John G. *Conrad and Impressionism*. Cambridge University Press, 2001.
"Introduction." *A Historical Guide to Joseph Conrad*. Ed. John G. Peters. Oxford University Press, 2010.
Joseph Conrad's Critical Reception. Cambridge University Press, 2013.

Purdon, James. "Secret Agents, Official Secrets: Joseph Conrad and the Security of Mail." *Review of English Studies* 65/226 (2015): 302–20.

Purdy, Dwight. "The Manuscript of *Victory* and the Problem of Conrad's Intention." *Journal of Modern Literature* 10/1 (1983): 91–108.

Raleigh, Patrick Henry. "Henry Patrick Raleigh (1880–1994)." *Illustrator's Lounge*, March 8, 2016. http://illustratorslounge.com/editorial/henry-raleigh-1880-1944.

Ray, Martin. "The Landscape of *The Secret Agent*." Moore (ed.), *Conrad's Cities*, 197–206.

Reid, S. W. "American Markets, Serials, and Conrad's Career." *The Conradian* 28/1 (2003): 57–99.

Reiss, Tom. "The True Classic of Terrorism." *New York Times*, September 11, 2005: 35.

Richardson, Brian. "Conrad and Posthumanist Narration: Fabricating Class and Consciousness onboard the Narcissus." *Conrad in the Twenty-First Century: Contemporary Approaches and Perspectives*. Ed. Carola Kaplan, Peter Lancelot Mallios and Andrea White. London: Routledge, 2005. 213–22.

Ricœur, Paul. "The Metaphorical Process as Cognition, Imagination, and Feeling." *Critical Inquiry* 5/2 (1978): 143–59.

Rigby, Kate. *Writing After Nature. Australian Humanities Review*, 39–40 (September 2016): http://australianhumanitiesreview.org/2006/09/01/writing-after-nature.

Roberts, Andrew Michael. "Conrad, Theory and Value." *The Conradian* 22/1 (1997): 178–202.

Roberts, Cecil. "Joseph Conrad: A Reminiscence." *Joseph Conrad: Interviews and Recollections*. Ed. Martin Ray. London: Macmillan, 1990. 124–31.

Robinson, Fred Miller. *The Man in the Bowler Hat: His History and Iconography*. Chapel Hill: University of North Carolina Press, 1993.

Rooney, Ellen. "Form and Contentment." *Reading for Form*. Ed. Susan J. Wolfson and Marshall Brown. Seattle: University of Washington Press, 2006. 25–48.

Ross, Stephen. "*The Nigger of the 'Narcissus'* and Modernist Haunting." *NOVEL: A Forum on Fiction* 44/2 (2011): 268–91.

Rothenstein, William. *Men and Memories: Recollections of William Rothenstein, 1900– 1922*. New York: Coward-McCann, 1932.

Royle, Nicholas. *Veering: A Theory of Literature*. Edinburgh University Press, 2011.

Rude, Donald. "Joseph Conrad's Letters to Eugene F. Saxton: A New Archive at Texas Tech University." *The Conradian* 14/1 (1989): 47–66.

Ruppel, Richard. *A Political Genealogy of Joseph Conrad*. Lanham, MD: Lexington, 2015.

Rushdie, Salman. *Midnight's Children*. London: Penguin, 1991.

Russell, Bertrand. *The Basic Writings of Bertrand Russell*. Ed. Robert Egner and Lester Denonn. London: Routledge, 1961. 221–26.

Contemplation and Action, 1902–14. Ed. Richard A. Kempel, Andrew Brink and Margaret Moran. London: Routledge, 1993.

"Knowledge by Acquaintance and Knowledge by Description." *The Problems of Philosophy*. London: Williams and Norgate, 1912.

"On Denoting." *Mind* 14/56 (1905): 479–93.

"The Philosophy of Logical Analysis." *History of Western Philosophy*. Abingdon: Routledge, 2009.

The Philosophy of Logical Atomism. Abingdon: Routledge, 2010.

Portraits from Memory and Other Essays. New York: Simon & Schuster, 1956.

Said, Edward. *Beginnings: Intention and Method*. New York: Columbia University Press,1985.

"Conrad: The Presentation of Narrative." *NOVEL: A Forum on Fiction* 7/2 (1974): 116–32.

"Conrad and Nietzsche." *Joseph Conrad: A Commemoration*. Ed. Norman Sherry. London: Macmillan, 1976.

Joseph Conrad and the Fiction of Autobiography. New York: Columbia University Press, 2008.

Salmons, Kim. "Anarchic Appetites: Vegetarianism in *The Secret Agent*." *The Conradian* 37/2 (2012): 35–49.

Schmitt, Cannon. "Tidal Conrad (Literally)." *Victorian Studies* 55/1 (2012): 7–29.

Schnauder, Ludwig. *Free Will and Determinism in Joseph Conrad's Major Novels*. Amsterdam: Rodopi, 2009.

Schneider-Rebozo, Lissa et al. (eds.). *Conrad and Nature: Ecology, Environment, and Animals in the Writings of Joseph Conrad*. New York: Routledge, 2019.

Schwarz, Daniel. *Conrad: Almayer's Folly to Under Western Eyes*. Trowbridge & Esther: Macmillan, 1980.

Shapiro, Kenneth and Marion Copeland. "Toward a Critical Theory of Animal Issues in Fiction." *Society and Animals* 13/4 (2005), 343–46.

Simmons, Allan. *Joseph Conrad*. New York: Palgrave Macmillan, 2006.

"Reclaiming Conrad from His Editors: The Case of *An Outcast of the Islands*." *Conradiana* 46/1 (2015): 39–52.

"Representing 'the simple and the voiceless': Story-telling in *The Nigger of the 'Narcissus'*." *The Conradian* 24/1 (1999): 43–57.

Simons, John. *Animal Rights and the Politics of Literary Representation*. New York: Palgrave Macmillan, 2002.

Skinner, Stephen. "Obscurity, Apophasis, and the Critical Imagination: The Unsayable in *Heart of Darkness*." *Conradiana* 42/2 (2010): 93–106.

Slovic, Scott. "A Roundtable Discussion on Ecocriticism." *The Future of Ecocriticism: New Horizons*. Ed. Opperman Serpil et al. Newcastle-upon-Tyne: Cambridge Scholars, 2011. 459–79.

Smith, David. "The Hidden Narrative: The *K* in Conrad." *Under Western Eyes: Beginnings, Revisions, Final Form*. Ed. David Smith. Hamden: Shoe String Press, 1991. 39–82.

Smith, Hobart and Rozella Smith. "The herpetology of Herman Melville's Moby-*Dick*." *Bulletin of the Philadelphia Herpetological Society* 30 (1982): 9–14.

Stallman, R. W. "Time and *The Secret Agent*." *Texas Studies in Literature and Language* 1/1 (1959): 101–22.

Stanley, H. M. *The Autobiography of Sir Henry Morton Stanley*. Ed. Dorothea Stanley. Cambridge, MA: Riverside Press, 1909.

Stape, John. "Conrad the Impressionist." *English Literature in Transition* 45/4 (2002): 481–83.

"'Gaining Conviction': Conradian Borrowing and the *Patna* Episode in *Lord Jim*." *Conrad: Intertexts and Appropriations: Essays in Memory of Yves Hervout*. Ed. Gene Moore, Owen Knowles and John Stape. Amsterdam: Rodopi, 1997. 59–80.

The Several Lives of Joseph Conrad. New York: Vintage, 2007.

Stein, Richard. "Dickens and Illustration." *The Cambridge Companion to Charles Dickens*. Ed. John Jordan. Cambridge University Press, 2001.

Stevenson, Robert Louis. *Travels with a Donkey in the Cévennes*. Ed. Christopher Maclachlan. London: Penguin, 2004.

Strawson, P. F. "On Referring." *Mind* 59/235 (1950): 320–44.

Sutherland, John. *Can Jane Eyre be Happy? More Puzzles in Classic Fiction*. Oxford University Press, 1999.

Is Heathcliff a Murderer? Oxford University Press, 1996.

Who Betrays Elizabeth Bennet? Further Puzzles in Classic Fiction. Oxford University Press, 2000.

Tagge, Anne. "The Butterfly Hunters." *Conradiana* 28/3 (1996): 182–89.

Taylor, David. "What Is Ecocriticism?" *Defining Ecocritical Theory and Practice: Sixteen Position Papers from the 1994 Western Literature Association Salt Lake City, Utah – 6 October 1994*. ASLE.

Towheed, Shafquat. "Geneva v. Saint Petersburg: Two Concepts of Literary Property and the Material Lives of Books in *Under Western Eyes*." *Book History* 10 (2007): 169–91.

Vasari, Giorgio. *The Lives of the Artists*. Trans. Julia Conaway Bondanella and Peter Bondanella. Oxford University Press, 2008.

Vint, Sherryl. *Animal Alterity: Science Fiction and the Question of the Animal*. Liverpool University Press, 2010.

Walkowitz, Rebecca. *Cosmopolitan Style: Modernism Beyond the Nation*. New York: Columbia University Press, 2006.

Warodell, Johan. "Beyond the Butterfly: Three Hundred Animal Species in Nabokov's Fiction." *Nabokov Studies*. In press.

"Conrad's Painterly Drawings." *English* 61/1 (2017): 45–69.

"Conrad's Unpublished Map of His Congo Journey: A Note." *The Conradian* 42/2 (2017): 64–68.

"Query: Joseph Conrad's Unpublished 'Map of Russias'." *Notes & Queries* 64/4 (2017): 681–82.

"Three Hundred Animal Species in Woolf's Fiction." *Notes & Queries* 67/1 (2020): 138–40.

"Three Hundred Fifty Animal Species in Melville's Fiction." *Leviathan* 22/3 (2020): 68–74.

"An Unpublished Conrad Drawing of Winnie Verloc?" *Notes & Queries* 62/3 (2015): 454–56.

Watt, Ian. *Conrad in the Nineteenth Century*. Berkeley: University of California Press, 1979.

Essays on Conrad. Cambridge University Press, 2000.

Joseph Conrad: Nostromo. Cambridge University Press, 1988.

"Pink Toads and Yellow Curs: An Impressionist Narrative Device in *Lord Jim*." *Joseph Conrad Colloquy in Poland, 5–12 September 1972*. Ed. Róża Jabłkowska. Warsaw: Polish Academy of Sciences, 1975. 11–31.

The Rise of the Novel: Studies in Defoe, Richardson and Fielding. Berkeley: University of California Press, 1957.

(ed.) *Conrad: The Secret Agent. A Casebook*. London: Macmillan, 1973.

Watts, Cedric. *Conrad's Heart of Darkness: A Critical and Contextual Discussion.* Amsterdam: Rodopi, 2012.

"Introduction." *The Nigger of the 'Narcissus'.* Ed. Cedric Watts. Harmondsworth: Penguin, 1988. vii–xxx.

Joseph Conrad: The Secret Agent. Humanities-Ebooks.co.uk, 2007.

Wells, H. G. *The Invisible Man.* Ed. Matthew Beaumont. Oxford University Press, 2017.

The Island of Doctor Moreau. Ed. Darryl Jones. Oxford University Press, 2017.

The Shape of Things to Come. Ed. John Clute. London: Penguin, 2006.

The War of the Worlds. Ed. Darryl Jones. Oxford University Press, 2017.

White, Andrea. "Conrad and Modernism." *A Historical Guide to Joseph Conrad.* Ed. John G. Peters. Oxford University Press, 2010. 163–96.

Williams, Porter. "The Matter of Conscience in Conrad's *The Secret Sharer.*" *PMLA* 79/5 (1964): 629–30.

Wölfflin, Heinrich. *Kunstgeschichtliche Grundbegriffe: Das Problem der Stilentwicklung in der neueren Kunst.* Munich: Hugo Bruckmann, 1917.

Principles of Art History: The Problem of Development of Style in Later Art. Trans. M. D. Hottinger. New York: Dover, 1950.

Woodward, David. "Introduction." *Art and Cartography: Six Historical Essays.* Ed. David Woodward. University of Chicago Press, 1987. 1–9.

Woolf, Virginia. *Jacob's Room.* Ed. Kate Flint. Oxford University Press, 2008.

"Joseph Conrad." *The Common Reader*, vol. 1. Ed. Andrew McNeillie. London: Vintage, 2003.

Mrs Dalloway. Ed. David Bradshaw. Oxford University Press, 2000.

Orlando. Ed. Rachel Bowlby. Oxford University Press, 1992.

Yates, Norris. "Social Comment in *The Nigger of the 'Narcissus'.*" *PMLA* 79/1 (1964): 183–85.

Yelton, Donald. *Mimesis and Metaphor: An Inquiry into the Genesis and Scope of Conrad's Symbolic Imagery.* The Hague: Mouton, 1967.

Index

Lightning Source UK Ltd.
Milton Keynes UK
UKHW010636110322
399901UK00002B/18

9 781316 512197